Embracing the Dance of Eden

Second Reformation Understanding in Biblical Thinking
from Perspectives of God's Eternal Present
and Creation's Unchanging Principles

Advantage™
INSPIRATIONAL

Charles Alexander

Embracing the Dance of Eden by Charles Alexander
Copyright © 2009 by Charles Alexander
All Rights Reserved.
ISBN: 1-59755-212-7

Published by: ADVANTAGE BOOKS™
www.advbookstore.com

Library of Congress Control Number: 2009904957

Cover design by Pat Theriault

First Printing: June 2009
10 11 12 13 14 15 10 9 8 7 6 5 4 3 2
Printed in the United States of America

Dedicated to:

Pastor John Briscall who encouraged me as a writer;

Pastor Jonathan Gibson who encouraged me as a theological-practitioner

and

Fr. Len Hagel who encouraged me as a teacher.

ACKNOWLEDGEMENTS

And in thanksgiving to God for:

Christine Rohs and Doug McLeod for their meticulous text-proofing and editing suggestions; the Rev. Douglas Skoyles who introduced me to the writings of Vladimir Lossky and John Meyendorff; Canon Dr. Michael Green who has inspired me as a friend, and in his gifts as a theologian-practitioner; Ralph Carter, who introduced me to the writings of Dr. Hugh Ross; Dr. Titus Matthews (former Dean of Physics, University of Calgary) who gently helped me stay on a track honoring the integrity of both faith and science in their own right; Bill Reimer of Regent College bookroom, Vancouver, who offered sage advice concerning the book publication industry. Grateful thanks to Prof, Dr. George Egerton (University of British Columbia) who is a great encourager to me and who offered me perceptive advice in preparing the manuscript for this book. Also to the people of St. James,' Calgary, and St. Mary's Gate, Victoria, who, in a variety of ways, helped me consider deeper perspectives of the Big Story of the Bible. To my beautiful wife Verna, who is a wonderful partner in our shared ministry for the Gospel of Jesus. In a variety of ways, all of these wonderful people have motivated me to view the biblical story from 21st century perspectives. Finally, to our glorious Lord God who woke me on many occasions with insights I didn't understand!

Table of Contents

INTRODUCTION

Eden's joyous dance is the story of God's embrace with His chosen Bride. From a panoramic perspective, we may see that the people of the dance are often very ordinary people; they experience moments of ecstatic embrace, they dance the wrong steps, they invent their own steps, they disobey, they despair, they reach great heights, and they reach the lowest depths. Their most significant struggle is in allowing God to take the lead steps of the dance. Ultimately, the dance is the story of God's absolute sovereignty: The Lord of the Dance once more leads the right steps while embracing His adoring bride in the arms of His engaging love. In the story of the dance, we will see some astounding conclusions arising from looking at the Bible through a new set of lenses. Instead of viewing the Bible in the light of *two covenants, one old and one new,* we shall look at the Scripture from the perspective of *three theological seasons.* Coupled with a view of attempting to observe *biblical time* from the perspective of God's eternal present, the Bible reveals some *startling answers* to very old questions. Questions of free will, eternal life, the resurrection of Jesus, and last things may never be answered the same way again!

****

Possibly, today is a time closely akin to the days of building the tower of Babel. No one can stand eyeball-to-eyeball with God and dialogue with Him on an equal level. We have built enormous towers of knowledge. For some, such attempts symbolize the desire to meet Almighty God on their own terms. *Paradoxically, we see clearly in this story that the only people who can embrace the dance of Eden are those who are willing to bow the knee in worship.* We now know that the rate of increase in knowledge is much more than doubling every year. The question is one concerning how well we use such knowledge. It would seem that the authentic biblical scholar enjoys a personal relationship with God, and is therefore intimately acquainted with the Big Story of a people living in close relationship with their Lord.

Somehow, it would appear that 21st century people are much more sophisticated and knowledgeable than were their forebears. Is that so? Actually, Hugh Ross, a Christian astrophysicist, tells us how much the world of physics has changed since the 1990s. Consequently, "...the community of scientists now considers the idea that God created the universe 'a more respectable hypothesis today than at any time in the last hundred years. Denial of theism among astronomers is now rare, and even the few dissenters hint at the strength of the evidence."1

My good friend, and former parishioner, Dr Titus Mathews, who is a previous dean of physics at the University of Calgary, hastens to remind me that physics and faith are both disciplines in their own right. God cannot be proven through scientific tools. Or, as Mark Worthing also puts it, "...neither do I wish to imply that science can 'find' God - that is, conclusively verify either God's existence or nonexistence." 2 However, he does go on to say that the two disciplines need not be entirely divorced from each other. "For Torance, therefore, any attempt to explicate knowledge of God apart from the structure of space-time which God created is inevitably irrational."3 In this book, I will not attempt to violate the tools with which both science and faith operate, but simply to help one discipline glean a better understanding from the other. And so, we may well ask, "Is science the only legitimate way to address questions of progress? Is there a credible place for the entire area of *biblical revelation*?"

In the mid 1960's, Michael Caine starred in the troublesome movie entitled, "Alfie." It's not simply that Alfie reminds us of the selfishness within ourselves, but that the story reminds us of certain common failings persisting throughout the entire human story. Reflecting on this thought, I began to wonder if the Bible in some way did the same thing.

Rather than there being two stories, one old and one new, I want to suggest that the Bible is really telling us of *one Big Story*, a story of humanity's response to God. The story seems to be disjointed at times; nevertheless it is one Big Story.

For example, in the famous servant passages of Isaiah (Chapters 42 and 53), the Suffering Servant is identified by the Jewish people as the suffering and *remnant nation of Israel itself*. They may have a good case. When we examine some of the passages leading up to those famous chapters, a cursory look at such verses as 37:31-32, 41:8-9 and 43:1-3, 10 all appear to make Israel's claim for the Old Testament to stand alone a credible one. But is there something much deeper to ponder? We are aware that Matthew directly quotes one famous servant passage (Isa. 42:1-4) in order to make the deliberate point that Jesus Christ really is the unique and prophetic remnant fulfilling all those passages (Matt. 12:17-21). Is it possible that the covenant promises, and its universal unity, beginning with Abraham, are clearly fulfilled in one *remnant person?* Maybe that one person really is representative of the Suffering Servant of Isaiah? If the Bible actually speaks of one Big Story then, surely, the entire book would begin and end with Jesus as the prime subject.

In order to glean a clearer picture of this proposal we shall have to *view it in the light of God's relation to time itself.* We will also need to pursue a basic view of time, particularly as we understand it today. How does God connect Himself with time? What does it mean for God to exist in the *eternal present?* Our basic questions in this regard almost accidentally draw us into some very fascinating areas of questioning.

What about free will and predestination? Is God really a sovereign God? Does He change His nature because of humanity's enfolding history? How does our view of time change our appreciation of the meaning of the cross, or the meaning of the resurrection? Can there really be a place called hell? What is the relation of time to spiritual gifting? How does the meltdown in creation's relationships affect the way we must think of latter days? Is there a tangible connection between, "It is very good" (Gen. 1: 31), and the Bible's view of new creation? (Rev.21:1-3) It will be almost unavoidable to hold together the idea of there being one Big Story in the Bible without noticing how easily these questions just naturally appear in both parts of the one Big Story.

In our pursuit of the meaning of biblical time, I will be exploring the following paradigm: I entitle it, *Moments of Light.* It will certainly force us to look at the questions mentioned, but many other questions will also emerge.

We note that physicists continually persist in their search for a "theory of all things."4 Similarly, we may also ask if it is a futile search when trying to find ultimate meaning in one Big Story of the Bible. But, quite possibly, a single theory may be found in this simpler paradigm; it may occur by applying it to *the breakdown of creation's relationships.* If so, then we ask: What is the place of humans in this primary meltdown? Must we now discard the Bible's basic tenets? And, will our exploration of its Big Story show that the Bible is no longer worthy to hold the exalted position it once held?

I will tell the story as one who has been profoundly affected by the discovery of its meaning. But, in order to maintain my own credibility, does this mean that I have to admit to a loss of credibility for the Bible? Sometimes, the God of fundamentalism holds great difficulty for me. However, in the writing of this book, I am persuaded more than ever, that *the Bible holds supreme authority in all matters pertaining to the fundamentals of the Christian faith*. Unlike an Agatha Christie novel, I have decided to lay my cards down at the beginning of the story.

Introduction

1. Ross, Hugh, Creation and Time, p.130. NavPress, Colorado Springs, Colorado 80935. (1994)
2. Worthing, Mark W, God, Creation, and Contemporary Physics, p.4 Augsburg Fortress, 426 S Fifth St., Box 1209, Minneapolis, MN 55440 (1996)
3. Worthing, Mark W, p5
4. Kung, Hans The Beginning of All Things, (English translation J. Bowden) Eerdmans,Michigan 4905 p.1(2007)

Chapter One

GETTING ON THE SAME PAGE

In order to avoid confusion in communication, we will need to have a common understanding of certain terms and concepts we will use. I used to be a journeyman electrician. Like many other vocations, there were certain assumptions involved in doing that job. As in most trades and disciplines, when working together, electricians had to learn the basic terminology, and the common purpose associated with a particular task. For one, we had to have a *common understanding of the words* we used and the principles which those words conveyed. When things weren't going the way they were intended, and when trouble-shooting, electricians usually reverted to an examination of *first principles*.

For example, if all the lights went off in a large factory room (with the switches on!) we didn't systematically examine every individual light bulb. *We would check the source first.* It was only when we were satisfied that the primary source was intact that we would proceed with an *isolation process* within the system. Nothing can operate, as designed, if the parts are not properly connected to the *source, and to each other.* Getting to the roots for the analysis and solving of difficulties will be a primary theme throughout this book. *In other words, what do we learn from creation principles?* Unfortunately, as Christians, we often focus our thinking on secondary issues; often to the detriment of examining our source relationships.

When expressing divergent views, we must ask: Are we all really speaking from the same understanding of Gospel story principles? (Gal. 1:6-7) It's a very important question for today! So, to continue with our electrical example, we could say that no matter how much electrical energy we think should be applied to a cooking stove, the conclusion would be quite meaningless if the apparatus in question were really a gas stove! That matter would be a question for people of another field, or religion! But, if we are speaking about one story in the Bible, not two, we are dealing with unique parameters to the exclusion of others. Let's look at some of the terminology employed in this book.

Moments of Light

The term that I call *Moments of Light* will figure prominently throughout the entire book. It's all about *what was revealed* through certain historical points in the story of Israel, and the New Israel which followed.

> *The term speaks of a datable period (or rather, event) in history at a time of God's appointment. In it, God reveals that the meaning of the event has profound theological significance for the entire story.*

It is not so much a matter of the amount of time involved, but the *meaning* of the event, itself. Always, in these Moments of Light, God *reveals* something of His nature and purpose for His creation. For example, the entire incarnation of Jesus Christ may be described as a *Moment of Light*. Somewhere back then (whatever point it was in the process of creation) God said, "Let there be light." We need to know what that event means in terms of God's revelation to us.

Chronos may be defined as the succession of time from one datable point to another. Kairos may be defined as a time of God's appointment. For example, in Galatians 4:4 the Apostle Paul tells us that *at the right time* God sent His Son into the world. Both of these words are very important for our consideration of the term, *Moment of Light*. But they are not enough to offer the full depths of its meaning. In a wider sense, we are saying that the very structure of this book addresses the idea of *theological time* from the perspective of three seasons we call, creation, redemption and restoration. In the process, numerous questions will arise. But, when our unique term is applied to the entire biblical story, some very exciting perspectives begin to emerge.

Miracle: May be described as: divine involvement during the normal course of nature. Somehow, God's involvement does not completely conform to the laws of the natural world of science, knowledge, and reason - as we know them. By its very nature, it is always an act "from above."

The 25-30 "fine-tunings" physicists identify in the creation process of the earth, or the raising of Jairus' daughter from the dead, are good examples (Mark

5:21-23, 41-42). However, on the one hand, much too much is sloppily attributed to the concept of the miraculous. Miracle and mystery are not the same word. Sometimes the word is attributed to situations that are just simply extraordinary. On the other hand, *both fact and miracle are absolute necessities in the understanding of the Gospel story.*

We can't appreciate the significant depth of the meaning of *mystery* unless we ponder why biblical writers insist that miraculous events took place at some points in history. However, God doesn't play dice with the lives of people. Did He decide who would survive the Titanic? Did that answer satisfy questions of God's nature to relatives of those who didn't survive?

Without dismissing the subject, *faith, reason, and fact* are all elements that are necessary to understand the Gospel story. At least, that's the case if we want to approach the subject with a modicum of integrity. The question of miracle is a pivotal dividing point separating conservative and revisionist thinking today. Indeed, for many revisionists, the acceptance of the very idea of miracle equates with the abdication of independent thought.

Apostolic: Here, we are not limiting the word to a particular order of ministry. For example, long after the death of Jesus, the Apostle Paul speaks of ordinary, anointed people being involved in apostolic ministry (Eph. 4:11). The word *apostle* is simply a Greek word (apostello), which means, *to send.* In that sense, God is apostolic: a sending God by virtue of sending His Son into the world (John 3:16). Similarly, Jesus sent His community into the world with an apostolic commission (Matt. 28:19-20). But we read that the sending God had already given an apostolic commission to His children in Eden during the very early days of their creation (Gen. 1:28).

It is here that the important charismatic element of the charge is made possible. The authority to carry out such an astounding commission would not be possible unless the Adam-Eve community had also been given the *power* to perform their task (Gen. 2:7). Similarly, neither could the community of Jesus have exercised the necessary power to mission without the personal experience of a Pentecost (Luke 24:49).

Sign: Let's think of the word "sign" as, an observable appearance of a reality it conveys. In the big picture of the Gospel, a sign is an act or a situation that demonstrates something of the very nature of God, and of His kingdom. Whenever we read of signs and wonders in the Bible, we are drawn, not only to the possibilities of life intended for Eden, but what reflects the very nature of God's kingdom. Signs are all about the dance! Wedding rings may well be a visible sign that a man and a woman are committed to a lifelong and exclusive relationship. However, the ring does not convey anything in itself. So, if my wife lost her wedding ring, she would still be married to me; whether she likes it or not!

Similarly, if we think of creation as a sign, we see that creation actually conveys that which it promises. For the Christian, Jesus is most certainly not simply a symbol of life and truth: He *is the Life and the Truth!* (John 14:6) He conveyed all that He signified by word and action. So what is the reality we want to signify in this book? The reality is all about the character and life of the kingdom of God, *as expressed in essential relationships*! What we are to realize throughout the pages of this book is that *signs* may also appear as *Moments of Light*.

Revelation in the context of time

At first sight, the meaning of this word seems to be obvious. Its roots are found in the word, apocalypse (apokalupto), which means *to reveal, or to unveil.* But the most important consideration in the exploration of our biblical journey poses the question: *Where does its revelation originate?*

Judaeo-Christian revelation is all about how God took the initiative to reveal Himself, and how He has shown something of His own nature in the process.

You may notice that I have begun using the masculine gender to describe God. It's not because God is a man anymore than He is a woman! Jesus told us that *God is Spirit* (John 4:24). Masculine language is employed for the purpose of making a clear distinction between natural religion and revealed faith. (Nature is often thought of in the feminine terms of birthing life.) In other words: God is totally independent of the nature He created. *Yet, Jesus told us to address God as Father* (Matt. 6:9). God is not an impersonal force out of Star Wars. You don't say, *"Daddy"* to Steven Spielberg's universal force (Gal. 4:6).

It's not for us to project our psychological needs onto God in order to conform Him to our image, or our needs. However, we do have to struggle with the understanding of *the God who reveals, and names Himself.* How are we able to name anything that is higher than ourselves? God doesn't have to, because there *is nothing* higher than Himself (Isa. 45:23). This means we are called to worship Him, *as He is, not how we think He ought to be.* We've discovered that such an idea is one of the marks of natural religion, *and that is why, all too often, when we begin our thinking from natural bases, truth (or God) becomes whatever a particular culture or individual desires it to be.* That kind of thinking sits well with the Post-Modern mind!

It's going to be very important, right from the beginning, to make a distinction between a view of revelation emanating from natural thought (good old Mother Nature), and the revelation which reveals something of the nature of our eternal God. Also, we consider how the revelation is made manifest by *God's own initiative.* Actually, distinctions may not always appear to be simple because God created old Mother Nature anyway. For example, if I made a robot and dolled it up to look like me, it would let an observer see something of who I am, but, fortunately, not a great deal! *So, creation does tell us something about God, but the very nature and character of God requires significantly more inspiration than watching stars on a clear night.*

The Bible does admit to the fact that *something of God's nature can be seen in His creation.* For example, the psalmist said:

> *"The heavens are telling the glory of God; and the firmament proclaims his handiwork" (Ps. 19:1).*

Elsewhere, King David ponders the thought:

> *"O Lord, our Sovereign, how majestic is your name in all the earth! You have set your glory above the heavens... What are human beings that you are mindful of them, mortals that you care for them? You have made them a little lower than God, and crowned them with glory and honor. You have given them dominion over the works of your hands; you have put all things under their feet (Ps. 8:1, 4-6).*

God's wonderful mountain-cathedrals, or the verdant streams meandering through rolling pasturelands, are clearly not sufficient to reveal to us what God wants us to know of His nature and character. However, they do tell us *something* of God and His love for beauty and order. Some further explanation is necessary.

Natural religion: From the very beginnings of civilization, humans have needed to grapple with forces they didn't understand or control. People figured that all the activity that is experienced in nature, whether good or bad, was directed by some sort of controlling force. Every force, like lightning for instance, was associated with a particular deity. *In other words, nothing happened unless some god made it possible.* So the old Anglo Saxons said that the deity Thor, (from which we get Thursday) was responsible for the lightning bolts which zapped their turkeys. Fear gets into the picture quite quickly.

This concept of natural religion must be raised once more when we consider methods whereby we interpret God's revelation today. *What we see in natural religion is that humans not only fear unknown forces, but they tend to produce gods that look, feel, act, or smell like something they know from nature - or from themselves!* One example that immediately comes to mind is the incident where God is credited with using a utilitarian and deceitful method in order to secure His own purposes (1Kings 22:19-23). This literal interpretation may well conform to the primitive and anthropomorphic character of natural deities. (The process of God's self-revelation was still rolling!)

But is this deity really consistent with the nature of the God whom Jesus reveals?

Clearly, there are instances when the God whom Jesus reveals is *not* consistent with earlier biblical views. For example, rather than following a deity who calls us to annihilate our enemies (Josh. 10:40), Jesus tells us to love our enemies (Matt. 5:44). The Bible records a gradual progression of how God reveals His own nature. This revelation is made complete in the Word become flesh (John 1:14). We will also see that Jesus really shakes people up when they can't get past nature, or even their own aspirations, when trying to explain the character of God.

Because there were so many unmanageable forces, *natural religion was therefore polytheistic - that is the belief in many gods.* It's interesting that the rather sophisticated Roman authorities persecuted Jews and Christians because they were *atheists.* These strange people believed in only one God! They were *monotheists*! Not surprisingly, the nature, or the characteristics of imagined deities became a reflection of all that could not be understood or *controlled*. But the gods didn't just take on the characteristics of natural forces; *they also took on the characteristics of the people who worshiped them. This is called anthropomorphism*. Not surprisingly, from the aspirations of ancient Egypt to the polytheistic religion of Rome, their deities usually *looked like people!* Sometimes, these gods looked like a mixture of person and animal. But this simplistic jaunt brings us to an important basis of how natural religions actually worked.

Natural Religion and Manipulation: Natural religion wasn't simply about submission to whatever the deities wanted; *it was all about getting them to do what you wanted!* How did they do that? They bribed the gods! It was all about *manipulation*. Tickle the gods and they will oblige. So, from the very beginning, we see that there were two forms of sacrifices. Both were designed to *create appeasement*. One was the offering of nature's own produce, such as fruit and vegetables, but the other was the offering of a life, like Mama's clucking chicken, or Johnny's yapping billy goat.

Of course, good old Mother Nature represented new life, fertility, reproduction, a good harvest next year, and a cute baby next spring. After all, in a simple agricultural society such as they knew, that was what life was all about. Not surprisingly, there was a simple and natural dimension to natural religions. *Everything was cyclical.* The seasons came and went in predictable order, and the sun came up every morning. In another part of the world, the sun god was persuaded by some Egyptian priest to wake up every morning. The sun god had to be enticed by an appropriate sacrifice. Birthing, new life, harvesting, maturity, and the cycles of nature often took on a feminist dimension. Natural religion, therefore, usually possessed an inherently feminine characteristic.

Revealed faith: Not surprisingly, when culture, or natural religion, is the source and determiner of truth, we are led to believe *that truth, concerning the nature of deity, is somehow related to contemporary situations and community needs.* There are no absolutes! (Does that sound familiar today?) By their very nature, absolutes cannot be defined; hence the need for revelation, not natural aspiration. Determining the nature of these deities becomes a little complicated, and also contradictory. That's especially true when we realize that cultural values change about every eighteen to twenty years in the western world.

Similarly, in the West, those principles are often used to decry the possibility that there may *be absolute truths or values*. This may be aided a little by the moguls of the media in promoting a globalized world economy. Political values, rather than religious absolutes, serve to put every value on the same level of truth. And so by avoiding the temptation to make God in our own image, we really do have to struggle with an integrity desiring to pursue the manner in which God chooses to reveal Himself. We, therefore need to know something of the *manner* in which He decides to name Himself (Exod. 3:14). To name a deity gives the worshipper some degree of control. How are we thinking, if we believe we can name God?

Recognizing such problems in the bases of natural religions, Judaeo-Christian writers display a number of reasons why God is described in the masculine. Masculine language is employed for the purpose of making a clear distinction between natural religion and revealed faith. In other words, *God is totally independent of the nature He has created*. God eternally transcends nature. He does not reflect the nature of creation; it is creation, at least in the beginning, that is a reflection of His nature. Actually, biblical literature shows us that God acts in both masculine and feminine ways. Clearly, we can't just label God with a characteristic or gender that suits us at any particular moment.

> *The Self-naming God reveals His own requirements as being consistent with His nature; they are designed to keep us in relationship with Him and with others.*

This concept of the morality of personal relationships is a huge dividing point between natural religion and revealed faith. Not surprisingly, the Apostle Paul shows us how faith that is based in nature leads mortals in exactly the wrong direction:

> **"For the wrath of God is revealed from heaven against all ungodliness and wickedness of those who by their wickedness suppress the truth. For what can be known about God is plain to them, because God has shown it to them. Ever since the creation of the world his eternal power and divine nature, invisible though they are, have been understood and seen through the things he has made.**

So they are without excuse...Claiming to be wise, they became fools; and they exchanged the glory of the immortal God for images resembling a mortal human being or birds or four-footed animals or reptiles" (Rom. 1:18-21, 22-23).

Now, that brings us to a very important factor in the whole story of God's revelation.

The Bible as revelation

When trying to put together crucial elements that provide a big picture of the biblical story, some aspects of biblical compilation will not receive a lot of attention. For example, there may well be two different *traditions* that speak about the creation. Many scholars are of the opinion that Chapters one and two of Genesis have different sources - they were written at separate times in history, and by people desiring to express a particular aspect of God's revelation. Priests would emphasize something about the importance of sacrifice, while prophets may emphasize something of God's revealed Word to His people.

More importantly, we see that the first chapter of Genesis records what God actually did in creation; and it then proceeds to introduce the human factor into the harmonious equation. The second chapter is much more about relations with God and other people. *In terms of our present purpose in outlining the Big Story, I don't think that anything of significance is lost by not addressing questions concerning who wrote what and when.* This would be a lesser problem when considering that many of our problems of biblical interpretation lie precisely at the door of ignorance concerning the bigger story which unfolds.

Nevertheless, we do note that many scholars suggest Moses could not possibly have written the entire Pentateuch - the first five books of the Bible. They do make a good point. For example, how could he have written about his own death, or humbly declared himself to be the greatest prophet of all time? (Deut. 34:10) Regardless of who wrote, or edited, the five books, we may well understand why they are attributed to Moses, given the enormous power of the oral tradition of those days. This tradition is no longer very strong in our modern, Western culture.

A very fine scholar, who was a good friend of mine until he went to be with the Lord, offers this simple principle of interpretation. "In such a context, it is necessary to stress that ultimately the authority of the books of the Law is to be found in their source in God-that is, in their character as revelation."1 Peter Craigie, a brilliant Old Testament professor, was fully aware of, but not overly distracted by questions of authorship. I believe that to be a good position. It is in this vein that we cursorily note apparent contradictions, such as we see in comparing 1 Samuel 31:4-5 with 2 Samuel 1:6-10, or Matthew 27:5 with Acts 1:18. Clearly, a variety of traditions have helped biblical compilers to glean a bigger picture.

> *So our concern is not so much about various traditions that may or may not have given us the Bible. Our interest is in what have been received and recorded faithfully as being important contributions to the whole revelation of the Big Story.*

The Church community has accepted a final canon of scripture that has left us with an impressive, real, and consistent Gospel story, supported in facts of history.

Maybe a good way to explain this process of revelation is by way of an orange illustration! It's a good way of reconciling the God of war (Who is so apparent in the Old Testament) in contrast with the more peace-loving God of Jesus. If we take this orange and begin to take off some of its peel, we would see a little of the orange underneath. We would know something of its texture and character. The more we would continue to peel, the more of the orange would be revealed. Eventually, all of the orange would be exposed. But the orange did not change in the process of peeling. At some point this illustration would break down, because the fullness of God can never be known. Only God can fully know God! He is ultimately unknowable (1 Co. 2:10-11). God does all the peeling! However, Jesus did say that, if you have seen Me, you have seen the Father (John 14:9). In other words, He is saying that, if you want to know God, then you need to know Me. It isn't the other way around. The Word of God is a Person; it is Christ (John 1:1). In this sense we may say, without equivocation:

> *The Bible records God's sovereign purposes by His involvement with the world, through the story of creation, redemption, and restoration.*

How we think of the Bible as revelation: I am not using the word, *story,* as if it were a record of some sort of historical musing, but a continuing saga *of a community as they celebrated the meaning of their dance with God.* It was a story that was intended to be passed on to chronicle the future enabling of a community embracing the dance of Eden. Peoples of different cultures and times tell of their fundamental beliefs and values in a variety of ways. When we consider this, we must begin to read the Bible from the perspective of a *Jewish person* desiring to communicate matters of importance. The fact is: Jewish people believed that God revealed certain fundamentals by becoming involved in their history. In other words:

The Bible is really a Jewish story, and is told in a Jewish way.

The Jewish mind doesn't think in the same way as the Greek (or Western) mind. "Specifically, their world was not one dominated by rationalistic philosophy, although the emergence of classical philosophy was taking place in the Greek world in the latter half of the Old Testament period."2 At his bar Mitzvah, a contemporary Jewish boy recites a story, beginning with the words, "My father was a wandering Aramean…" He knows who he is because he is part of an historical chronicle. The God whom he believes in is active in the Jewish story. There isn't a great deal of philosophy involved here.

A notable exception to what is being described is found in the person of Gregory Palamas. He was a fourteenth century pietist engaged in the eremitic tradition of the Byzantine Church. Having received a first-class education in classical Greek literature, nevertheless, he preferred the spirituality of Hesychasm. This was an approach of earlier desert fathers who had their origins in the fifth century. It was an apophatic tradition (negation). Here, there is a lessening of the positive and exclusive use of sense and reason (kataphatic). The silent approach to God was much more preferred. This was the favored method of the Desert Fathers in discerning the knowledge of God's self-revelation. "Palamas refused to give any credence to what the ancient philosophers said of the knowledge of God. He developed a realistic doctrine of supernatural knowledge, independent of any sense experience but granted in Jesus Christ to man."3

We see that the Greek, or Gentile, mind is more likely to articulate essentials of life from a rational perspective. Greco-style writers of today are more likely to lean on their analytical inheritance. It was a tradition begun through people like Aristotle and Plato. In answer to the question, how do you know that God loves you? the Jewish boy will tell a story while his Greek friend may debate the relative merits of love through the reasoning of words, such as agape, philia, and eros.

Let's face it. The Greek response is more likely to be the way we moderns of the Western techno-communication age prefer to think. It's no wonder, when Western people of this inherited mindset look at a controversial passage of scripture, that they often prefer to view it through Western, rational eyes. God didn't reveal Himself to Jewish people as if He were addressing the nation of Denmark, or a Parisian convention of philosophers! A modern Dane doesn't think the same way as did an ancient Jew! *So it's very important for us to get into the heart and mind of the Jewish believer.* In other words, the Jewish person is a *person of memory! He, or she, knows the meaning of personal identity because of the engagement in a common story* (which also requires a high degree of intellect in its translation to life situations). So Judaeo-Christian theology is tied to *real events of the Big Story.* In other words, the essential belief of these two faith communities was tied to verifiable events enabled through *Moments of Light.* The most significant point we note here is that the best of *Jewish scholarship has rarely ever been divorced from the story of Israel as a community.* (This will be an important consideration when we trace the nature of authority in the New Testament.)

You may want to check out the different techniques the Apostle Paul employed when offering his apologetic to the faith. It's almost possible to see his mind shifting gears when he speaks to the Athenian debaters on Mars Hill (Acts 17:20-34) and then, sometime later, when he makes his defense to a hostile Jewish crowd in Jerusalem (Acts 22:1-20). What we see here is that, in one instance, Paul makes identification with a crowd by starting his address from the basis of natural religious thought. It's very *propositional*! In the other instance, he immediately identifies with a Jewish crowd by identifying with their *common story,* and then by enlarging upon that same story with a Christian apologetic. *Maybe it isn't coincidental that both Jews and Greeks held one annoying irritation in common: the question of Christ's resurrection.* We'll certainly get to that later!

The Bible as revelation for today: Present day revisionists tend to view faith statements in the Bible as emanating from *evolutionary processes inspired* *and transmitted through the mores of culture.* Consequently, the word *miracle* rarely enters their vocabulary. With such a philosophical basis, it isn't surprising that faith statements may be ignored, *or re-symbolized* according to current understandings and values of culture. On the other hand, a blanket literalist approach (i.e., every word of the Bible has been dictated by God to scribes, prophets etc.) is likely to produce a more *fundamentalist* approach. Of necessity this method would entail a defense of every biblical word and concept as being equally valid for all time. However, a much more difficult, but rewarding approach, is an historical one that struggles with the methodology, such as Jesus adopted as a Jewish person speaking to Jews.

Jesus wanted to view all biblical thinking in the light of creation principles. That is: what God intended at the beginning. In that light, He expected us to understand the plain sense of what He was saying.

Clearly, He felt that the revealed *principles* of creation were valid and necessary *for all times and cultures; at least, in the light of the kingdom principles creation represents.* And so, when a group of Pharisees criticized Christ's disciples for plucking corn on a Sabbath day, Jesus reminded them that, "The Sabbath was made for humankind, and not humankind for the Sabbath" (Mark 2:27). Similarly, when confronted with questions on divorce, He immediately focused His questioners back to creation principles (Mark 10:2-6). This approach was not a license to interpret scripture in whatever way was convenient, but to struggle with the meaning of the *Big Story, as God intended in the first place!* What did His hearers have in mind when Jesus spoke of Jonah being in the belly of a whale? Were they hearing it as a literal story or as a theological story? Or was it both?

Of course, we are immediately drawn to questions concerning the closed nature of revelation. *Does God still speak today?* Actually, scholars, of a variety of persuasions, speak of God continuing to reveal His will and purposes for the present. Some would say that God is a growing God. He is growing in His own nature because He is influenced by the changing insights and attitudes in His creation. But what does this say about the Judeo-Christian God who knows the beginning from the end? (Isa. 46:10) He is the God whose creation purposes will not fail?

In a more liberal view of revelation, we observe a God who continues to speak through the varieties and changes of human culture. In that sense, such people accept additions to, or revision of, the former revelation. (Whatever happened to our illustration of the orange?) Conversely, in the more conservative position, God also continues to speak. He may even use changes in knowledge and culture to reveal His will. For the charismatic-minded, the revealed voice of prophecy has not become silent. However, the conservative and charismatic nature of the gospel reveals God's *will without adding to, or negating the former revelation; particularly as found in Jesus.* Yes, the earth is round and it runs around the sun. We didn't know that for sure until long after the canon of the Old and New Testaments were agreed upon. *But when you understand the peeling of an orange, such knowledge is easily adapted.*

Our conclusion here is really quite simple. *All revelation which is truly of God will be consistent with His nature; particularly as we continue to see Jesus at the heart of the Big Story*(John 14:9). We will not spend time on this rather large area of discussion here. However, one thing of utmost importance must be stated. A revelation *that is truly of God, and of fundamental value to the faith,* never reveals something of doctrinal importance that is contrary to the *revelation passed down by Christ's Apostles.* (See Jude verse three.) For example, what is truly and *uniquely distinctive* between monotheistic faiths is that the nature of the one God is, and always has been, of a Trinitarian nature. This was clearly *new knowledge* revealed in Jesus; not a change in God's nature. New Testament scholars could not avoid this startling revelation. That is why we are part of the Apostolic Faith. *The nature of God, the revelation of the faith, and the way it is relationally acted upon, are all intrinsically connected.*

Do other religions claim to possess a book based in revelation? Yes, they do, and furthermore, some of these religions claim that the words of their book were given by direct revelation from God. Or, quite possibly by someone very close to Him! Now, I don't want to get into a harangue about comparisons here; I simply want to raise one point which will be relevant for our purposes. I haven't the slightest intention of demeaning any other book or religion at all. Let freedom of choice remain, but also, *let truth prevail*! I'll mention two books here, but only to make my point a little clearer. One is *The Koran,* and the other is *The Book of Mormon.* Interestingly, both of these books hold a similar premise when claiming revelation to be the source of their faith.

There are two things common to the understanding of both books:

1. The writer (note, *one writer* in each case) claimed to receive his particular revelation from a messenger of God, *at a particular time (or period), and in a specific place,*
2. Both religions claim that their book represents the *final revelation of God,* and therefore is superior to that of all older and subsequent religions!

In the first instance, Mohammed, while sitting under a tree (some say in a cave), claimed that he received a visitation (or a number of visitations) from the Angel Gabriel. The period in question was the 7th century A.D.; it was near a place called, Mecca.4 The fact that this was but the first of 114 visitations claimed in Islam will not alter the conclusion we shall assert.5 *The Koran* (Qur'an) is the result of Gabriel's dictation. The principle of revelation coming to one person, at one period, and in one area, is intact.

In the case of *The Book of Mormon,* Joseph Smith (again, one man) claims to have received the words from golden plates which were delivered to him by an angelic figure named Moroni. Smith claimed there were two witnesses, and also that the translation of this indecipherable language took place over a period of three years. However, the rendition to an understandable language was supposedly made possible by special glasses provided for him. (This translation process, i.e., the special glasses, was likened to the Urim and Thummin of the Old Testament.)The golden plates and the glasses were then taken back to heaven. It is claimed that these visitations began around the year 1804 in the United States.6

By way of contrast, we note that *the Bible is actually a library consisting of 66 books* (the sum total of Old and New Testament literature). As such, there are probably at least *50-60 authors of these books. Also,* the period of time for their writing took place *over the course of about 1200 years!* The Bible, as we assert here, is one Big Story. We are truly amazed by the consistency of a Big Story which is a revelation of God's workings in the story of creation, redemption and restoration. No other book in the entire world has received such a measure of internal scrutiny and criticism. Actually, much of the Bible's documentary evidence is much closer to the actual recorded events than that of other reputable books, such as Plato's Republic. Yet, the Bible's long, many, and factual claims are truly amazing, and are more easily datable.

A process of revelation: Maybe, at this point, I would dare to suggest a simple way of considering what may be a credible process of biblical revelation:

1.   The true revelation of God's nature is always revealed by *the initiative of God*. Clearly, the parameters of theological thought must always be stretched. However, it is imperative, in these days of theological confusion, to discern where the *boundaries* of revealed faith end, and where the aspirations of evolving culture begin. There are absolutes in the Christian faith which are not dependent upon cultural processes! Most often, God reveals Himself in a particular context, and a culture, concerning present or future events. As such, *cultural considerations are not totally divorced from the revelation process.* If it were, then what would be the context for the revelation? Mostly, God speaks through His prophets about real-life situations; in turn, they predict, or interpret, the events in the light of God's revealed will and purposes (Amos 3:7; Heb. 1:1).

2.   The revelation becomes the *common experience of the community through which God reveals Himself.* As Christians, we do relate to a book; the Bible. However, *the Christian community was not initially founded on the basis of following a book, but the following of a Person.* Of course, the person is Jesus. And so we read in the first chapter of Acts that the choosing of an apostle to replace Judas necessitated that he be chosen only from those who had a personal history with Jesus, and had been an eye-witness to His resurrection. The most essential reality of the faith was given credibility by the *factual experience* common to its founding community. Without this commonality of experience, there would be a danger of cultic individualism being a major determiner of the faith. (Jesus, as both God and Man, and the subject of the resurrection, stands apart as the source of the historical faith.) These requirements, based in factual and common experience, are one reason why the individually subjective thoughts of poets and mystics have not contributed to the Creedal statements of the faith. All revelation in the community is tested in the community according to a common, revealed understanding of the nature of God.

In the Old Testament, it isn't uncommon for God to reveal Himself to an individual (such as a patriarch like Abraham, or a prophet like Jeremiah) but that revelation is always intended to be *addressed, tested, and lived out within the life of the community*. Of course, we observe similar constraints in the New Testament, e.g., 1 Th. 5:20-21. Therefore, in the New Testament it is very difficult, if not impossible, to discern any place where a revelation, intended for God's community, was exclusively claimed and accepted by one individual.

In the New Testament, no one is granted such exclusive and monarchical authority. Jesus never granted it to one individual. *Surely this would fly in the very nature of God existing in the community of the Trinity!* One such claim is made of Peter in relation to Matthew 16:18. However, apart from some pointed interpretations of this verse, the very same accounts in Luke, Chapter 9 and Mark, Chapter 8 do not infer that authority, associated with the revelation of Christ's divine nature, was given to Peter alone, but *to all the apostles*. (We note that the very same confession was also made by Martha before Jesus raised her brother from the dead - John 11:27.) As in the nature of the godhead, Jesus did not give monarchical authority to one person alone, but *to one community*. And that authority was intrinsically manifested in the character of agape-love which we see enveloped in the words of John 3:16.

3. The assimilations of written records are discerned in the community *and are approved, or rejected, on the basis of the authenticity of its common experience and revelation of the knowledge of God* (2 Pet. 1:20-21).It was up to the community, not an individual, to formulate and interpret the written record of the historical revelation. The *written record* is not a private revelation given to one person (2 Pet. 1:20-21). Recorded revelation has become the common experience of the revelation over time. That's also a reason why individual Christian mystics and poets have not figured largely in the transmission of basic and essential revelation. In the transmission of the Judaeo-Christian faith tradition; individual gurus do not receive prominence at all. What we see here is a reversal of the claims made in some other religions. In those situations, *the book* comes first. Subsequently, it points individuals to a common following of the book's requirements. In the Christian revelation, the Word comes first. It is the Word who reveals His words and life to the community. A subsequent existential element

comes after. All those people living after the record is produced share experience which parallels that of the earlier community. For example, throughout the ages, a theme of, "Jesus Christ is Lord, to the glory of the Father," is common to the experience of the entire historical community. We cannot place the written word above the experience of the community, or vice a versa! The Church cannot be divorced from its belief, or its belief from the community. *The community of God exists in the playing out of God's revelation.*

The Bible and theological language: There are a variety of *literary forms* making up the biblical story. These forms are often found in the major segments of the Old Testament: The Law, The Prophets, and The Writings. However, literary devices are employed throughout the entire Bible. Usually, it is easy to discern literary devices such as the poetic, apocalyptic, allegorical, analogical, metaphorical and mythological. (Incidentally, many Westerners are afraid of that latter word, and that's often because they understand its use differently than did those ancient writers. Because of such fears and confusion, I often prefer to replace the word *myth* with the term *theological story*).

John Stott warns of this when he pleads that readers of the Bible should always *look for the natural meaning of a passage*: that is, to discern the meaning that the writer wanted to communicate, "For sometimes the natural meaning is figurative rather than literal."7 Also, he asks that we try to understand that classical Greek and Hebrew thought forms are expressed in the secular language of the day.8

We must remember that the Bible wasn't written specifically to be a scientific nor an historical book. Both elements are clearly present. However, it's also clear that, whenever a chronology is presented, we are intended to take *time* seriously. The Bible speaks primarily about God, and the fact that language is employed to speak about Him means we are reading language that conveys theology, i.e., reasoning about God. So all the *literary devices the Bible employs are intended to be conveyors of theological truth*. Wonderful examples of how this approach more naturally occurs may best be found in the parables of Jesus. However, Jesus never spoke of His impending death and resurrection as something other than being factual. Clearly, the Bible does not specifically answer questions that could not be posed in the past (e.g. matters of overpopulation or medical ethics). However, it does furnish us with sufficient evidence of *the nature of God* to help the Church struggle with how God may want us to deal with such issues.

Some may still ask the question: *Why do Christians need a New Testament?* Actually, the answer may be summed up in one simple sentence:

If the revelation of God's nature and purposes were complete in the Old Testament, then there would be no need for another testament!

We will encounter more questions on this biblical journey. Augustine once said that the New is in the Old concealed, and the Old is in the New revealed. We will have to agree with Augustine if we are able to demonstrate that *the Bible is really one Big Story!* Clearly, we will have a need to appreciate the Big Story of the Bible if we are to deal with these questions. We are soon to discover how fascinating and exciting God's purposes for creation are interlaced throughout the Bible. Quite possibly, some considerable new light will be shed on scripture as we apply our unique paradigm of *Moments of Light* throughout its pages.

Chapter 1 Getting on the Same Page

1. Craigie, Peter C, The Old Testament, Abingdon Press, Nashville. TN p.216 (1986)
2. Craigie, Peter C, p.302
3. Myendorff, John. *St. Gregory Palamas and Orthodox Spirituality*, p.109. St. Vladimir's Seminary Press NY., (1974)
4. Kramer, Kenneth. *World Scriptures*, Paulist Press, New York, pps 250-251, (1986)
5. Rifkin, Ira. *Spiritual Perspectives on Globalization,* p.44. Skylight Paths Publishing, Vermont. (2003)
6. Kennedy, Richard, *The International Dictionary of Religion,* Crossroad, New York, pps 48-49 (1984)
7. Stott, John R.W, *Understanding the Bible,* Zondervan edition. P.221 (1959)
8. 8. Stott, John R.W, ibid. p.227

Chapter Two

IT'S ABOUT TIME

TIME AS THE FOURTH DIMENSION

Albert Einstein referred to *time* in this manner because it is related to the three physical dimensions of height, breadth and width. We're not getting into scientific theories of space-time, or the bending of light, or the effects on matter when traveling at the speed of light; for our purposes, we don't need to! But we do need to have some appreciation of the nature of time, particularly as it relates to us. Stephen Hawking asks us to remember that, "In the theory of relativity there is no unique absolute time, but instead each individual has his own personal measure of time that depends on where he is and how he is moving,"

One way of saying this would be to suggest that it may take me eight hours to fly to London; but from where you live, and at the same speed, you may do it in 30 minutes. On the other hand, if I could travel a hundred times faster than you, then I would certainly be the first to arrive. Nevertheless, speaking in more absolute terms, Steven Hawking goes on to say, "The situation, however, is quite different in the general theory of relativity. Space and time are now dynamic quantities: when a body moves, or a force acts, it affects the curvature of space and time, and in turn the structure of space-time affects the way in which bodies move and forces act."2 For the purposes of the Big Story of the Bible, in the world in which we live, there is no need to include this general view of time.

Nevertheless, we can't achieve our purposes if we are clearly violating basic rules of science; *at least, as we know them*! For example, we do know that light travels at the rate of 186,000 miles per second. So if we look at the nearest star through a telescope, we are actually looking at Sirius the way it reflected light four years ago. *It takes that long for its reflection to reach us!* If it were possible to arrive at that star in just an instant, and if we dragged a big telescope with us, we could look at the earth and see what we were doing four years ago. God can do that! Can you imagine looking at a planet a million light years away? It may not even exist anymore! For us, as Hawking reminds us, it doesn't mean that we could *suddenly appear* on Sirius and look at the Earth as it was four years ago.

Einstein's Special Theory of Relativity shows that if we travel into space at the speed of light our bodies are going to change! The faster we go, the quicker our teeth will ache, the sooner our eyes will pop, and the more quickly our faces will look like a melting marshmallow. In fact, if we go fast enough, *time, itself, will seem to be distorted*. We may actually come back to earth looking younger than our grandchildren! So, in our four-dimensional universe, we can't travel at the speed of light. (Unless you are on the spaceship, Enterprise, and travelling at warp speed!)

In contrast, we certainly can't say the same thing about God. After all, God is Spirit (John 4:24). He is therefore not subject to the fourth dimension of time. And, He most certainly doesn't exist in the form of matter. If all creation exists in Him, then *He doesn't change*, and He knows perfectly well what will happen four thousand, or four million years from now! That's because *time exists in Him.* (Col. 1:17). He, as its Creator, isn't subject to it at all! In other words, in the instant that space and matter began, time also began. But, in contrast, we humans are still subject to time because, as physical beings we are part and parcel of those basic laws of nature. We exist in the dimensions of height, width and depth, and are therefore subject to the fourth dimension of time. Maybe this would be news to Isaiah, but *he did pen that remarkable revelation which stated that God is able to declare the beginning from the end, and His purposes will not fail (Isa. 46:9-10)*. He really does know the future, including ours!

Science knew very little beyond that of a four-dimensional universe until very recently. Mathematicians, applying their skills to something called the string theory of basic particles, discovered that, "… in the attempt to quantify the theory it proved that a consistent mathematical description of these strings is difficult; scientists arrived at eleven or more space-time dimensions and a thousand different possible universes, without being able to explain why it was our universe in particular that became reality."[3] What we are speaking about here is what may become mathematically understandable, but in practice, very, very difficult in reality. Without entering into the realm of the bizarre, we shall consider (somewhat lightly) how a Spirit-filled Adam and Eve effectively could become stewards of God's entire creation. Would they have possessed the ability to explore the possibilities of moving through more than four dimensions? Would this have been essential for them in order to exercise global authority? Who knows?

In order to accomplish this seemingly impossible task, I would venture to raise questions of how they may have been able to exercise some degree of control in the management of time. How could they possibly take charge of what was going on in South America or Tibet when they were limited to a four-dimensional world around the Euphrates? Is it possible that Adam and Eve needed such an ability in order to accomplish His commission? Did they experience something of *multi-dimensional ability?* Is it possible that, when we see some parallel examples in the Bible, they were also signs of what was *once possible in the Eden community*? We shall spend one entire chapter considering the relationship between the event of Pentecost and the charismatic nature of the Spirit's inbreathing into the people of Eden.

By spelling out some of the *essential relationships* which signaled the creational harmony existing under Adam and Eve, we shall have a clearer understanding of what has gone wrong. In the concluding section on restoration, we shall be looking at a way of viewing eschatology. In other words, what is really happening in latter days in relation to life in Eden? Here, I shall be pointing out the reasons why the teaching of Jesus must be held paramount. Other literature, symbolic or otherwise, will be given honor, but held up to the light revealed by Jesus.

DOES GOD REALLY EXIST *IN* TIME?

Yes and No! Yet, the answer would seem to be obvious. If God created the elements which allow the dimension of time to exist, then God must have preceded time. A book which records four views on the meaning of time is simply called, *God and Time.* The editor, Gregory Ganssle, in his introduction to those four views, makes this statement, "…God is atemporal. He experiences all of his life at once in the eternal present. Nothing of his life is past, and nothing of it is future. God possesses his life 'all at once.'" 4 Quite honestly, it's not my purpose to debate the relative merits of the four views in this book, but I must say that I will present a biblical view of time very close to this one. It will be interesting to see how God acts when He already knows what is going to happen. *God is never surprised*! (However, this does not mean that God does not delight in, or is pained by, the moment.)

To God, past, present, and future all exist in the same "Moment." In other words: *Everything - past, present, and future - exists in the "Eternal Present" of God.* God, in His "eternal *nowness*," sees the finished story of the dance, even though, through the limited eyes of chronological time, it has not yet been played out. God is Spirit (John 4:24) and therefore is not restricted by the dimension of time. Another way of saying the same thing is that *God unchangeably exists in the eternal now, and He incorporates past, present, and future into Himself.* Or, it may be said that God is pained by Adolph Hitler's Holocaust, while He also views the demise of the dinosaurs, and the landing of the first man on Mars.

John Poklinghorne, a renowned Christian physicist, notes the aforementioned classical view before offering his own insight on a non-static perspective, "God relates to the whole of cosmic history' at once...A God incapable of exercising a timeless free response to a multitude of temporal free actions is just a God condemned to react to things as they happen, doing the best he can but continually having to revise his plans in the light of changing circumstances. Only God who sees all that was, and is, and is to come, 'at once,' is able to produce the best for his creation."[5] However, a little later in his book, while previously recognizing that God continues His involvement in the creation process, paradoxically, Polkinghorne also sees God limiting Himself to the unfolding natural processes He initiated.

The following statement is clearly predicated upon his assumption that God's incarnational outpouring of Himself (kenosis) also entailed laying down the eternal nature which was not subject to future time, or any time. "I also believe that by endowing his creation with the power of true becoming, God has permitted a kenosis of his omniscience, parallel to the kenosis of his omnipotence. Even he does not know the unformed future, and that is no imperfection in the divine nature, for that future is not yet there to be known." [6] (Christ, *in His humanity,* laid all things down, yet this fact did not prevent Him from gleaning from the Father the *predictive* elements of His prophetic ministry. E.g., Matthew chapter 24) The pursuit of this paradox may indeed leave room for those who believe God to be of a changeable nature; and that is precisely because He does not see the future! God, who is Spirit, is not limited to creation's dimensional characteristics. And it is in this vein we can understand how God actually does communicate something of His knowledge to us by means of *predictive revelation*. How else could the prophets speak about the future? As far as our universe is concerned, all history, all that is present, and all that is future, already exists *in* God. So we see that, in God's *Eternal Present*, grief exists, joy exists, knowledge exists, and perfect peace exists! But it all exists in God's *Eternal Present*. Let me employ a contrast of the *human, limited experience* of time. The illustration is quite simple.

My elderly friend, Anne, used to be the secretary of a church in which I was the pastor. Later, she became a pivotal part of our healing ministry at St. James' Church, Calgary. Some years later, Anne suffered from Alzheimer's disease which eventually caused her death. In my frequent visits to her at a nursing home, we arrived at a point where we no longer had common ground for sharing memories of life. No longer did we have a common past. Also, Anne was no longer able to project what our common story meant for *the future*. She was no longer capable of planning an event for tomorrow. No longer did we share a common story or a hope.

All she knew was that a friend, no longer associated with a memory of her past, came to visit. Our time together seemed to bring life to her day! However, in a matter of minutes after I left, she had forgotten our visit. Anne lived totally and absolutely in the now. Of course, her *now* held little or no memory. Clearly, for her, the present had no connection to the past or the future. We did hold a common story, but in reality, it meant very little because our story no longer was connected by a common memory. Clearly, the human experience of time is always in connection with someone else, some other event, or some common place. It is always relative to something else.

In contrast, God doesn't have Alzheimer's! As Spirit, *His eternal now encompasses all time for all ages!* And it isn't relative to anything. The *fullness* of the entire human story always exists *in* Him. And when we look at elements required for time to exist, we will realize that *it cannot be any other way!* The amazing thing is, without an understanding of time, ancient prophets of God understood this truth!

Let's jump right in here with a quotation from the Apostle Paul when writing to Colossae. Talk about revelation! Like all other prophets, Paul probably knew little or nothing of the science of time; yet this text may give us some idea of how God's present is everlasting:

"He himself is before all things, and in him all things hold together" (Col. 1:17).

Of course, Paul is speaking here of Jesus Christ through whom everything has been created (Col. 1.16, also John 1:3). Therefore, if everything holds together in Christ, and if everything has meaning in Christ, then we may say something which sounds the very opposite to an earlier question, *All creation is in God; therefore all time is in God!* Obviously, Paul is not speaking here of anything resembling *panentheism* i.e., a belief that at least something of matter is, and always was a part of God. That would make *matter and time* both inseparable from God, and therefore immortal. (But that is precisely a belief found in some Eastern religions.)

If all things hold together in God, is it then a logical next step to ask, If there is a Designer of the universe, must not the Designer also have had a *purpose* for His creation? Did He succeed? (Isa. 46:10) However, the elements of *faith and empirical data, plus the initiative of God revealing Himself in the human story are all needed.* Placing God at the centre of all things, the Apostle Paul gives us a theological perspective. For him, *God is the pre-existent One who exists in perfection before creation, and therefore before time began.* Without God's sustaining power and purpose, nothing can hold together. What we may say is that *God gives meaning, and He continually gives meaning to everything that exists.*

In this eternal sense, the pre-existent Jesus is truly the Cosmic Christ. He straddles the pages of all time (John 1:3). *He, alone, draws all time into Himself.* As the Creator of time, and the focus of its meaning, nothing can be hidden from God, because it is all *in Him.* God is fullness and perfection; therefore His nature cannot be changed by the changes and variations of time.

Actually it is very important to say this because it's fashionable today, with one view of time, to speak of the *"Growing God."Here, God is changed by external pressure and circumstance. He learns something from His own creation.* (Such an idea would presume that God has no awareness of future time, and, in some sense, ties God's very existence to the creation itself.) Roots of this thinking may be found in a type of process theology that had its beginnings in 19th century British Idealism. "God is the world-process...He is no static perfection...we are to think of God as the perfect in process, as a dynamic progress from perfection to perfection..." 7 Somehow, that statement, by itself, is self-contradictory. How is it possible to move from perfection to perfection? How can He be the perfect in process? Of necessity, it would mean that God evolved into a further stage of so-called perfection, being influenced by the next stage of creation's evolution. Doesn't this also make the Creator somehow dependent upon His own creation? Hugh Ross offers a 21st century perspective: "The remarkable advance of research reveals a God who lives and operates in the equivalent of eleven dimensions of space and time. Such extra-dimensional capacities are more than adequate to resolve the doctrinal conflicts and paradoxical issues that have divided the church and perplexed both believers and unbelievers for centuries."8

Obviously, the above view is not going to be expressed in this book because I feel that an understanding of God's unfolding revelation, in the context of the Big Story, just doesn't reveal this kind of God at all! *This growing God only finds perfection in relation to His creation.* Isn't that the very basis of primitive religion? However, I should say that some people take a slightly modified view. The old view of *impassibility* (the idea that God, in part or passion, cannot be moved in any way by His creation) has been challenged by what is often called *modified impassibility.* Now, in similar fashion, it is being described by one person as the *Open View.*

Clark Pinnock speaks of God as, "...a most moved, not unmoved, Mover."9 God can have passions and feelings that are influenced by the people He has made.10 Clearly, I realize that a little of what I present will be congruent with Pinnock, but my thesis cannot allow for conclusions such as his. Pinnock's thinking will definitely not agree with the nature of time that I will pursue throughout this book. Let me illustrate with just one of his quotations:

> *"Though God knows all there is to know about the world, there are aspects of the future God does not know. Though unchangeable with respect to his character and the steadfastness of his purposes, God changes in the light of what happens by interacting with the world."11*

For Pinnock, the movement of change within God is possible because the future hasn't happened. And God doesn't know what it is! Of course, this would mean that, in some sense, God's so-called changeable nature is somehow dependent upon movement in His creation. Then, how could God exist in absolute perfection prior to His work of creation? I'm not interested in attacking Pinnock. I admire the fact that he is forcing evangelicals to re-examine their thinking - *even if his postulations don't really work!* He leaves me with two glaring problems. They force me to conclude there is a major inadequacy in his train of thought:

1. 1. I need to be convinced that he has grappled with the *scientific nature of time* at much broader levels than he demonstrates in his book. God, *who is Spirit*, is the creator of time, and is therefore not subject to the dimensions which make time possible. Admittedly, I am purposely not delving very deeply into this area either, but I am not asking others to come alongside of my thinking, solely on the basis of hypothesis. We do have biblical data, which takes us to all sorts of charismatic realms of what is unknown - to us!

2. I wish that he had produced more *biblical data for his premise.* Let me simply give two examples:

    1) The God who is revealed in Isaiah knows the "end from the beginning, and from ancient times things not yet done" (Isa. 46:10, 65:24). In other words, *there is nothing yet to come that is not in the knowledge of God.* For a writer who knew almost nothing of the nature of time, isn't that statement an amazing revelation? As we dabble into the nature of time, we may easily understand why.

    2) Much of the prophetic literature in the Bible is not simply of a *forth-telling* nature, but of a *foretelling and predictive nature!* For example, after 1800 years of diaspora, the nation of Israel was re-established in the Middle East. This was the result of a massive return from many nations of the world. It had been prophesied! (Jer. 29:14) *Wasn't God the source of this prophecy, and also many other predictive utterances?*

We move on with our thoughts, supplemented by Hugh Ross when he reminds us, "It is reasonable to conclude that the universe must have been caused by an ENTITY who transcends matter, energy, and all the space-time dimensions associated with matter and energy."12 He goes on to say, "In Hawking's words, time itself must have a beginning. Proof of the beginning of time may rank as the most theologically significant theorem of all time, assuming validity of the theory of general relativity."13 Ross devotes the rest of the chapter to postulate how Einstein eventually was right! I am laboring this point from biblical and scientific perspectives in order to debunk the idea of God's changing nature moving from perfection to perfection. It is a sentimentalist notion. The entire postulation is circumscribed by our limited view of what I, in blanket fashion, call, Moments of Light. As we consider the nature of time, we will see that the idea of God's changing nature just doesn't work.

Pursuing the Big Story, *and in the light of God's unfolding revelation,* a different perspective on time will emerge. We are going to see that, in order for God to grant freedom of choice, He doesn't sacrifice His knowledge of future events. How will this view affect the varying views on predestination?

Will God's chosen vulnerability to human decisions mean that His original and sovereign purposes will become modified or defeated?

God may exhibit an emotion of sadness at the effects of human decisions, but His sovereign purposes and His ontological nature never change, no matter how created beings respond.

> *"...for the sake of the faith of God's elect and the knowledge of the truth that is in accordance with godliness, in the hope of eternal life that God, who never lies, promised before the ages began" (Titus 1:1-2).*

> *"...I am God and there is no one like me, declaring the end from the beginning and from ancient times things not yet done, saying, My purpose shall stand, and I will fulfill my intention" (Isa. 46:9-10).*

Clearly this God, the Alpha and Omega of life, really does know the beginning from the end. God may well be moved. (Jesus invites us to pray in order to cooperate with God.) He can exhibit passion (of His own free choice).

But it is totally absurd to assume that He has to forfeit or modify His eternal knowledge, or His unchangeable nature, in the *process.* After all, *creation is a reflection of the nature of God, not the reverse!* God is the One who exists throughout all eternity. The universe, and therefore time, was a creation of the God who eternally exists. But God is complete in the perfection of His Trinitarian nature!

We arrive at this view precisely because: First of all, contrary to the light of Christian revelation, we are often coaxed to a view of time that actually *diminishes* the essential revelation and biblical paradigm of the Big Story. Nor is it feasible to subscribe to a view that contravenes *demonstrable empirical laws of material science.* God is Truth and He delights in our discovery of its realities. The exploration of this Big Story and its purpose is consistent with most modern views of time, and will also speak for itself.

Second, we *don't use Old Testament literature as if it were a complete revelation of God's nature.* Many do, including some who participate in debate concerning matters of time and of God's individual election. And that's why they can't get around problems of their own making. However, there are many Old Testament scriptures that are perfectly consistent with revelation in the New Testament. If we are to pursue this Big Story, then we need to follow both Old and New Testaments with great care.

The Bible does speak about time extensively! The fact is that we cannot possibly understand the meaning of creation, redemption and restoration - the essential components of the Big Story - without an understanding of time. Otherwise, we are going to find ourselves enmeshed in a spiritual fairyland of sentimentalism!

TIME AND NATURAL THOUGHT

Questions regarding the meaning of time have long existed amongst thoughtful proponents of natural religion. It is important to raise this matter because, in holding a particular view of time, there really is a relationship between the nature of time in the universe and fundamental principles of belief. The major question concerns the point at which time began. A cyclic and naturalistic view of the universe would assert that the planet earth, in particular, has always existed and will continue to exist forever. It is immortal.

"Instead of having a beginning, time was thought to consist of endless eras, repeated over and over again for eternity."14 In other words, as in the patterns of nature, all things exist in cyclic fashion. The static universe, as Einstein once thought, was either expanding or contracting. A repetitive and cyclic view of time may easily become a natural corollary and, indeed, continues to remain an intrinsic and basic principle for Eastern religions, such as Hinduism or Buddhism. The belief in reincarnation is a good example. There is no doubt that both of these ancient religions had a profound effect upon the later sophistication of Gnostic thinkers. For example, Plato believed in a static universe, and he taught his students that everything was destined to be repeated in cyclic fashion. Much later, Augustine, bishop of Hippo in North Africa, (354-430 A.D.) expressed his disapproval of this repetitive and predestined view of life. It denied the uniqueness of Jesus Christ, and the thought that subsequent, predestined actions would negate the need, or ability, to choose Jesus Christ and His call upon people's lives. For him, time began at the moment of creation.15 But when was that?

In the mid-seventeenth century, the learned James Usher, Archbishop of Armagh, began his very lengthy work of determining this date on the basis of biblical manuscripts. Eventually, he believed he had found a fixed and indisputable point to refine his chronological schema (i.e. the date of Nebuchadnezzar's death - 562 B.C.). For Usher, Augustine was right, and so his date for the beginning of time was October the 22nd 4004 BC at 6pm!16 However, although Oxford and Cambridge Presses were producing Bibles, and inserting this date alongside Genesis 1 until the very beginning of the 20th century, science had not yet discarded the belief in a static universe. In many disciplines, such as geology, archeology, and biology, new questions and time frames were unfolding. But *space* was to become the major frontier upon which the questions of time were to be played out.

In order to fix a date for the beginning of time, and by accepting that the universe had been in a condition of expansion, or in subsequent contraction from the very beginning, Albert Einstein produced a formula which he felt would still preserve the notion of a *static universe*. However, quite quickly, he realized that, in stating this position, he had made his "biggest blunder." And so, in 1917, he produced his cosmological constant. It was a formula designed to explain a constant rate at which the universe would expand until something, like gravity, would reverse the process. However, the age of the universe turned out to be considerably less than the 13.4 billion now accepted by most natural disciplines.17 Much earlier, at the time of his death in 1882, Charles Darwin had not settled on the static universe theory. Nor had he accepted the proposed younger date of a universe being just a hundred million years old.

Although never intended to be a book of science, the astounding power of biblical revelation made known a *Creator* who exists before time began (John 1:3). The Apostle Peter was surely correct in asserting that a thousand years is as one day in God's view (2 Pet. 3:8).What does 13.4 billion years mean to God? The expanding universe is precisely what God intended. *If it is true that humanity occupies only about two seconds on the chronological clock of the universe, so what?* God will accomplish His purposes for humanity in His own way, and in His own kairos time. "God is Spirit" (John 4:24). He is not subject to the factors of time that He brought into being.

TIME: A LAYPERSON'S VIEW

For our biblical and gospel purposes, by accepting the concept of time as part of our four-dimensional universe, *we need not go beyond the fact that God reveals His purposes to us in the context of time as it is played out in this universe.* Here, we also see that time is contingent upon other factors. In the four-dimensional perspectives in which we quite narrowly think of our life, of our purpose and existence, *time is not an abstract notion.* Why does it take me eight hours to fly to London? The reason is obvious. There's a lot of *space* between Calgary and London. But, if there's no such *place* as the planet earth, then both Calgary and London could not exist as distinct entities either. If there is no space between Calgary and London, then there is *no distinction* between them, and hence no need for the places to have distinctive identities. *There must be measurable space in order to define distinct places in relation to one another.* A very tiny blob of matter, which once exploded in all directions, was truly the reason for the beginning of time. *Space between two points, or places, introduced the reality of time.*

In order for me to get to one place from another, I have to pass through space (or distance). And, no matter how fast I travel, it will take a certain amount of *time;* which is also relative to space and speed of travel. Even if I walk just one step, I have crossed space, and it has taken a measurable time to do it.

There's a very simple principle here: It really doesn't matter what the distance is between two points, it takes time to cross that space.

In other words, because there is place and space, there is also time- no matter how fast it's traveled! (Except at the speed of light!) There is also a measurable distance on the circumference of the sun or the moon. There is time involved between two points and the space between. All material things are like that. Therefore, in order for the earth to spin around the sun, there is going to be time involved. In chronological terms, we call that measure of time, "one year." In simple terms it's now possible for us to think of an easy and simple principle:

Time is related to Space and Place.

This very simple principle will be of the utmost importance when we consider the dimensions involved in discovering the meaning of a place called hell. We humans live in a material, four-dimensional universe, and so, in these natural terms, we are subject to an equation such as the one proposed. Imagine if Calgary didn't exist, or never did, then it would be totally meaningless to postulate how much time it would take to travel from London to this non-existent place. *So, if we take either place or space from the equation, then we have lost a means whereby we can think of the dimension of time.* The consideration of time *requires* the dimensions of both place and space. The point that I am getting at, with regard to this book at least, is that, as far back as we may think of life on this planet, all parts of that description were in place.

> *There was no such thing as time until God caused space and place to exist. "Let there be…" At that inexplicable "moment," by the power of the Word, there was a mighty explosion. From that millisecond on, there was a continuing separation of place and space. So time began! And time increased with the further emergence of place and space!*

We have always thought in terms of place, space and time, therefore:

> *in all our thinking about existence, we cannot think of time again without relating it to place and space. Nor can we think of place and space without including time.*

A THEOLOGICAL WAY TO VIEW BIBLICAL TIME

We have already alluded to a connection between *creation, redemption, and restoration*. The Bible story may best be understood by viewing it through the paradigm of those *three theological timeframes*. This paradigm has its meaning in a story. God has entered into, and has become involved in this living story. Using a broad brush of our *creation principles*, we may see that the simple use of the word *creation* means that we are gleaning its primary principles from a particular point in history:

Creation: There is a definite point at which God says, "It is very good." He is satisfied that *all which emerged at this one particular point is exactly what He intended*. There were no surprises! And this beginning of the biblical story is when He spoke into His creation. It's a word which summarizes *all that God purposed* when He decided to make the world. (The key to our thinking here will centre on the power of the Word of God.) What is the connection between the Word of God and His activity in creation?

We may start from a particular point at which creation stands as a sign. In itself, it is a sign pointing towards God's purposes for the world. Many of these purposes and principles are *signed* in the story of a place called Eden. The story of Eden therefore provides much of the beginning and substance for all good theological thinking. Jesus did it all the time! How often did He remind us to go back to creation stories? e.g., Mark 10:5-6. *If we don't know what the original purposes of creation were, then how can we possibly understand the ramifications of what has gone wrong?* Is it possible that conservative evangelicals begin their thinking in the wrong place? Is it also possible that liberal thinkers begin at the wrong place? For many, and most often, the gospel story has its genesis from *redemption principles onwards*. Do modern revisionists make a similar mistake when their thinking begins with *justice principles of restoration*? Could it be that the starting point for Jesus is often the very point which made religious people angry?

As a starting point for our exploration of theological principles, we will certainly ask such questions as: In what way does paradise relate to, "Let there be…"? What practical implications are there in relating creation to restoration? How do the latter days relate to creation's principles?

I am suggesting that these three words in question may admirably sum up a theological view of time enabling us to peer, ever so tentatively and awesomely, into the mind of God. They help us to see the Bible as one big package. In summary, *creation is all about what God intended in the beginning.*

Redemption: This word is often used to mean, *to buy back*. It's a word that will need some explanation. The redemption story is really a chronicle of how God set about the task of *rescuing the purposes He intended in the beginning. Rescue* is a good word. The whole point of ransom "...is our rescue from a perilous predicament through the very costly self-giving of Jesus. Rescue and costliness are the point."18 It speaks equally about a salvation extended to humankind *so that, in some measure,* humanity's *stewardship of all creation could still be a signature of what God designed.* How may we know the meaning of salvation unless we can see how far we have moved from God's creation purposes? *Of course,* alongside salvation is the word *deliverance.* This word speaks of *being delivered from the* ultimate *consequences of a creation gone wrong.* (Col.1:13)

The much longer story of redemption has its climax in the very costly offering of Christ's death on the cross. It is here we will be drawn into addressing questions such as: Was He really dead for nearly three days? How is it that God can offer redemption to those who died before His awesome sacrifice? How could redemption be offered to all those who died after Christ? How may redemption be offered to those who have died without ever having heard the Gospel? Or, how does the power of the cross radically affect our lifestyle, motivation, and the meaning of justice in our time?

Restoration: The concept of restoration lays wide open the questions concerning human freedom; particularly as it relates to the sovereignty of God. *It's all about how God has brought about the restoration of all that He intended in the beginning of creation.* The climax to this story is the resurrection of Jesus Christ from the dead. In an astounding revelation to the prophet Isaiah, God reveals that *He does know the beginning from the end; His purposes will not fail* (Isa.46:10). Given our modern understanding of time we marvel at how the writer of this passage (apart from God's revelation) could possibly understand what he was writing. How does this fact affect certain modern thinking which limits God's view of the future?

By taking this perspective of a theological process, some firm-standing positions of *both conservatives and revisionists* are held in question. For example, is the forensic view of conservative evangelicals adequate for finding a central focus for the faith? Is the centrality of the cross the most important tenet of the faith? We are proposing that the major creation principles *are really all about relationships.* So we will look carefully at what those relationships are and how they are played out; even during latter days. The reason why relationships are a primary principle of creation is very simple. *In Trinitarian life, God is a relational being!* Then, does God intend relationships to be at the very heart of all He has created? Or, is He telling us that some sort of legal standing is of the utmost importance?

This question is truly imperative today when we consider that modern revisionists also gravitate to a position where a legal piece of paper (such as one denoting that a baptism has taken place) is sufficient for full entry *and position* within the Christian community. In itself, that position may not be all bad, but can it possibly be acceptable to God when there is not an equal commitment to walk in the *revealed pathways of His holiness?* Most certainly, in the Bible, moral standards of behavior, and certain abilities, are clearly required for those in leadership (1 Tim. 3:1-13). We see this question to be particularly poignant when essential principles of revelation are ignored.

This is certainly a sensitive issue when we read of behavior which the Bible shows us to be threatening to the maintenance of God's *essential relationships.* Deviation from this behavioral path is also seen to be highly offensive to the awesome holiness of God. Is it ever a biblical principle that we may come to God *on our terms?* Is it a godly way of thinking to focus on the meaning of restoration being *simply the pursuit of justice?* How can our present, multitudinous views of justice possibly be valid when God's revelation for personal transformation has been ignored? What is the real nature of justice? I want to suggest that, by focusing our thinking on one or other of these two words (redemption or restoration), the meaning of the Big Story of the Bible (creation, redemption, and restoration) is seriously diminished. The Gospel, in whole, must include the meaning and exploration of *all three words.* But what does all of the above mean in relation to God's purposes for creation? Let's look at some of those purposes.

Chapter 2   It's About Time

1. Hawking, Stephen, p.33 *A Brief History of Time,* New York, (1990 edition)
2. Hawking, Stephen, ibid, p.33
3. Kung, Hans p.15 *The Beginning of All Things* Eerdmans Publishing, Grand Rapids, (2007)
4. Ganssle, Gregory E, (ed) *God & Time-Four Views*, IVP Press, Illinois, p.23 (2001)

5. Polkinhorne, John, *The Faith of a Physicist,* pps.59-60, Fortress Press, Minneapolis, (1996)
6. Polkinghorne, John, p.81
7. Macquarrie, John *Twentieth Century Religious Thought,*p.28 SCM Press, London N1, (1983)
8. Ross, Hugh, *Beyond the Cosmos,* p.46. NavPrerss, Colorado 80935, (1999)
9. Pinnock, Clark H, *Most Moved Mover-A Theology of God's Openness,* p.3 Baker Academic, Grand Rapids, Michigan, (2001)
10. Pinnock, Clark H, ibid, p.116
11. Pinnock, Clark H, ibid. p,32
12. Ross, Hugh, *The Creator and the Cosmos,* p.97 NavPress, Colorado 80935 (2001)
13. Ross, Hugh, *The Creator and the Cosmos,* p.102
14. Gorst, Martin, *Measuring Eternity,* p.4. Random House, 1540 Broadway, New York, NY 10036,(2001)
15. Gorst, Martin, p.6
16. Gorst, Martin, p.34
17. Gorst, Martin, p.283
18. Green, Michael. *The Empty Cross of Jesus,* p.62. Inter-Varsity Press, Illinois 60515, 1984.

Charles Alexander

CREATION

Charles Alexander

Chapter 3

WHEN TIME WAS A FRIEND

AND GOD CREATED

"In the beginning God..." (Gen. 1:1) When was that? Who knows? It's actually the writer's way of employing theological language to say:

> *There was a beginning to creation, God existed before creation came into being; the transcendent God was complete in His nature before He began the work of creation and Time began when the power of the Word caused creation to come into being. From the substance of energy-matter which God had caused to exist, time began, but as yet, was not completely ordered.*

Tom Maloney, a Liverpool comedian and school teacher, tells of a boy in class who was once asked the meaning of God's ontological nature. In superb theological fashion, and as only a child can answer, he replied, *"God always was, is, and always will be, was."* Similarly, in the Gospel of John, the writer can't define the word *beginning* in relation to the work of the Word:

> **``In the beginning was the Word, and the Word was with God, and the Word was God. All things came into being through him, and without him not one thing came into being" (John 1:1-3).**

John doesn't use the word, *was* as an aorist verb (a simple past tense), rather, he employs an *imperfect tense*. It's his way of saying that it's impossible to determine a beginning for the Word, Himself. This is the living Word whom John is to declare as being the incarnate Christ. There is no doubt that the writer is clearly identifying the Word with the Genesis God of creation. In Second Peter, the writer expresses a similar thought:

"...by the word of God heavens existed long ago and an earth was formed out of water...." (2 Pet.3:5).

How did the biblical writers know that water came first? In other words, God's existence cannot be restricted to our concepts of time. For, as creatures, time has its essential nature connected to a four-dimensional universe. *Before there was space and place there was God!* He is the self-existent God whose identity and nature is complete. And God remains complete - entirely apart from His creation. The God of Judaeo-Christian thinking exists eternally, *before (if we can employ the word) anything else.* Ancient religions usually speak of their deities being connected to some form of material existing somewhere in space. It's a little like some scientists who, answering one problem by creating another, are desperately looking for basic answers from other planets as a way of answering bewildering questions concerning earth's creation. In ancient Babylonian thinking, the gods take hold of existent chaotic stuff in space; then they reshape it the way they want it. "Marduk divided the dead body of Tiamat into two parts. 'Half of her he set in place and formed the sky therewith as a roof.' Next he established the earth, the residences of the gods, and the constellations."1 These deities really don't have any meaning or existence apart from nature. Such thinking may also provide a basis for pantheistic belief. (Pan means "all," while theos means "deity" or "god"). So everything is god!

Here, deity and creation are intrinsically connected; one cannot exist apart from the other. In that sense, creation itself is eternal, and always will be, was! Consistent with the cycles of nature, time itself goes round and round in circles. (That's why *reincarnation is at the very heart of many natural religions, and this natural view is becoming more popular in the Western world.* As we shall see, with a right understanding of the words, it will be impossible to believe in reincarnation and the resurrection at the same time.) But the ultimate goal in pantheistic belief is to lose all sense of personal identity in order to become absorbed into Pan, into the *all* of everything. However, in some Hindu thought, everything material is an illusion anyway; *nothing is real!* (This thinking was to become influential in later Gnostic thought.)The force that gives this illusion is called, Maya. 2

PHYSICS AND ANCIENT SPIRITUALITY

Strange though it may seem, similar thinking does exist today, but with major roots in early twentieth century thought. However, there's been a brand of humility that has edged its way into the scientific world ever since the advent of Quantum Physics. Most scientists now engage with the word *mystery* in ways they never have before. And so, in recent years, we now hear such language reaching far beyond Enlightenment thought. It speaks of scientists *never able to answer* all the questions they pose. In today's world of science, the more predictable, macroscopic laws of physics (about big, cosmic things, such as Newton's laws of the universe) can no longer be considered to have sole or primary sway. Conversely, in the micro world of particle behavior, many of the givens are found to be unpredictable. In the mid 1920's, Werner Heisenberg's Uncertainty Principle helped us to appreciate the unpredictability of particle behavior. Nevertheless, there are many today who would give *disproportionate weight to New Physics*.

Physicists are generally agreed that Newtonian and Quantum physics are both important; they need each other. (As a physicist friend once told me, "Both disciplines were needed to put a man on the moon.") Those of whom we speak, when exalting micro over macro science, tend to downplay the notion of a transcendent God; especially as the creator of all things. However, many do think there may be an existent force, like a universal mind.3 *Some, in this vein, may more easily gravitate to a monistic spirituality which speaks of the "oneness" of all things.* It's close to the Star Wars belief in some kind of natural force. This impersonal force represents a form of *universal oneness*. In spiritual terms, this has paved the way for many Westerners to adopt principles of Buddhism into their spirituality. Subsequent efforts in the West to unite all religions on the basis of this oneness will ultimately fail. There may be a modicum of institutional success; however, Christian integrity cannot but maintain the view which holds all things together in the life of the Trinitarian God.

Since the 1990's modern physicists who believe in an ever circular, directed universe have become a rarity. *The Big Bang appears to be a demonstrable fact, and as a growing number of physicists now concede; because there was a beginning,* *there must also have been a Beginner, or a Causer.*4 Francis Collins (the head of the Human Genome Project) laments the fact that many North American Christians tend to divide people into believers in God, or believers in the evolutionary process.5 Clearly, most deeply committed theistic physicists cannot accept this simple polarization; they believe God was present and involved in all the stages of the evolutionary process.

Natural views concerning an ever-repeating, cyclical universe are in sharp contrast to the Judaeo-Christian revelation of a linear universe. There is a beginning leading to an end. And the end is known by God. He is the Alpha and Omega. Here, God is the Creator of everything, and yet, absolutely *distinct from everything He has made.*

GOD DOESN'T NEED US AT ALL!

The point we make here, concerning Judaeo-Christian thought, is that God exists eternally; He has no need for anything at all. *God doesn't have to create in order to be God*! He is complete in His oneness! The New Testament is even clearer about the reason why God had no need for anything else in order to complete Himself. God exists in the complete and perfect relationship of love expressed in Three Persons; One God in Three Persons - Father, Son and Holy Spirit. Trinitarian views of God in Christian thinking have been in sharp contrast to that of other monotheistic religions.

Trinitarian thought is very clearly a dividing point in the understanding of God's essential nature. Without entering into this very long debate, let us say something very quickly and simply. If God's *very nature* is that of love (1 John 5:8, not simply that God performs acts of love), then there has to be an *object* of that love. Love must also be *received* if it is to exist in perfection. *Otherness* is an essential ingredient of perfection in the nature of love. The *distinctiveness* of Persons within the Trinity is therefore seen with the Father (as focus, and as Jesus taught, Matt. 6:9) loving the Son and the Spirit; the Son loves the Father and the Spirit; and the Spirit loves the Father and the Son. Therefore, each of the Persons receives love as well as gives love to the others. It's like a circle of love with the arrows going in both directions. *It is completeness in a focus of otherness.* If this were not true, then *this* monotheistic God may well have an egocentric nature. "Egocentricity is the death of true personhood. Each becomes a real person only through entering into a relation with other persons, through living for them and in them."6 God is not One Person; a self-loving deity. Nor is God a duality; a mutual admiration society. Actually, New Testament writers never try to explain the "how" of God living in Trinity of Persons. Indeed, they avoided trying to explain what is always, and always will be, an incomprehensible mystery.

This view of a monotheistic God, aided by a few anthropomorphic brush strokes, would give rise to a possessive deity, and a jealousy, which is directed towards His creation. But also there are a lot of other things; such as going to war against those who don't believe in your god. Eternally, God exists in the perfection of oneness in community: *One God in Three Persons existing in the relational perfection of love, will, and action.* There are no arguments or secrets within the godhead!

God didn't need anything; creation was a choice, not a necessity. Many years ago I heard an evangelist attempt to answer the question, "Why did God make the world?" He replied, "God did it because He was lonely." *Not a good answer at all!* Certainly, God doesn't need us! A reply such as this means that *God needed to create*; He had a need beyond Himself; He would not be fulfilled apart from creation. The God of the Bible is completely self-existent, "Creation is therefore a free act, a gratuitous act of God. It does not respond to any necessity of divine being whatever. Even moral motivations which are sometimes attributed to it are platitudes without importance."7 So God didn't *have* to do anything; *He decided to create.* Why He made this decision, God only knows!

In the process of creating, God was *not diminished* in any way. A little bit of Him did not become intrinsically, and forever, connected to nature. God is always complete; He exists eternally apart from nature. This means when God creates, it doesn't, of necessity, mean that a little part of Him is lost in the thing He created.

God is the eternal, self-generating energy of love.

Frank Wilczek, the 2004 Nobel Prize winner in physics, shows us that the idea of self-generation is not a concept unique to the world of theology. Electric and magnetic fields, filling what was once thought of as empty space, "…can animate one another in turn, giving birth to self-reproducing disturbances that travel at the speed of light. Ever since Maxwell, we understand that these disturbances are what light *is*."8 And so, if God decided to create a hundred universes, His self-generating energy means that He is always complete. *He doesn't need to be in, around, outside or on top of what He created.* When some think that a little bit of Him is lost in there somewhere, they are thinking in terms of *panentheism.*

Another way of saying this is to suggest that, even if the universe does lose its thrust from the Big Bang, and it then begins a reverse fall, it won't come back to God. It will come back to nothing! If it came back to God, then the constituents of time would be insinuated into His nature; elements that were not there in the first instance. God is Spirit! (John 4:24)

> *However, many in the scientific community now agree that the universe will not come back on itself. It continues to move outwards at an ever increasing rate and will continue expanding forever. 9*

Some scientists suggest there may be limits to this expansion. However, Denyse O'Leary, a science journalist, summarizing the conclusions and implications of the Big Bang, records her findings in this statement, "The universe will continue to expand because it does not have enough gravity to contract. The expansion may even be speeding up because of an antigravity force."10 Interestingly, the biblical and theological perspective is one of creation being sustained by the power of God's Word alone (2 Pet. 3:5). God is still active in His universe! He is not a deistic god who does a job, then whisks away on some cosmic excursion!

When the New Testament speaks of God creating through the power of the Word, it is spelling out what is already inferred in the Old Testament. If God existed before anything else, then *He must have created by the power of His will and Word alone.* To a physicist, matter and energy are interchangeable, and therefore the same thing. The writers of Genesis and of 2 Peter didn't know that! The explanation, for some scientific believers in God, is that, by the power of His will in creating energy, a very highly compressed amount of matter came into being. This matter, containing an enormously large amount of energy, would soon burst its pent-up energy to begin the process of a physical creation. God's love, will, and actions are consistently the same. It's often put this way: *God created ex- nihilo - out of nothing!* Basil the Great (a fourth century Byzantine bishop and theologian) said, "He calls all things from non-existence into being; once things are created He keeps them in existence."11 In other words, God is the sustainer of all things.

As an astrophysicist, Hugh Ross not only speaks of God's sustaining power in His universe, but that His creativity is observable by the fact that *He was consistently fine- tuning every facet of His creation. He did that in order to make it habitable for humanity.* "Recent research shows that at least twenty-five different characteristics of the universe must be exquisitely fine-tuned for life's essential building blocks to exist...We can conclude only that the Cause of the building blocks of life is unimaginably intelligent, creative, capable, and caring."12 If physicists are correct in asserting that there was something like twenty-five to thirty "fine-tunings," then we may venture a theological statement: *In the process of creation's stages, God continued to speak into the development of earth's formation.*

A twentieth century theologian adds to this thought, "God makes the world make itself ... and this in spite of the fact that the constituents are not for the most part intelligent. They cannot see beyond the tip of their noses, they have, indeed, no noses to see beyond, nor any eyes with which to fail in the attempt. All they can do is blind away at being themselves, and fulfill the repetitive pattern of their existence."13 Actually, this statement raises more questions to my mind.

The Knowledge TV Network began a series on January 31st 2008; it was simply called, 'Time." In the second session (Feb.6th) the assertion was made by the host that, 570 million years ago, a mysterious thing happened. "An explosion of life forms suddenly appeared in the oceans." If we assume, as Christians, that this was also a point at which God was speaking into His world, then He must have had a plan for this process. Would this mean God had also planned for humanity to suffer the same fate as all other species; it would become obsolescent? If that is true, then surely, God is also responsible for the horrible processes and events which terminate life. However, in the Genesis story we see that humanity did die, outside of Eden. *But it was not in God's purpose for humans to die.* (The Genesis Chapter 3 narratives make that clear. Isn't that an amazing assertion? It goes against all that he has experienced of life.) Death proved to be a matter of choice by those passing on their DNA to subsequent generations. There is a little more involved than blinding away in isolation, but we'll get to that later.

> *In the very substance of His Trinitarian being and nature, God is a relational God.*

We are going to see that, because creation's essential meaning is *in God*, then we understand why creation itself will be called into a primary condition of relationships. That's its very nature; it reflects something of God's own nature. *Therefore, the Gospel itself will have a particular and primary focus in what I am calling, "essential relationships."* However, the creation story, by itself, doesn't say a lot about *why* God chose to create the universe.

Maybe it was for the unbridled joy of sharing the wonder of creation with the creatures that would inhabit it! (Rev. 4:11 KJV) Even though God is omniscient (knowing all), maybe it was for the sheer pleasure of watching life grow and change. (Parents enjoy watching their child grow, even though they know it will also become an adult.) Maybe it was to enable a created being (in some ways like Himself) to enjoy and utilize the utter delights of His creative genius. Maybe it's because He loves variety. After all, He had already created a heavenly and spiritual host. But that was an immaterial creation which wasn't subject to the time constraints of a four-dimensional world. One thing is certain:

> *An intelligent Creator would not have created without a purpose in mind.*

Surely, if all time exists in the Spirit-God, then we may postulate that He knew everything that was to happen with this new enterprise! (Most certainly, Isaiah would have believed the statement we see in Isa. 46:9-10.) If so, *then why did He create the world at all?* Why did He create a world that would produce the Holocaust in which six million Jews were exterminated? Why did He create a world whose inhabitants would dispassionately stand by while thousands of Ethiopian children died of starvation? Why did I have to bury two- year-old Tommy who died of cancer and blood disorders; a condition directly inherited from his alcohol- and drug-captive parents?

Unfortunately, some of our recent popular books on Christian life are not helpful to me in the struggle to know the God revealed by Jesus. For example, one Christian writer says, "God prescribed every single detail of your body...Because God made you for a reason, he also decided *when* you would be born and *how long* you would live...choosing the exact time of your birth and death...God also planned *where* you'd be born...Most amazing, God decided *how* you would be born...It doesn't matter that your parents were good, bad or indifferent. God knew that those two individuals possessed *exactly* the right genetic makeup to create the custom 'you' he had in mind."14 How may I possibly use those statements in response to the enquiry of Tommy's aunt who adopted him, or the friend who asks why he was born blind, or to another suffering the horrid effects of brain malnutrition, or the parents of a dead child who was killed on the sidewalk by a drunken driver? My question to God is: "I know *You* were not the cause of all this suffering, but why did *You bother* creating a world; especially when you knew of the immense pain that was to follow?" That will be my big question when I meet the Lord, one bright day! I'm sure this book won't answer that question. However, maybe we have to continue with *what* He did in order to glean some understanding of the *why*. Like Job, I feel that the alternatives are more likely to leave me unnecessarily annoyed and confused.

As we look at the life and message of Old Testament prophets, we are going to see why such questions are very important. They battled hard and long with questions concerning the effects of natural religions. The same problem most certainly exists in mainline Christian churches of today. A dominant philosophy of natural religion is reappearing. Although we know considerably more of the science of genetics, of DNA compositions etc., in a different way, the same thing must be said: The only way we should begin to take natural religion seriously is when scientists can create human genes out of a lump of clay. Or, or even better, out of nothing! Of course, this would mean that they would have to create that lump of clay! Only then may humans think of deifying themselves. Or, in the feminine character of *natural religion,* address themselves in terms of female deity; the matrix of a *cyclical* universe!

It is hardly ever likely that questions of purpose and values for living will be resolved by scientific equation. Yet, the human quest for meaning and truth will never be extinguished. The created will always long for identification with the

Creator! Maybe it is not too preposterous to suggest that, in our Post-Enlightenment era, we no longer need to give much credence to the blanket and feely prognostications of certain philosophers. For example, the 19th century philosopher, Ludwig Fuerbach, believed that religion was no more than human needs projected upon the clouds. Undoubtedly, with such motivation, *the deities that emerge from this approach are much more likely to appear as reflections of our own wants and needs.* However, the integrity and meaning of this very complex being, we call human, must be maintained. We maintain integrity while moving along a pathway demanding an exploration of truth.

> *Truth is truth no matter where it leads! Christians should never be afraid of what is empirically true!*

For our theological purposes, in discerning the nature of our Creator-God, we must admit, once again, that science will not, and cannot, by itself, lead us to God. Without doubt, science will never be able to describe the ineffable nature of the Creator. At some point, beyond basics of scientific endeavor, we will, paradoxically, be forced to tread *two* parallel pathways:

> *The first is the quest for scientific certitudes, and the other will inevitably be a traversing of the pathway of faith.*

Maybe that's the reason why the priests of mystery today are more likely to be found amongst scientists than amongst our revisionist clergy! It will be the latter pathway that will force us to consider, not so much the results of our human search for God, but the historical realities of *God's search for us.* Here, we enter the well-focused paradigm of God's gracious Self-revelation! By far, it is this pathway that will lead us to deeper understandings of the existence and nature of God. Here, we tread into an astounding arena of revelation. We begin to appreciate how the awesome Creator-God has entered into the historical paradigm of the human story. But the primary purpose of this book is to discern *what it is* that God has chosen to reveal to us. It is in this Self-revelation, that God makes known to us His nature and purposes for creation.

"LET THERE BE…"

Everything begins through the power of God's Word. *His will, His actions and His Word are seen to be consistently the same.* As God thinks and speaks, things begin to happen! His Word is living and active (Heb. 4:12). Try to put a timeframe to that! (You cannot until some physical characteristics are introduced into the picture.) The opening verses of Genesis present an initial picture of apparent *disorder and darkness*! So, as God is responsible for the Big Bang, then what is to happen from that point on is connected to what God has already created. In Hebrew texts the word, *ruach,* meaning breath, wind or spirit, is used to describe the Spirit hovering over this, as yet, unordered state (Gen. 1:2 - NIV). However, we must never think of this chaos as a state of erratic randomness which has no purpose, nor is it one which cannot be moved in an orderly direction. According to the Genesis writer, the Word comes into action in the creation, and in the ordering of the planet earth. But this does not preclude that God wasn't already speaking into the chaotic process. We must never assume that God was *not* responsible for the creation of this disordered state; He was.

What we are saying here is that *the apparent state of disorder is what is observed before the Light of God shines upon creation. Subsequently, by God's order, the Light of God illuminates the process in which God brings about recognizable order, form, and time.* The Genesis writer understands the Word of God to be the agent bringing about order and distinction into creation. (It is difficult to distinguish a complete separation of the work of the Spirit from the work of the Word.) Nevertheless, we are to see throughout the Bible that metaphors of chaos are often employed to describe something other than God's completed purpose. *For example, the sea is often a metaphor describing chaos, or resistance to God's purposes* (e.g., Ex. 14:15). The imagery of sea stands in contrast to that of rivers of life flowing from Eden and which denote God's Presence and promises (e.g., Josh. 3:17). In the process of creation, the Spirit is brooding over the water in order to accomplish His purposeful design from the genesis of seemingly unordered beginnings. In many, many, ways, the work of the Holy Spirit continues in the work of bringing order from apparent disorder.

"LET THERE BE LIGHT."

It was the First Day! That is a theological statement. (And for our theological purposes, we might just as easily think of "day" to be *Moment*. The creation story is remarkably poetic in character. Here, we should not think of the word *day* in the chronological framework of a twenty-four-hour period. Rather, the word introduces us to three very important theological concepts:

First, this is our introduction to the perception of time as it relates to the successive stages of *what* God has created. Our concept of time and its separation begins here! In a world possessing the dimensions of place and space, time is now present. *This is a physical universe* and, as far as we know, unlike anything of the orders which God had previously created.

Second, our scientific view that it was only matter-energy, and empty space that existed in the beginning of creation, is now seen to be erroneous. Frank Wilczek tells us that the electromagnetic disturbances that existed in the beginning, "…*are* light. So the equations predicted the existence of new kinds of things - new kinds of matter, if you like - that weren't known at the time." 15 So then, the very nature of God, Light, was impregnated upon creation at the very moment of its beginnings. Now, therefore, instead of thinking in terms of hours and minutes, the Genesis writer begins to introduce us to certain realities of *what* God has done or revealed. This event is truly to be our first consideration of a *Moment of Light!*

Third, "Let there be…" is a theological statement that introduces us to the revelation that life forms, which God calls into being by the power of His Word, are now able to exist, and be sustained in their environs. Something had to occur in the created world *before* those particular life forms could exist (Gen. 1:20-23). The awesome wonder of divine inspiration is clearly evident. What began on the First Day would be sustained and connected to *the natural lights of the Fourth Day*.

According to Rev. 21:22, there is no Fourth Day Light in the new creation. *First Day Light is the everlasting constant of new beginnings*. It represents an eternal discovery of the inexhaustible revelation of God's Holy Presence. The writer of this Genesis passage knew absolutely nothing of the Big Bang or the 25-30 fine-tunings which were necessary for life forms to exist and be sustained. He was clearly divinely inspired in stating how, by the power of God's Will and Word, a*lone, God was intimately the instigator of every stage in the creation of the universe!*

Speaking in theological terms, a Christian physicist may say that God *spoke* at least 25-30 times in order for the world to exist as we know it today! Similar thinking is already evident in the New Testament (Titus 1:2; 2 Tim. 1:9). In our description of time, we may consider God's successive commands in His fine-tuning of the Earth. They are to be the successive *moments* of speaking into His creation.

Immediately, we are riveted by the thought that *God is light* (1 John 1:5). A New Testament thought is, "God dwells in unapproachable light" (1 Tim. 6:16). He is also the "Father of lights" (James 1:17). In the conversion of the Apostle Paul, we see that *God is the life-changing power of light* (Acts 9:3-5; John 8:12). If there is to be meaning emerging from this dark and seeming disorder, then it has to be the work of the Spirit. All sense of meaning may only be seen in the light of God Himself.

Natural light does not appear until the fourth day. Fourth Day Light speaks of the reflection of nature's lights and the distinction of days and seasons. Obviously, it is not the primary light in which God calls His people to walk. *From a theological point of view,* we may say that the awesome light, which accompanied the initial moments of the Big Bang, is the energy of God's Shekina glory! It was that glory which shed light upon the disorder of dark and raw nature (Gen. 1:3). All meaning for creation has to emerge in the awesome light of God alone! *The beginning, the heart, and the end of the biblical story is the glory of God!* And so, from theological perspectives, we see that:

> *By the power of the Word, all creation is initially baptized in the illuminating light and glory of God's creative and sustaining Presence. From the moment of its beginning, the universe became a sacramental sign of God's creative love. It conveyed something of the very nature of the Infinite into the created finiteness through which blessings would appear.*

I must confess that I have struggled with the naming of my foundational paradigm. In many ways it may have been perfectly appropriate to name it as *Moments of Revelation.* Maybe that concept would be easier to grasp. The meaning of First Day is powerful. Hence, it would have been the illumination of God that *revealed* what He had begun, in contrast to the primary stages of creation. However, and upon reflection, I felt that the most lasting and powerfully poetic expression of the word *moment* may better be remembered and understood in relation to the word *light*. This will become more apparent when we begin to see historical events connected to the light of the first day. Somehow, we cannot gloss over the fact that creation was initially baptized in the light of God's glory.

Here, in this early stage, we have an amazing coincidence, or a magnificent stroke of revelation. As we have noted, physicists tell us that energy and matter is the same thing. Clearly, the writer is recording something he cannot possibly understand. The power of God's Word sheds the energy of light upon the first millisecond of creation's exploding energy. But the Source which enabled the existence of this tiny ball of matter was caused by the Word of God. ("All things came into being through him, and without him not one thing came into being" John 1:3.)

> *It is the light of God which first illuminates all that becomes possible in the process of creation.*

The Light of God exists long before the physical order of creation begins to emerge. It is not eternally connected to, or dependent upon, the substance of creation. God is Light! God's purposes have begun. In His sovereign nature they will prevail!

Obviously, from theological perspectives, it was not a continuous baptism of fire, but one which served to further and sustain all of God's purposes for creation. Initially, it was a signature event which denoted the primary difference and separation between *darkness and light*. Gen. 1:2 tells us that, before God's process of order emerged, darkness prevailed. Without this particular glorious light, creation could have continued in disorderly directions! The event provided many concomitant metaphors throughout the entire Bible (e.g., 1 John 1:7). In natural terms, although the brilliance of Baptismal Light may possibly have faded, Fourth Day Light governed the principle of the separation of day from night. Will First Day Light ever appear again? In our quest for the meaning of light we shall see how the emergence of a new order will answer this question.

John, like a good Jewish writer, presents an astounding thought when likening this principle to Jesus. (It's very difficult to accept that he was really writing for Greek Gnostics.) Speaking of Christ as the Living Word, John writes, "The light shines in the darkness, and the darkness did not overcome it." Speaking of John the Baptist as Christ's forerunner:

> **"He himself was not the light, but he came to testify to the light. The true light, which enlightens everyone, was coming into the world" (John 1:5, 8-9).**

John is speaking of new creation (John 1:12-13). He is announcing that in Christ, the light of the world, a new order is being introduced into the old order. It is a new creation, made possible only by the brilliant energy and Light of the Creator.

Now, what would that mean to a Jewish reader? Similarly, Paul speaks of a people who have been rescued from the powers of darkness in order to receive their inheritance with the saints in light (Col. 1:12-13). The writer to the Ephesians speaks metaphorically of disorderly behavior becoming visible when exposed to light (Eph. 5:1-9). In fact the Bible often contrasts, metaphorically, darkness (a chaotic condition that is an unfinished work in God's planned order) with light (*a state that is consistent with the finished brilliance of His own nature*). We are about to see that the continuing *power of God's light will be sustained in the principle of what we are calling, "essential relationships."* In other words, the entire order of creation will be held in equilibrium through the power of God-enabled relationships. These relationships are a reflection of their source, i.e., the Triune relationships eternally existent in the Creator. *This principle will be at the very heart and life of the gospel story.* In fact, we may say that the gospel story *is* about essential relationships.

The writer then moved through the various stages of creation. His use of the word *day* becomes the acknowledgment that *time has now begun (although, from scientific perspectives, he may not have known that). What we are to observe is that each so-called day was a Moment of Light.* The physical dimensions are now there to have produced the fourth dimension of time. So, as we move on through the various stages of creation, we note that each major facet was preceded by the words, "And God said." The power of the Word was responsible for every stage in creation. After each stage, "God saw that it was good." We are also called to observe how the natural light of the *fourth day* provides the process where time, days and seasons, are able to be *measured because they are governed by changing light.* The writer of this passage had no idea of the scientific implications of *fine-tuning* when creation moved in its rightful order! In other words, everything was going according to God's plan.

> *Creation was just the way God originally thought of it. And this would certainly also mean that God was involved with the fine-tuning of all creation's stages.*

He wasn't simply waiting to see what emerged from His initial command. Nor was He waiting to see what planet would best suit His purposes. "The whole cosmos was assembled step-by-step over billions of years and across billions of trillion of miles just for us!"16 Obviously, the biblical writer is describing the earth's shape according to the ancient three-tier view. We would only get upset today if we felt that the writer was compelled to write in scientific terms. All that the writer wants us to know is that, however it was done, or however long it took, *creation came into being because God said so.* The order finally emerged precisely according to His design and purpose. God was not surprised by the result!

FINALLY!

Finally, we come to the words, "Then God said." (Something was about to happen of an astounding and wondrous nature.*)* *For all time, this act of God would change the entire shape of inter-relationships within the total schema of His plan for creation.* The earth was ready for humanity, and humanity was ready for the earth. The time was now ripe; the conditions were ready for God's ultimate relational purposes to be played out upon His creation:

> *"Let us make humankind in our image, according to our likeness" (Gen. 1:26).*

When I was in theological college, an Old Testament professor explained the use of the plural as being a simple literary device. It was the *royal plural*, just as the Queen of England would use it. In major speeches she always says, "We" instead of "I." This gives the idea that she is representing something bigger than her own person. I'm a lot less convinced of that explanation today. What could

God be representing that's bigger than that of His own Person? "By myself I have sworn..." (Gen. 22:15; Isa. 45:23).

Quite possibly, as monotheism was not clearly articulated by Israel's writers in its earlier period, the polytheistic concept of the 'Most High' or the God above all gods, (El Shaddai) was the highest deity upon which most primitive seekers focused their sense of awe. However, at the time of Isaiah of Jerusalem, monotheism was being loudly proclaimed in Israel (Isa. 37:16). (Just from a reading of the very intimate 23rd Psalm I have yet to be convinced that King David was not a monotheist.) *Is it possible that the Genesis contributor was actually inspired to write of God in a magnitude, or character, larger than he could personally imagine?* What had he experienced of God's supernatural Light? This entire principle of foretelling revelation puts the revisionist followers of Enlightenment methodologies somewhere into distant shadows!

When God *decided* to make humanity in His own image, He must have been revealing something of His own nature, and of His own power in the process. Was He saying that He wanted His own nature, and His abilities, to be reflected upon the face of creation in a special way? Was this process to be spearheaded through a gifted authority given to humanity? There are enormous ramifications here:

> *If God gave to humanity the authority to rule over everything in creation (Gen. 1:28), then humanity must also have been given the ability to do the job!*

God had made creatures which were uniquely able to focus all things that exist into synchronous harmony. This new community would be the primary medium which pointed to God as the very centre of harmonious relationships.

All creation was subject to these unique creatures! (Gen. 1:28; Ps. 8:6; Heb. 2:8) Imagine the astounding possibilities that are at play here! *The Spirit, who breathed on the disorder of matter, also breathed into the human form. It was now able to exercise a powerful measure of governance and order into God's creation.* This community would have power and authority of First Day Light. There was not a time limit placed on this embryonic community; God's inbreathing of His own life was *eternal*. The Genesis Chapter 1 account, which records the command to be *fruitful and multiply*, meant that their own offspring would also be privileged with this unique relationship as "sons of God" (Gen. 6:2). Indeed, this race of Adam was intended to posses the power to hold all things, all places, and all time under his and her rule. (The command is given in plural terms - Gen. 1:28). Surely, such a command would have *required* that the community had the ability to operate above the level of what we now accept as the natural. Nothing else in all nature received the inbreathing of God, nor was it given *the authority for such a universal responsibility,* and without time restraint. What other creature could have received it? So we must consider that this ability had to be of a supernatural nature! It didn't evolve. Maybe God was fine-tuning for the thirty-first time!

Are there certain elements of multi-dimensional ability here? (Gen. 2:7) Maybe it is a far-reaching question, but the thought does raise other questions. Would this inbreathed ability to reflect God be an *essential gifting* to make possible the performance of this global task? For all the earth to be *under his/her control,* must this community be endued with a God-given ability to rise above the time constraints of place and space? We shall pursue this matter further. What we may assume, to this point, is that the Adam community, in terms of its unique power over creation, was totally focused on *using this inbreathed power to honor God's kingdom rule. In the process, they would partner with God in the playing out of His purposes.*

In particular relation to time, we may glean something in the first *sign* of Jesus (John 2:1-11). When taken as a literal event, *by the power of the Word alone,* the instantaneous changing of water to wine must rank as a natural impossibility. Similarly in Acts Chapter 8 there is that strange story about Philip and the Ethiopian eunuch. After the eunuch's baptism on the roadway, how was Philip suddenly found to be in Azotus? Certainly, in the life of Jesus, we do discern a particular measure of control over time (John 11:6). Were they signs of what was once possible in Eden? What would this commission really mean if the original Adam were indeed *restricted* by the constituents of time? How could he rule over all the earth if he had to *leg it* or *jet it* from the Garden? After all, at this stage in his existence, and from theological perspectives, time was never considered to harbor any problems! *It was certainly not an enemy,* nor was it an obstacle to his everlasting purposes. *Nevertheless, if we don't place the focus and meaning of the Adam community squarely in the nature of the kingdom of God, we may leave room for ramblings into the area of the bizarre.*

The Genesis writer most certainly didn't think of God in Trinitarian terms, but we have spoken of the perfection of God's love expressed in the Three Persons of the godhead. In contrast, although God has no need to express His love by creating a universe, *human beings are totally connected to the earth from which they were formed.* That's the main theological point the writer is making by saying that humans were created out of the clay of creation. As we shall see, and with all due respects to Origen, *they were not originally spirit-beings sent down to a physical creation.* (He called this little jaunt, the trans-migration of souls.)17 God was not to say, "Spirit you are and to spirit you shall return." Recently, I watched a TV sitcom where a little girl completely baffled her daddy with the question, "If we are all intended to go to heaven, then why should we start off on earth?" That very same question was asked many years ago by pioneers of Gnostic philosophy! It was God's plan for every *unique*, physical person of this inbreathed community to live *forever* in a material existence.

In this way, and at the right time in the process of humanity's creation, God breathed into this creature. And, from that time, the nature and creative possibilities of God were reflected upon all creation. We'll get to the above questions later. Suffice it to say right now that the first Genesis account simply declares that God created humankind in His own image (Gen. 1:27). The second account speaks little of the how. In fact, all the biblical accounts of creation are much more concerned with the *why* than the how. But one thing stands out with the intensity of a flashing neon sign. When God finished this little job, He said, "…it was very good" *(Gen. 1:31). God was completely satisfied with the product and order that had emerged.* It was no random accident! However, we must make note of a particular observation found in the first Genesis narrative:

> *God did not say "It was very good" until Adam and Eve were able to understand, and perform their place and purpose within God's schema of creation.*

John O'Keefe, a renowned modern astronomer, marvels at the complexity of the universe and arrives at an astounding conclusion. He is amazed by humanity's relation to it. "We are, by astronomical standards, a pampered, cosseted, cherished group of creatures; our Darwinian claim to have done it all by ourselves is as ridiculous and as charming as a baby's brave effort to stand on its own feet and refuse his mother's hand. If the universe had not been made with the most exacting precision we could never have come into existence. It is my view that these circumstances indicate the universe was created for man to live in."18 Not every believer, occupied in the arena of science, would totally agree. Some would deny with O'Keefe by suggesting that Darwin never claimed the human status to be self-achieved. However, they may well agree that God intended a special place for His human reflection. They were a product of First Day Light!

Francis Collins, the renowned geneticist, is also a committed Christian. He notes: "Evolution, as a mechanism, can be and must be true. But that says nothing about the nature of its author. For those who believe in God, there are reasons now to be more in awe, not less."19 Again, I must repeat that the various Christian perspectives on the *how* of creation should not cause us to be angry at, or derisive of each other. The truth of these questions and findings brings honor to God, not defensiveness. In the meantime, we press on further with the questions of *why*.

One thing is certain, the Adam community was clearly the most unique creature amongst all that had ever existed. Here was an inbreathed creature which was *both physical and spiritual in nature*. In that sense, Adam could truly be the priesthood for all creation. Standing between the eternal, I Am, and the time-governed, created, he was uniquely able to offer all creation to God in joyous worship. This creature, in both genders, was truly the priesthood of creation.

But, at that particular point in creation, was it really finished? We'll see!

Chapter 3   Creation: When Time was a Friend

1.   Finegan, Jack, *Myth and Mystery,* Baker Book House, Michigan, p.34 (1989)

2.   Kramer, Kenneth, *World Scriptures,* p.26, Paulist Press, New Jersey, (1986)

3.   Davies, Paul S. *God and The New Physics*, p.223 Touchstone Books, Simon and Schuster, New York, (1983)

4.   Ross, Hugh, *Creation and Time,* p.129, NavPress, Colorado 80935 (1994)

5.   Collins, Francis, S. *The Language of God,* p.206, Free Press, NY 10020 (2006)

6.   Ware, Kallistos, *The Orthodox Way,* p.34, SVS Press, New York, (Reprint 1986)

7.   Lossky, Vladimir, *Orthodox Theology,* p.52, St. Vladimir's Seminary Press, New York, (1978)

8.   Wilczek, Frank, *The Lightness of Being,* p.6. Basic Books, Park Av. S, NY, (2008)

9.   Ross, Hugh, *The Creator and the Cosmos,* pps, 63, 63, 95, NavPress, Colorado Springs,(1993)

10. O'Leary, Denyse, *By Design or by Chance,* Castle Quay Books, p.35 Kitchener. ONT (2004)

11. Basil the Great, *On the Holy Spirit,* p.38, St. Vladimir's Press, New York, (1980)

12. Ross, Hugh, *Creation and Time,* p.76

13. Farrer, Austin, *The One Genius,* p2, S.P.C.K., London (1987).

14. Warren, Rick, *The Purpose Driven Life, pps* 22-23 Zondervan Press, Grand Rapids, (2000)

15. Wilczek, Frank, *The Lightness of Being,* p.186

16. Ross, Hugh, *Creation and Time,* p.139

17. *The Oxford Dictionary of the Christian Church,* p.129, Oxford University Press, Revised Edition, Editors, F.L.Cross and E.A. Livingstone, (1983)

18. Strobel, Lee, *The Case for a Creator,* p.191, Zondervan, Grand Rapids, Michigan, 49530 (2004)

19. Collins, Francis, *The Language of God ,* pps.106-107

Charles Alexander

Chapter 4

FIRST DAY LIGHT ON A GLORIOUS PRIESTHOOD

Before we begin to describe the peculiar characteristics of the remarkable creature we know as human, there is need to broaden our theological picture a little more. It is very important as we tread this road *to understand that the accounts surrounding humanity's creation are primarily a theological story*. In order to walk this road we will need to place the two accounts of creation, not in opposition, but in *apposition* to each other. So I will meld the two stories in order for us to discover the bigger picture of their meaning. It's a bit like a 3D movie; you can't get the full picture until you look through both lenses of the glasses!

In the Judaeo-Christian way of thinking, how's versus *why's* are clearly different questions. Often, people who pursue scientific disciplines help us to appreciate the differences. "...if the universe is expanding, there may be physical reasons why there had to be a beginning. One could still imagine that God created the universe at the instant of the big bang...."[1] Here, a little tongue in cheek, Stephen Hawking is interested in the origin of time. He offers a scientific theory of how it all began, but wisely leaves it to others to suggest why. We can see very quickly that the greater interest of biblical writers is about the question, *why?*

At the very outset I want to present a thesis that will shape the entire direction of this book. We have seen that *God, by His very nature, is a relational God; His Light is pivotal in shaping new directions in the biblical story of relationships*. In the perfection of His Triune personhood, He created the universe with the stamp of His own nature upon it. In other words:

The planet earth, and everything in it, is intended to exist in a synthesis of interdependent and harmonious relationships. These relations are a reflection arising from the very nature of the Trinitarian God. The Creator is a relational God, and plans all nature to be a reflection of His glory.

Clearly, the motivating force that keeps all things, and all relationships of creation, in harmonious syntheses is the power of love. Why is that? It's not simply because God does acts of love; it is because "God is love" (1 John 4:8). His very nature is love. Therefore, all creation is intended to harmonize together in a synthesis of loving relationships emanating from God's nature - as He has revealed Himself. We must hasten to add that these relationships are not held together in a sloppy way. In other words, they are not brought into effect by our individual perceptions of how a love relationship is carried out. For example, Jesus once said to His disciples, "You are my friends if you do what I command you" (John 15:14; italics mine). We are talking about God here. The God, who is love, knows more about the how of love than do we. These relationships, holding together by the power of God's love, may be summarized in the following four ways:

RELATIONSHIP WITH GOD

What we are to see here is that humanity is not, and cannot be, fulfilled until it is in harmony with God, with others, with creation, and with itself. The heart of worship finds sweet fulfillment in what we are calling *Essential Relationships of creation.* God is the source and focus of all creation. It's only a matter of good sense that, as the Alpha and Omega of life (Rev. 1:8) all created things must have their meaning and purpose in Him (Col. 1:17).

Primarily, we know who we are in relation to Whose we are!

In the first account of creation we are simply told that God created humankind in his own image (Gen. 1:27). In what is probably a further tradition, a similar thought is posed in this way:

"Male and female he created them, and he blessed them and named them 'Humankind' when they were created" (Gen. 5:2).

Very clearly, we see that God created *both male and female in His own likeness* (Gen. 5:1). In other words, both male and female are created with the ability to reflect the power, the nature, the purpose, and the light of God's glory upon creation. "The glory of God is man fully human, fully alive," said Irenaeus.2 *Clearly, humanity could never find fulfillment and meaning apart from an intimate relationship with the Original - the very Source of life.*

Questions of man's essential connection with matter, or with creation itself, are clarified in Gen. 2:7. He is fashioned from the very substance of the earth; from dust! Now, that's exactly the way wild animals were created (Gen. 1:24, 2:19). The significant difference between animals and humanity is not brainpower, nor the ability to use finger with thumb; it's the inbreathed life of God! *All other creatures mostly live and move by instinct. However, humanity moves in the extraordinary reflected power of an intimate relationship with God.* They walked together in the Garden (Gen. 3:8). It is a blissful picture of harmonious relationships. The advent of Eden's full humanity was truly a *"Moment of Light"* upon creation:

> *God's essential purposes for humanity cannot be divorced from creation itself.*

To be ruled by the Spirit is the only guarantee that humanity can exercise stewardship of creation; to maintain order in God's creation (Eph. 5:18). When God created people He produced something entirely unique. But this creature was fundamentally connected to the earth. And so, in some way, humanity is designed to be connected to the earth, precisely because it is formed from the very stuff of creation.

> *So the inbreathing of the Spirit (Gen.2:7) is fundamentally connected to the empowering for universal and essential relationships.*

In further passages from Genesis, we see a clear distinction between the Adam community and other creatures that are not gifted by God in the same way. In the early Byzantine Church, they used the term Theosis to describe this unique relationship. By this inbreathing, the community of Eden had become divine in reflecting the glory of God upon creation. Adam (whose name, for theological purposes, will now represent this entire relational and embryonic community) is clearly seen to have a personal and intimate relationship with God. But essential roots of his identity and meaning are also expressed in his ability to accomplish God's purposes for the earth.

In Gen. 6:1-2 we see that the *direct descendants* of the Eden community are described as, *"the sons of God."* All other creatures, or persons, in the first six chapters of the Bible (human-like or not) are *not* afforded that designation! We note that Adam was not originally born in Eden, but that God placed him there! (Gen. 2:8) Where were his origins? It is the sons of God who have a unique connection and relationship with Him. It is the sons of God who inherit the God-given commission to maintain God's order in creation. God does not have grandchildren! He has a distinctive, first-hand, and direct connection to the Adam community. Similarly, in the Gospel of Luke, the genealogy of Jesus is traced back *to Adam, "son of God"* (Luke 3:37).

> *"When God created humankind, he made them in the likeness of God... When Adam had lived 130 years, he had a son in his own likeness, in his own image..." (Gen. 5:1, 3).*

In the prologue of John's Gospel, the Jewish writer picks up on this human distinctiveness which is played out in direct and intimate relationships:

> *"But to all who received him, who believed in his name, he gave power to become children of God, who were born, not of blood or the will of the flesh or of the will of man, but of God" (Italics mine; John 1:12-13).*

And, as we shall soon suggest, that is why there was need for an apostolic mission from Eden from the very beginning.

RELATIONSHIP WITH GOD'S COMMUNITY

The Hebrew word Adham is really a plural noun, which would be interpreted as, *"mankind."* In Gen. 3:20 we read that Eve means, *"mother of all living."* From a Genesis perspective, I want to suggest that *this description of Eve is more likely to be in reference to her being the mother of the "children of God."* This is a relational distinction! It is logically difficult to see how Eve was the mother of the population residing in the land of Nod. (Gen. 4:16-17) We note that this was the place where their son Cain found a wife. "…most scholars are convinced that *Homo Sapiens* come from what was not a very large group of early human beings in tropical/subtropical warm Africa…around 200,000 years ago…In the late Stone Age, probably far more than 100,000 years ago, this *Homo Sapiens*, presumably in small hordes, made his long way over the globe. "3

In Genesis, other people or human-like creatures did exist at the time of Cain and Abel. Some believe that, at one time, Neanderthal creatures cohabited with humans about 40,000 years ago.4 However, it's very hard to imagine that female Neanderthals would ever attract the fancy of the sons of God! (Gen. 6:2) "…Neanderthal man…was probably not a direct descendent of *Homo Sapiens,* but at any rate a relative." 5 "We should never forget that Aborigines, 'bushmen,' Asians, Europeans and Americans are not different species of human being but form a single human species, the same human race…Under our skin we are all Africans." 6

The Apostle Paul appeared to believe that all people of the earth were of the line of Adam - or, at least of a common nature (Acts 17:26). *However, Adam and Eve represent a special community in a particular time who live in a unique relationship with God.* Possessing a special inbreathing, which resulted in a unique *relationship and responsibility,* the children of Eden were clearly distinct from anything else in all creation.

In the first apostolic commission in the Bible (Gen. 1:26-28), we realize:

First of all, that this priestly and apostolic charge, (to bring the world to the worship of Almighty God) and given to both Adam and Eve, is also a commission to bring all people into the *community of the sons of God.* The entire Adam community had been commissioned as a Royal Priesthood. They were a royal community in that they were directly related to the King of all creation and had been commissioned by Him.

Secondly, after their fall from grace-filled relationships, Adam and Eve subsequently passed on a *nature incapable of effectively sustaining this apostolic commission.* Some sort of a *devolution process* had set in.

Thirdly, for the purposes of God to be sustained, the inbreathing of the Spirit would have to be transmitted to his descendent community again and again. (We will never understand the meaning of Pentecost apart from these creation roots.)

In Gen. 4:16-17, Cain leaves his homeland and settles in the land of Nod where he sired Enoch. Of course, Enoch is the prototypical figure signifying the promise that human life was originally intended to last forever (Gen. 3:3). We are to see that Enoch's home was to be a new creation. Maybe the terminology, sons of God (Gen. 6:2), could be interpreted to mean, children of an Eden community living in the purposes of God. The underlying principles of modern Darwinism are moving into more and more disciplines, most of which demand more serious investigation.7. We really do need to question the implications further. Indeed, we may do well to consider more the reason *why,* outside of grace, humanity has become a product of some sort of moral and physical *devolution!* One writer describes some problems of atheistic Darwinist's exponents from this perspective:

"First, there is the problem of their need to see Darwinism as a biological Theory of Everything. Darwinists insist on the implausible origin of life from non-life for the same reason as many of them insist on Social Darwinism. If there were any aspect of life that was not explained by Darwinism or other naturalistic, no-design theories, Darwinism would have to base its claims on evidence. And the state of the evidence is not good.

"Then there is the problem of their bad behavior. For example, Richard Dawkins, the well known atheistic Darwinist claims - on behalf of Oxford chair and as Professor of the Public Understanding of Science - that 'if you meet somebody who claims not to believe in evolution, that person is ignorant, stupid or insane (or wicked, but I'd rather not consider that)...'

"Third, there is the problem of underlying agenda. I have never heard such hard-line, aggressive promotion of atheism under the guise of science as I have heard from the Darwinists. It is, at best, amusing to hear Darwinists charge that the creationists have an underlying religious agenda, when the Darwinist's own anti-religious agenda is pretty obvious...

"Fourth, Social Darwinism (sociobiology, evolutionary psychology, and whatever the next rebrand will be called) is a Bad Idea that should just be abandoned. Every time Social Darwinism rears its ugly head, many people learn about Darwinism for the first time. They discover that learned professors think that less educated people are inferior...The chief danger from compulsory teaching of Darwinism is that any dissenting view may begin to sound reasonable by default. However, a view cannot be assumed to have merit simply because it is not Darwinism."8 One wonders if both this writer and Dawkins have really had serious dialogue with informed theistic evolutionists!

For the purposes of this book we must remember that the goals before us are of a primary theological nature. Here, we are principally concerned with the God-given nature which makes it possible for humans to live and worship in God's universal community. As such, we are not particularly concerned with the evolution versus Intelligent Design debate, or of the many varieties of Darwinism. Incidentally, in the world of science, many acknowledge how the proponents of Intelligent Design have shown something of the enormous complexity of the universe, but that, in itself, ID has not produced new discoveries in the field of science. Indeed, Francis Collins declares that "Intelligent Design fails in a fundamental way to qualify as a scientific theory." 9 However, we reiterate that our primary purpose is to look to the Self-revealing God who has involved Himself in the Big Story of the Bible. Further, He has done so by revealing something of His own nature and purposes for creation. In our contemporary world, it is important that we briefly consider some other principles arising from creation.

Human Sexuality:

Unfortunately, in many mainline church circles today, rarely is this subject debated on the basis of biblical principles, but rather in the area of sentimentality and cultural pressure.

> *God, who is otherness, never intended humans to discover their identity in the context of sameness.*

Whether or not this matter is debated as having emanated from revelation or from culture, or both, is a matter of debate. What I am suggesting here is that it seems to have emerged as a matter of *theological order*. Actually, we see in the Trinitarian nature of God that, for love to be genuine, it is not played out in an individualistic fashion either! *God is absolute completeness and oneness.* In His very nature, we see that love always has a focus of otherness. The Father, who is not the boss in the Trinity, loves the Son, the Son loves the Holy Spirit, and the Spirit loves the Father. God is the perfection of love given and received. Consequently, we may say:

*The significance of our identity and life is determined in differences
which make up the relationship of unity. There are three Persons in
one God, but each Person exhibits the difference of otherness.*

Let's face it; we really are people who need people! The extraordinary stress
and mental sickness of the modern Western world may show us that *we need to
relearn the creation principle that we exist in mutually dependent relationships.* There
are five things appearing which seem to point to an action plan devised by God:

First of all, *the work of looking after Eden requires the effort of more than one
inbreathed type of person* (Gen. 2:15). Here, we see the beginnings of community
as reflected in the nature of God. The gifts that God gives to people are shared
throughout the whole community. In the New Testament, we read that *people
need each other in order to accomplish God's purposes!* (1 Co. 12:7, 14, 18-22).

Thomas Smaille offers one reason why there is also need for difference in
gender focusing the primary community of family:

"An only son in his mother's house can easily become first and central; in his
father's house he is more likely to be kept second and subsidiary. He will not only
have a helper behind him, but a norm, a corrective, a protector over him. He will
know the safety of being second, of not being the one round whom everything
revolves, but of being dependent on somebody else who is 'greater than I.'"10

Second, we see that the creation of Eve is not an afterthought; man cannot
exist in health and harmony without the *otherness* of woman. *Man cannot be
alone!* Nor can the woman, having been taken from out of his side (Gen. 2:18).
Now, she stands with him, side by side. If God exists in the otherness of three
Persons, how can this inbreathed creature exist meaningfully in isolation of
personhood? This is not a cultural fad. Clearly, in order to accomplish God's
purposes for creation, unity is expressed through *distinction in gender, nature and
function.*

Third, man's *identity could not be realized by relating to nature alone.* That
sort of focus would probably have led to self-idolatry, or in making God into an
image reflecting man's own perceived needs (Gen. 2:20; Rom. 1:21-25; Ex.
20:4). Clearly, the Apostle Paul introduces the idea of self-idolatry into the
homosexual debate. (Indeed, the basis of such thinking would easily relate to that
of natural religion.) There is a side of us that longs to be fulfilled in the *difference*
provided by the opposite sex.

So then, completeness is discovered in *difference, not sameness*. For this reason, a child, in order to express confidence in his or her sexual identity, needs to experience good role modeling of *both male and female parents. This is clearly a creation principle.* A number of my Christian, homosexually-oriented friends, have told me that this biblical principle has been a major factor in their willingness to live a life of struggle in fulfilling the will of God. Like heterosexual people, kingdom-focused discipleship means putting the wants of self under control. It's a concept hardly understood in our Post-Modern world. Surely, the mistaken notion that Jesus said nothing about same-sex relationships arises from ignorance of His creation-centered theology. In relation to questions about divorce, *Jesus really did speak about homosexuality* by outlining God's creation purposes. From this perspective, it is absolutely inconceivable for Him even to countenance the institute of marriage in terms other than between a man and a woman (Mark 10:6-9). In the very physical intimacy of sexual oneness, how can they become one flesh?

We must not linger in an area coated in a veneer of sentimentalism. Unfortunately, when same-sex issues are often left in this, or in a political arena *which does not countenance creation principles at all,* then creation theology is abandoned. The assumption that some sort of homosexual gene exists has absolutely no scientific basis whatsoever. Speaking of the very low percentage of homosexual leanings in identical twin males, Francis Collins concludes, "...sexual orientation is genetically influenced but not hardwired by DNA, and that whatever genes are involved represent predispositions, not predeterminations."[11] *Even if there were predeterminations,* then such a discovery would merely prove that, in sin and brokenness, there has been a radical change in certain predispositions of the entire human condition. That is why all sincere Christians identify with the struggle for holiness in themselves and all others in their struggles. Therefore, heterosexual Christians can do nothing less than to come alongside homosexually-oriented people in their own *struggles* (1 Co. 6:9-10; Gal. 6:1-3). To come alongside (as we see the Paraclete doing in John 14:16-17) does not mean that such unhealthy behavior is affirmed. Clearly, in our arrogant nature, we admit that we are all lepers!

Fourth, we see that throughout creation (except possibly for worms!) *the different physical makeup of two sexes is required in order to procreate.* "Be fruitful and multiply, and fill the earth" (Gen. 1:28). Obviously, the physical structures of man and woman were designed differently. This physical difference facilitates a physical *intimacy* leading to procreation and the fulfillment of God's command to fill the earth. (Sexual behavior, other than this, depends on *mimicry* of God's design.) Clearly, in God's design, it was solely in the union of man and woman that two people could become one flesh. Isn't this the very reason why Jesus said, "For this reason (i.e., because the two are becoming one flesh) shall a man leave his father and mother and be joined to his wife" (Matt. 19:5, parenthesis mine). Not surprisingly, *there isn't even one verse in the entire Bible that supports the idea of God's blessing on same-sex relationships.* Human beings cannot bless what God has not ordained! Culture may persuade us to bless, but God's very nature and purpose does not honor it.

Fifth, *generally speaking*, there is a difference in *focus* between a man and a woman. The nature of both sexes is a primary motivator for this difference. The woman has a natural (but not exclusive) desire to be a nurturer, a supporter, enabler, and comforter. In that sense, she is usually the one who becomes primarily focused on the caring of the children of this relationship. She is mostly focused on the support, emotional and physical, which the man needs from their *peer relationship.*

For many today, traditional relationships and roles between a man and a woman are changing. This is particularly true in the area of who provides for the family. However, *generally speaking*, the focus for the woman is more *inward and local.* Maybe some roots go back to hunting and gathering, but the husband, in his very nature, usually possesses a *focus extending beyond the home.* (We may even say that his primary focus has apostolic pinions.) As the one traditionally equipped to be the provider and protector for the family, he is away from home more often. To this point, the male interest in things beyond the home has need to be larger than local. *The woman is not devoid of such knowledge, activity, or interest.* Nevertheless, for *theological reasons,* we must take seriously the differences in the natures that God has designed for His children. This is particularly true because both see themselves as contributors to a primary purpose extending beyond the home. And, in our theological interest, *the apostolic purpose of both Adam and Eve is equal.*

Both need each other in order for the commission to work. So what we see is that both apostolic and pastoral emphases are important for the work of their commission. However, the outward apostolic focus is different than the inner pastoral focus. When the pastoral focus dominates that of the apostolic focus, the community becomes inwardly centered; whether it is initiated by men or women.

The essential and healthier focus is lost. And so today, in the life of the Church, whenever we see that the apostolic focus has been diminished, numerous problems of identity and purpose arise, and confusion reigns.

Men and Women in Priesthood:

Clearly then, in the commission given to the Royal Priesthood of the Eden community, *both man and woman are priests. Generally speaking*, the man takes *leadership* in his particular expression of priesthood. However, the outward focus will not work without the nurturing and inner focus. We must not make firm rules of order where we note that God has chosen leadership in, normally, unusual cultural ways. For example, in the history of Israel, its people would have been in a very sorry state without the leadership of Deborah and Queen Esther. Historically, we now note that, although under social constraint, certain women of the past two centuries have made enormous contributions to the world of science. Given the opportunity, we would assume that women will more easily take leadership roles in their particular callings today.

Historically, men, in their providing and protective nature, more naturally take leadership roles; but not always! Today, gender roles are not quite so static. For example, many couples, convinced that the continuing closeness of a mother is vitally important for the healthy formation of their children, forfeit the material benefits of two incomes for a significant period of time. After that time, the woman often re-embarks, or sets out, on her own career or vocation. And so, from a theological point of view, in historic churches, there is absolutely no theological reason why a woman should not preside at the celebration of the Eucharist. *She is also a priest of creation.* (We will further examine the meaning of that term a little later.) But that may not mean she would naturally be the *leader* of a local church. Unfortunately, political rights have become the criterion, and not the *most effective way* in which a Christian community carries out its primary apostolic commission. The question of the most effective leadership must be paramount in the apostolic community where both men and women share in an equal priesthood of creation.

RELATIONSHIP WITH GOD'S CREATION

The *identity* of the Adam community is primarily *realized in a focus lying beyond itself.* Otherness is a primary requirement in the community understanding of its own purpose and nature. In Genesis Chapter 1, we see that this *otherness is primarily focused in God, and is expressed in a relationship with creation.* It's like another Trinitarian type of relationship, *except God doesn't need creation!* In both accounts of creation, (i.e., approximately Genesis Chapters 1 and 2) God places the Adam community in a material and physical context for a particular purpose:

> *Fashioned from the stuff of creation, humans are seen to be intrinsically connected to the earth; they are designed to be at home in the physical environment which God provided. Humanity needs the earth, but God doesn't. This is an essential principle of creation, and one which will not fail in the ultimate purposes of God.*

The purpose God had in mind is very clear. He commanded His children to fill the earth and have dominion over it. (We may even venture to suggest that this empowered community was to be a *sign to all creation* of the harmony and focus God had originally designed.) It was the beginning of a covenant relationship. Never, at any time, before or after, has there emerged another creature uniquely equipped by God's Spirit to take responsibility for the stewardship of creation.

> *Indeed, we may say that the biblical narrative on creation becomes one Big Story when it is connected to the apostolic mission given to the Eden community.*

Some people are very cynical about this passage of scripture. They think it gives license to plunder and ravage creation. *Nothing can be further from the truth*!

> **"Be fruitful and multiply, and fill the earth and subdue it; and have dominion over every living thing that moves on the earth"** *(Gen. 1:28; see also Ps. 8:6).*

The Septuagint use of the verb "katakurieuo" strongly suggests the interpretation, "*to bring under your control.*" It is very important to note here that the commission to subdue the earth (because the verb is used in the plural) *is given to both the man and the woman.* This commission is really quite remarkable: As far as we know or understand, humans are the only creatures who possess an ingrained life mission to preserve the species of other creatures. (What a strange perversion that such a passion often seems not to extend to itself!)

They are both required for an apostolic mission - i.e., a mission beyond the signature life of Eden. The commission is: *As sons and daughters of God, to raise a universal race living in an intimate relationship with Him and with all creation.* Clearly, for both man and woman, God's command is that they live with a primary *outward focus;* and quite probably, by exercising *different functions* in the command.

> *In this sense, the Adam community is clearly a community engaged in an apostolic mission. They are to become a prophetic sign to all peoples of the earth.*

We are drawn to Gen. 2:15 where it is recorded, "The Lord God took the man and put him in the Garden of Eden to till it and keep it." He was not created there, but when he was ready, God put him in an environment where he could live in signature of kingdom life.

> *God had already created the perfect arena for kingdom life into which humanity was placed; He did so in order for the Adam community to sign and focus the life of worship in a priestly ministry for all creation.*

With Eden as its base, *and also its sign to the world,* this is to be a community of proclamation; it is called *to offer all creation before God in a life of worship.* Both male and female share in this *priestly, outward purpose* they are given. Later, we are to see that it is Jesus, the Real Adam, who actually succeeds in fulfilling this priestly charge (1 Co. 15:24). It is to be the *"royal priesthood"* of Jesus, which will continue a signatory life work. As a royal priesthood, their worshipping work is to raise a universal people to become sons and daughters of God, and living in the priesthood and stewardship of all creation (John 1:12-13).

> *Clearly, theirs is a priesthood of creation; they stand at the pinnacle of all life offering all creation in unified harmony and praise to God:*

*"Let the peoples praise you, O God; let all the peoples praise
you. Let the nations be glad and sing for joy....The earth has
yielded its increase; God, our God, has blessed us." "Let heaven
and earth praise him, the seas and everything that moves in
them" (Ps. 67:3-4, 6; 69:34)*

The fact is that God intended to hang around to help them in their priestly
mission and in the enabling of *Eden as the primary sign of kingdom life.* God
doesn't partner a creature who interprets this mission as a charge to plunder His
creation. It is very clear that He is most certainly not like the deist god who
clocks off work and then moves on to take an indeterminate vacation. An
example of this continuing relationship of Creator to steward, of Lover to the
beloved, is highlighted in the picture of God walking in the Garden. God, the
consummate lover, is courting the responses of the beloved.

Actually, the question asked by God is a matter of checking out their
responses to the covenant He had established with them. "Where are you?" (Gen.
3:9) *It's a matter of both intimacy and accountability!* (Does this remind us of the
prophetic call to Israel?) God is right there, and He wants to stay! But it's more
than in simply helping His new pals with a caretaking job. We may only imagine
that God had raised that question once before. (Maybe on the occasion when
Satan stopped showing up for morning worship!)

We are to see in God's decision to give authority to his *"sons,"* that He
allows Himself to be vulnerable to the decisions humans will make. Here, Adam
and Eve possess both the authority and the power for the commission. Whether
or not we can describe this power in contemporary terms, we do know one thing
for certain: *The Spirit-enabled ability would have been absolutely necessary for
such an apostolic commission!* God allowed Himself to be vulnerable to the
decisions of Adam. But, in the choices Adam was allowed to exercise, he was also
vulnerable. Ego-driven decisions may have been attractive, but God's community
was called to work through the power of *loving persuasion.* In other words,
through means of invitation! Modern evangelistic efforts may do well to be more
firmly aligned to this creation principle

Authority without power is meaningless, and vice versa. So the power of God's
inbreathing is clearly given to embrace the ability to sign the Creator's purposes

for all He had made. This gift was given in order that work should become the worship of fashioning the world into images of kingdom life.

RELATIONSHIP WITH GOD'S IMAGE: THE SELF

Many psychologists tell us that a fundamental problem within humans is not so much that they love themselves, but that *they hate themselves!* The roots of this problem may well lie in the fact that the human search for meaning begins in the wrong places. In the agnostic and contemporary world-view of relationships, unfortunately, the reverse is the beginning and end of relationships: *They begin in a naturalist sense with the self* and evolve from there onwards. No wonder, when there is also a theistic dimension present, God, being conformed to our image, simply becomes the product or the enabler of human desires. In this sense, the idea that the philosophical premise determines the conclusion makes God the product of self-motivated feelings. Friedrich Shleiermacher, the late 18th century philosopher and theologian, understood this by asserting that human needs and feelings were placed at the very centre of religious thought.12

When Jesus commanded His followers to love themselves (Mark 12:29-31), which was understood by the expert in law to include loving their neighbors as themselves (Deut. 6:4; Luke 10:27), He was recalling them to a condition which existed in the original schema of creation. This extraordinarily complex and beautiful creature was never designed to know himself, apart from knowing others. *His predisposition to inner harmony would only be explored in the freedom to pursue the otherness of essential relationships.* With essential relationships in place, and with God as the primary focus, body, soul, and spirit are in harmony with each other; and not at *war* within themselves.

Earlier, we considered the fact that God was never diminished in the act of creating. In other words, He wasn't fundamentally connected to His creation. In the same way, He is not fundamentally connected to the creatures into which He breathed His life. This is a very clear distinction from the way of natural, Eastern religions. "The starting point of all their doctrines is that the spirit of man is a part of the eternal, universal, divine spirit, and is, therefore, by nature immortal. There is a 'spark of divinity' in every man...."13

Of course, this would mean that God became complete, once the spark returned to Him. Or, humanity is complete upon the return to the spirit realm of God. *But the reality is that this human creature was never intended to live in a world of spirit; he was intended to live in a physical environment with enormous spiritual potential.* His sublime existence is complete in his longing for partnership with God. Ps. 42:1 speaks of the human heart longing after God. This psalm proved to be a very moving experience when it was sung at the baptism of Augustine. Years later, in his *Confessions,* he wrote, "Thou hast made us for thyself and our hearts are restless till they rest in thee." 14

The Adam community is not only responsible to be in partnership with God by maintaining harmony, *but in itself.* It is an essential sign of how this harmonic equilibrium relates to the world. In our contemporary world we hear much of the idea that we have to start fixing our internal disorders by beginning with our own perceived needs. We have to spend our lives patting ourselves on the back. That requires a long arm and lots of wind! Television commercials persuade us to buy certain products, because "… we are worth it." In other words, in the worldly sense, peace within begins by looking within, and is normally accomplished through material consumerism.

This is a false premise! And the reason is primarily because the quest for serenity begins in the wrong place. It really begins with a relationship with God. This relationship is then expressed in relation to others; it moves further outward to the physical environment of which we are stewards. (God so loved the world.) The apostolic, sending God sends His children. *Resulting from the harmony of relationships, beginning with God, then community, and creation, we see that harmony within the self is almost a natural by-product.* What we observe in the creation story is an inner peace and a gracious harmony within the Adam community. No wonder, when the inner harmony of essential relationships devolves into disharmony within the human condition, *all nature* suffers the death, sickness, and disease of its resultant disharmony.

THE ABILITY TO CHOOSE

Eden, the home of perfect love, finds human expression in its sublime ability to make choices. We could not be really human without the ability to choose. "God said, 'You shall not eat of the fruit of the tree that is in the middle of the garden, nor shall you touch, or you shall die." Here is the first indication that life, which seems to have been designed for eternal existence, would be lost if this gifting were abused. It would not only be by making wrong choices but by *deciding* to make wrong choices. The ability to make choices is a good thing; but perversion of the good is possible. Obviously, such inwardly motivated choices, made in disobedience to God, have the capacity *to alter the synchronous harmony of essential relations*. Subsequently, we shall have to raise the question of whether choices are present in God's restored kingdom.

The Adam of Eden employed personal choices in many aspects of his stewardship. Adam even had choices about the things he could do to the Garden God had given him. Analogies often break down, but let me risk one for this particular context.

My wife, Verna, and I lived in a relatively new suburban area of Calgary, Alberta. In our initial scouting for new housing possibilities, we viewed a number of completed show homes. They were lovely, but the principle of the show home was, "What you see is what you get!" Actually, we were much more interested in a *"spec house."* This was a house with all the *basic essentials in place*, but *the builder had left room for modifications according to the creativity and imagination of the buyer.* But nothing of the basic intent of the designer could be changed without some consequence.

It turned out that most of the good ideas came from Verna! However, with my background and her creative input, we shared, and agreed on new possibilities for the house. In this situation, *we didn't create and build the house*. So in that sense *we were not co-creators with the builder.* However, we were given the opportunity to be *creative with the potential the builder had left open to us.* We may easily see that this view presents us with a scenario that *Adam and Eve were not commissioned simply to be caretakers of Eden, but given a charge to be creative stewards from which to model their apostolic function.* (They did not create the Garden of Eden - God did! Gen. 2:8.) Adam couldn't steward all this by himself; he needed Eve to complete God's purposes.

A HOLY PRIESTHOOD

The abundance of God's provision must have represented an exotic menu centered in "the Tree of Life" because the writer describes every tree as, "pleasant to the sight and good for food" (Gen. 2:9). God provided the means for the provisions, but Adam also had to *work for, and cultivate* this sustaining life from the ground.

"The Lord God took the man and put him in the Garden of Eden to till it and keep it. 'You may eat freely of every tree in the garden'" (Gen. 2:15-16).

But work was no sweat; it was worship! It was unbridled joy! Imagine that!

As we noted, Adam wasn't born in the Garden; he was placed there by God (Gen. 2:15). But everything they did in the Garden was in cooperation with God, and the whole of their existence was an offering of thanksgiving and praise.

The community of Eden was truly a priesthood of creation!

"…you have made them to be a kingdom and priests serving our God, and they will reign on earth" (Rev. 5:10).

So we see that *Adam's priestly relationship is played out in both communion and cooperation with God.* The Apostle Paul speaks of this living sacrifice as "spiritual worship" (Rom. 12:2). Here, the Greek word he chooses (latreia) is intended to convey the thought that all life is a sacrificial offering of worship. Also, the Apostle Peter describes God's community as, "a royal priesthood, a holy nation, God's own people" (1 Pet. 2:10). They are *royal* because they are *children of the King;* they are a *priesthood* because all of their *life was spent in offering creation to God in acts of praise and thanksgiving;* they are *God's own people because they are His sons and daughters in a relationship of awesome and joyful dependence.* They are a holy people (hagios-to set apart). They were separate and distinct from all peoples of the world.

"For you are a people holy to the Lord your God; the Lord your God has chosen you out of all the peoples on the earth…" (Deut. 7:6).

Eden is therefore seen to be the model and base from which the Adam race takes off for the fuller mission of "subduing the earth and filling it." It will remain in the memory of the Sons of God as the model of God's original purposes. Eden is the prototypical story which later finds tangible expression in a place called

Jerusalem - the physically identifiable place where God's Presence is to be found. Jerusalem, then, is later to become the city from which a commissioned community begins its mission. It is the Eden existing in signature of God's kingdom, and from which the universal invitation begins.

Chapter 4 First Day Light on a Glorious Priesthood

1. Hawking, Stephen *A Brief History of Time,* p.9
2. Ware, Kallistos, *The Orthodox Way,* p.64.
3. Kung, Hans, *The Beginning of All Things,* p.164
4. *Current Science,* Issue Feb.9th 2001 p.3
5. Kung, Hans, *The Beginning of All Things,* p.164
6. Kung, Hans, *The Beginning of All Things,* p.165
7. Strobel, *The Case for a Creator, pps.23,44-45,238*
8. O'Leary, Denyse. *By Design or by Chance,* pps. 238-240
9. Collins, Francis, *The Language of God,* p.187
10. Smaille, Thomas. *The Forgotten Father,* p.12. Ecclesia Books, Hodder and Stoughton, London, 1980.
11. Collins, Francis, *The Language of God,* p.260
12. *The Oxford Dictionary of the Christian Church,* p.1243
13. Robinson, John T., *In the End God,* p.89, Fontana Books,,London and Glasgow, (1968)
14. Marshall, Michael, *The Restless Heart,* p.78 William B. Eeerdmans, Grand Rapids, (1987)

Charles Alexander

REDEMPTION

Charles Alexander

Chapter 5

HOW DID TIME BECOME AN ENEMY?

THE PERVERSION OF GOOD

One fundamental principle of creation was that humanity could make free choices. Indeed, how could relationships of love be possible if the principle of free choice was not a reality? That's the essential nature which God implanted in Adam. With some reasonable assurance, we may say that *questions concerning the problems of evil are connected with God's decision to create a universe inherently free to be itself.* Are all the subsequent problems God's fault? This creation principle of freedom is precisely one with which the powers of evil can engage. Conversely, God "… has respected man's free will and has not forced Himself on man. Only thus could He produce beings who are not automata, but are akin to Himself."1

Satan was surely a creation of God.2 As a spiritual creation he existed before time began. (This will become a very important point when we consider the nature of his ultimate destiny.) The Big Story has never entertained the idea that there could be two gods.ii "There is no ontological evil."3 In the book of Job, Satan is described as one of the heavenly beings (Job 1:6), and *he appeared to have some sort of responsibility in connection to the earth,* and its inhabitants (Job 1:7-8).

What went wrong with him was a self-imposed egocentric process of *self-perversion.* Such a power-centered ego would not be content unless it could spread its self-centered perversion to others. In the process, *whatever is perverted will then look to him in admiration - possibly even in worship!* The self-perverted Satan was about to fly in the face of God by perverting the good in God's creation. He set his sight on the worshipful community of Eden! As the priest of creation, Adam was already capable of offering worship to God, and his apostolic purpose was universal. However, the right use of that power was tempered by the inbreathed nature of God in his life. Both *power* to perform and the very *character* of God were involved in the inbreathing. It was the *right use of that nature and power* which ensured an intimate relationship with God, but also with all that He had made.

In this context, freedom denotes a capacity to change or develop what already exists. (Adam didn't create the universe.) How else would a God of love operate? *If that were not true, then humankind would be just a little pawn in a game that God couldn't possibly lose!* (We are to see that the loving God, designing autonomous freedom, has allowed Himself to be vulnerable to the implications of creation's decisions.) But this part of the story didn't start with Adam, did it?

There is something very intriguing and interesting concerning the nature of evil. What we will see is, not so much *the ability of some diabolical creature to produce evil, but of its prideful need to pervert what is essentially good*. In Eph. 2:2 the power of evil is described as "...the ruler of the power of the air," but he may also be described as the *Prince of Perversion*. For example, many people remain loyal to institutions and nations long after their fundamental values of goodness have eroded. Dietrich Bonheoffer is a good example of a man who withstood Nazism, which had grossly perverted the honorable values of pre-war Germany. Many of his fellow clergy, with supposed biblical support, urged their congregations to "...accept the authority of every human institution..." (1 Pet. 2:13) Like many who speak prophetically, Bonheoffer found himself almost totally isolated and alone. Courageously, he also quoted Peter's paradoxical response to the religious establishment of his day:

"Whether it is right in God's sight to listen to you rather than to God, you must judge; for we cannot keep from speaking out what we have seen and heard" (Acts 4:20). This statement sounds remarkably like the response of Martin Luther in 1517. The occasion was when he addressed the pope with the words, "Here I stand; I can do no other." Eventually, Hitler (now dominated by hatred, vindictiveness, and ego-centered feelings of a Nietzsche superman) ordered his Nazi officials to execute Bonheoffer. They did it during the last few days of the war.

Loyalty is easy to pervert, especially in a crowd!

We see an example of perversion in one of the disciples of Jesus. Clearly, Judas Iscariot had the freedom to choose as his conscience or inclination led him. But in his handing Jesus over to the authorities, we are actually looking at a man who was possibly filled with honest, but sentimental intent. It caused him to become angry at Jesus. But why? Being generous, and giving him the benefit of the doubt (John 12:26), we may assume that there really was a time when *he had a genuine concern to help the poor.* Nevertheless, we remember that he never understood why Mary, with the approval of Jesus, *wasted* costly perfumes to anoint Him (John 12:5). He seems to have made other utilitarian decisions. They may have been out of *good motivation, but he never saw the bigger picture of Christ's mission.* Substance often gives way to sentiment!

What we are seeing then, is that a created spiritual being becomes self-perverted, through his own ego. Once able to live in the glory of God's reflected light, *Satan became an angel of darkness.* Nevertheless, knowing that the nature of God is one of Light, he sets out to counterfeit it. With great cunning, he appears as an angel of light.

> *"And no wonder! Even Satan disguises himself as an angel of light. So it is not strange if his ministers also disguise themselves as ministers of righteousness" (2 Co. 11:14-15).*

This raises a very important point. Is the devil responsible for everything that is evil? For example, we know that animals were tearing each other apart long before humans entered the stage of human history. Robert Capon suggests that it is a serious error, "...to fob off all the killing and eating to sin - to tie natural badness to moral evil, and to say that, if it hadn't been for sin, all the animals would have been vegetarians...We act as if only man were free, only man had knowledge, only man were capable of feeling."4 There really is a condition we may label as *natural evil.* Nevertheless, when we use the term natural evil, it does not equate with an immoral condition, but of nature pursuing its own natural course. Earthquakes *must* happen, but we don't ascribe moral questions to them unless people are killed. When a little child is killed by a drunken driver, it is not God who caused the death, but the actions of a driver out of control. Many of the questions we ask concerning evil events are not connected with the nature of God, but the nature of creation which has lost its bearings.

TACTICS OF SATAN

The Tree of the knowledge of good and evil is very important (Gen. 2:17). It represents the dreadful possibility that *Adam has all the ability needed to choose its enticing offerings - or no*t! Throughout the story of redemption, we are to see that one of the obstacles in the marriage dance is that the Bride will trip up if she doesn't follow the One doing the leading. From what we have seen to this point, we now understand that a paradox lies within the nature of Adam. Undoubtedly, *he was created good, but has equally as much freedom to choose evil.* Could it be otherwise if a loving relationship of trust existed between him and God?

Adam could have said, "No." And so, the perversion of God's original intent took place. Satan had license to roam the Garden. As some have suggested, this may not have been Satan's first attempt at messing up God's creation. For example, C.S. Lewis postulates, "It seems to me, therefore, a reasonable supposition, that some mighty created power had already been at work for ill on the material universe, or solar system, or, at least, the planet earth, before ever man came on the scene."5 "Much of the Old Testament is based on the assumption that certain supernatural beings have dominion over geo-political spheres."6 But the temptation story did not begin with Adam, did it? What I will call the *Eve Syndrome* displays the cunning tactics of Satan.

The story is seen to be a description of how Satan *exploits the gender differences between a man and a woman.* Amazingly, Satan was able to draw both the man and the woman into it. It's a way of operating that is sometimes considered to be solely in the realm of the feminine. (Even the writer to Timothy suggests this idea 1Tim. 2:14.) Both Adam and Eve were caught in it. *Both* are responsible for the desertion of their apostolic calling. It is a position which has a primary focus beyond themselves, and also their immediate environment.

The taking of the fruit may well represent *a process of turning inwards from a normal God-focus.* It's much more than a successful ten-minute *snow-job* by a smooth-talking, egotistical deceiver. In Job 1:10 we see that Satan taunted God about Job's false sense of security. Job has a hedge around him. Of course Job exhibits righteousness - *because there has never been anything in his life to test his ability to make choices!* What's the point of having that ability when there aren't any alternatives! *Here we see the willingness of God to be vulnerable to the very principles of a freedom He had purposely designed.*

The Eve Syndrome:

To a wandering desert people (as Israel became) a serpent is the most feared and natural enemy (Num. 21:6-7. It's no wonder that Satan is represented in this way. However, at this point in their story, the Adam and Eve community don't have cause to recognize a natural enemy. Everything can be trusted! *The cunning serpent first approaches Eve, not Adam.* However, it is vitally important to point out that, in contemporary life, *the Eve Syndrome is often adopted equally by men. Rightly lauding equality, men often abandon their unique gender characteristics of leadership.*

In the garden, the Genesis writer depicts the man who *represents the focus* of community decision. He is also the focus (not the power-seeking boss) of community life in God. On Adam's part, if he can't trust Eve, whom can he rely upon? In Eastern cultures of that day, as in many of ours, the man and his name provide the recognizable focus of the family (as the basic unit of community), and of its primary identity. And we note again that our present struggle is often in determining what theological principles simply *evolve from culture, and what revelation God wants to impart through culture - or in spite of it.*

The Adam community was much too bright and magnificent to be picked off quickly and easily. Here, the fruit of the tree represents a shift from a trust and dependence on God to a perverted reliance on the self. It was a perversion from the outward focus in God, to an inward focus in the self. It also represents the lie espoused by Satan that, *in being dependent upon God, humanity would be cheated of its natural ability to reach its divine, eternal potential.* Surely, as Satan reminds them, they have more than enough ability to decide what is good and what is evil; they don't need God to lay it out before them! To this point, they have clearly demonstrated their enormous abilities. What, on earth, are they *not* capable of? The ego is being tickled.

It is of enormous interest to note that the writer depicts Satan's primary target to be Eve. Yet, Adam (in Genesis Chapter 2), is seen to be the *focus* and the one ultimately responsible for the good order of the community. *The Eve Syndrome is a tactic, with regard to ethical or social issues, not normally based in substance, but couched in sentiment.* Sometimes, it lies in a self-perceived notion of what is right. Here, the revelation of the Word of God is relegated to a secondary place. The tactic continues to work today, when those who live or die on the basis of the *"Word of God"* are not challenged by present revisionists on the basis of the Word's authority. A subtle change in direction takes place when the dialogue is based in *individual feelings and subjective experience.*

Eve has a good heart! She doesn't want her husband to be deprived of anything that is good. *It is on the basis of sentiment that the Deceiver can play his cards.* Adam is not likely to distance himself from his wife's actions. He will stand by her because *she desires only the very best for him!* The subtle trap of sentimentalism was being set, and it was *through the one person who, with good intent,* may more easily fall into it. For example, we note that Lot's wife turned back to face Sodom. Probably, it was not because her primary motive was arrogant defiance, but a sentimental caring for her daughters who were losing their future husbands (Gen. 19:26).

In answer to the question of unfettered license, *without inevitable consequence, (Gen. 3:1),* Eve reminds Satan of God's warning, "God said, 'You shall not eat of the fruit of the tree that is in the middle of the garden, nor shall you touch it, or you shall die.' But the serpent said to the woman, 'You will not die; for God knows that when you eat of it your eyes will be opened, and you will be like God, knowing good and evil.'" That is often the tenor of modern discussions on values; particularly when they are influenced by the evolving mores of a globalized culture.

In other words, *"Take no account of the word of God; you cannot trust it; you have moved on from there. That was the past! God is the deceiver! Human beings are perfectly capable of finding their own way to immortality."* Here is the beginning of the notion that natural immortality is born from the womb of sentimentalism and natural aspiration. How can humanity ever die when it possesses such a natural capacity to produce life? If Adam had not been able to exercise amazing power from God, surely he could not have been tempted to use it wrongly.

Adam was standing by! (Gen. 3:6) His own ego was now being tickled. Satan had introduced a *face* to the situation. It was a beloved face. Revelation mattered nothing now. She was reaching! Adam knew it was just because she wanted the very best for him. (This is motivation that is all too easy to pervert.) She was a very good and loving wife! He did nothing to stop her! *It was a mutual decision. Adam was equally responsible for the decision! To do nothing is to be implicit in everything!*

Satan's deceptive tactic was to convince them that *salvation* (which was a word never in need of consideration) was not a word they would ever use in their vocabulary. (It is also a word that is now highly offensive to some modern revisionists.) They could live out their lives in their own way. Further, Satan's strategy was to delude Eden's community that, if things got difficult, this God would not seek them out in their troubles. However, the Genesis writer takes pains to show that the nature of God is precisely one of seeking out those who are estranged from Him.

NOTHING HAPPENED!

At least, not immediately! It just *appeared* that nothing had happened. Eve reached out, and there appeared to be no instantaneous consequences. That's the delusion which has impregnated itself upon the human psyche ever since. God had said that they would die if they made that particular self-focused decision. Right at that moment, Eve was still alive, and she was having a good time enjoying the fruit. Maybe it had all been a power ploy by God to keep them in a state of dependence. Maybe He had not wanted them to reach their full potential after all! Surely, they may even become capable of challenging God Himself! *But they were slowly changing!*

As seasons went by, Adam and Eve began to note some very strange changes. Eve was developing wrinkles! Adam was getting near-sighted! Neither of them could run around the bed like they used to! Many things, which they once considered to be ordinary, were becoming extraordinary. Adam didn't know it, but the commissioned steward of creation's relationships was slowly dying. Maybe something like a *DNA of death and decay had insinuated itself into the human condition.* An illusion of long life has become a defensive reaction to the reality of an inevitable death. "I am just 85 years young." The desire to possess a meaningful life for an extended time is always admirable. However, *in reality, old age is a terrible indignity; a poor impersonation of what once was.* In reality, the priest of creation had been rendered impotent. The commission from God was still valid for the human race, but the community no longer had the power or the character to perform it effectively.

Instead of bowing the knee in worship, their desire to stand alongside God, eyeball-to-eyeball, was growing! Maybe God didn't want them to know that they could stand so tall; and do it forever! (Gen. 11:4) *A perversion was settling in*: Nature itself, not its Creator, would become the focus for spiritual life. The game was up. Consequences for self-centered decisions were about to unfold.

God addressed the serpent with words of judgment. They were words that separated him from the divine purposes God had planned for him (Gen: 3:14).

God predicted the warlike nature of future relations with humanity. This passage has resulted in endless debate concerning its prophetic nature:

> **"I will put enmity between you and the woman, and between your offspring and hers; he will strike your head, and you will strike his heel" (Gen. 3:15).**

This is mind-boggling language! *No one ever referred to the offspring of the woman; it was always that of the man.* So what did God mean by this strange statement? It reminds us of the passage from Luke concerning the Annunciation (Luke 1:30-37).

Not everyone rushes to the conclusion that the passage prophetically looks towards a messiah from God. Many are likely to jump to the idea of a God-Man messiah that unfolded gradually.7 However, by the time the New Testament was written, there seems to be little problem with the idea that the birth of Jesus Christ made sense of the statement in question. Being fully God and fully Man, Jesus was a man, born of the will of God and also the seed of a woman.

Of enormous significance is the statement God makes to Adam. "Cursed is the ground because of you" (Gen. 3:17). Here we see that the cursing of the ground declares the fracturing of one more of the inter-relatedness of essential relationships. *The harmonious relationship of humanity with creation will now be a struggle throughout all time.* Adam will earn his living by the sweat of his brow. Work will be more difficult to offer as an act of worship, but will become a burdensome act of toil. In that toil, he will eventually return to the dust from which he was formed (Gen. 3:19).

Being rendered to dust meant that he returned to a state of permanent unconsciousness in connection to all things, including himself. As dust, time would have no more meaning for him. As dust, the necessary constituents of place and space would have no meaning. *Time could not exist without place and space.* "For the wages of sin is death…" (Rom. 6:23)

Plato thought that there was a spark in everyone that could never die because it was connected to the spirit of all oneness. He felt that the *"nexus,"* a bridge to the divine spirit, became crossable by means of intellectual enlightenment. (That's an idea not too far removed from Hinduism. That religion had a profound influence on later Gnosticism.)c However, the late Bishop John Robinson said that the Jews tended to think simply of soul and body. Nevertheless, he didn't feel there was an essential difference between the two concepts. The Greeks were really quite close to the Hebrews with their view of body, soul, and spirit. Like the ancient Greeks, Robinson also believed in *natural immortality*. Fortunately, at least, he admitted that natural, pantheistic thought would never be able to achieve personal and individual immortality.8 Unfortunately, in order to salvage his universalist view of immortality, he had to make some unsubstantiated, at least, questionable leaps when opting for his philosophy. iii 9

We are human beings in all the fullness of what it means to be human. We were never intended to be spirit beings with no physical connection to matter. As people, not spirits, we are connected beings: We are connected to God, to others, to creation, and to ourselves. With an intimate relationship with the source of life, we may say:

We know who we are when we know Whose we are!

Let us simply say that human beings are intended to exist forever in the harmonious relationship of body, soul and spirit. This New Testament view is expressed by the Apostle Paul:

"May the God of peace himself sanctify you entirely; and may your spirit and soul and body be kept sound and blameless..."
(1 Thess. 5:23).

ONE ACT, OR A PROCESS ?

One strike and you're out! Is that the kind of God Jesus is to reveal? It seems to be a little petulant that Adam is consigned to such a horrendous fate because of this one covetous and arrogant act. We have made a big issue in highlighting the fact that *freedom of choice is fundamental to the principles of creation*. However, we see a principle appearing in the New Testament which helps to clear things up. For example, when the Apostle Paul speaks of those who will not inherit the kingdom of God, he lists the activities of such people as acting in the present tense (1 Co. 6:9-11). In other words, these acts are continually being done, by choice. In this vein, we see that the Adam community was facing the consequences of the future, and precisely because of the free choices they had made. *It was not because they had been pre-determined to do so!* The matter of Original Sin is a very big subject; its influence in Western theology has largely been attributed to St. Augustine and reformers like John Calvin who enlarged upon much of the thinking of Augustine.10

In the extreme, the idea of original sin is not simply that we are born of a nature predisposed to sin, but that we are *incapable of making good, moral choices* without the initiative of God's grace first working in us. In some quarters, this is called total depravity. Christian thinkers, such as C.S. Lewis, are horrified by the notion of total depravity, "....the consequence is drawn that, since we are totally depraved, our idea of good is worth simply nothing. He (God) appeals to our existing moral judgement."11 Throughout the history of the entire prophetic ministry in Israel, God's messengers assumed there was some innate goodness in people that was capable of responding to the call for forgiveness and reconciliation (Rom. 2:4). So, with such a premise of depravity, uneasy responses are made to the suggestion that people, such as Gandhi, made some very good moral decisions, yet were not Christians. Often, the defensive response is that those decisions were made without the conscious understanding of the Holy Spirit being at work.

The idea of total depravity, connected to the doctrine of original sin, quite naturally led to further assumptions: Creation, apart from the prevailing grace of God, is incapable of presenting any of the good fruit of creation. Some support for this position may be found in passages such as Isa. 64:6. However, it would be legitimate to view this statement in terms of *what God's people had become;* truly, a far cry from the condition under which they were once included in the shout, "It is very good..." (Gen. 1:31) These problems find expression in roughly two schools that have divided much theological thought since reformation times. The two schools are Calvinism and Arminianism.[iv]

Rather than entering this fray, and for the purposes we are pursuing in this book, we temper these theological divisions *by going back to first principles.* We see that in the Garden, Adam, not driven by animal instinct, was given a unique human gift of free will. This was a gift which enabled him to *choose* either good or evil. That was the whole point of the tree of the knowledge of good and evil.

The consequences of his decisions have to be met (Gen. 3:14-24).

However, not at any time, is there an inference that one of the consequences will include the loss of free will. That's a creation principle which the God of love will not override! Nevertheless, we must also admit to the reality that *there now appears to be a predisposition within the human psyche, which more naturally turns to the self before it will turn to God.* Ask anyone who has raised children!

At some point in their life of decision, God declared the consequences of their actions. It is significant that, at first, they weren't very comfortable in parading their new-won condition of independence from God; so they tried to hide. *They were ashamed of their transparency.* However, no one can escape the ultimate encounter with God. Like the father of the Prodigal Son, God was waiting for His beloved to return to the intimacy of his primary relationship. He cried then, as He still cries after His lost children, "Where are you?" (Gen. 3:9)

> ***The Adam-Eve community did not simply hide from a searching God, but from the awesome brilliance of glorious Light which illuminated and exposed everything around and in them (1 John 1:7a).***

It's not that God didn't know the answer to His own question. *Adam, like us, needed to hear the question!* He needed to realize that a *perversion and a reversal* had taken place in his very nature.

> *In the loving nature of God's initiative, the primary direction of humanity's relational encounter would never be focused in the human search for God, but in God's search for His people.*

To spend life in an *inward* search for God *would inevitably lead* towards the futility of aloneness leading to nihilism. It is the fate of natural religion.

They couldn't stay at home anymore! Their model home and garden has been sealed off from their use (Gen. 3:24). No longer were they able to enjoy and use it as God had purposed. No longer could they be signatories of Eden's kingdom life. *Eden remains a dim memory of a kingdom model for the Adam community; but yet as a blurred memory within the psyche of all humanity.* The idea that life was intended to last forever still lingers on! It would seem that a process of *devolution* had really set in!

Is it possible that God's magnificent purposes for creation, and its priesthood, had failed? Was it not possible for there to be *Moments of Light* in the ongoing history of this Adam community? Was it no longer possible for God to find a people, or even an individual, able to be a sign of what once was? We are to see that:

From that very moment of His search, in every nook and cranny of the human story, the longing call of God echoes hauntingly throughout the cavernous corridors of redemption's story: *"Where are you? Where are you?"*

There was need for some kind of rescue. There was need for a hope that First Day Light would break through once again. The redemption story was shortly to begin.

Chapter 5 How Did Time Become an Enemy?

1. Latourette, Kenneth. *A History of Christianity*, p.8 Vol. 1. Harper and Row Publishers,New York, London, Revised Edition, 1975.

2. Lossky, Vladimir, *Orthodox Theology,*p.79, St. Vladimir's Press, New York, (1978)

3. Capon, Robert R. *The Third Peacock*, p.41. Image Books, Doubleday & Co., Garden City N.Y. 1972

4. Capon, Robert R. p.19

5. Lewis, C.S. *The Problem of Pain*, p.122 Collins Fontana Books, London, 3rd impression (1961)

6. Wagner, Peter C. *Warfare Prayer*, p.92. Regal Books, Ventura Calif. (1992)

7. Vos, Geerharder, *Biblical Theology*, p.44, Eerdmans, Grand Rapids 1948

8. Robinson, John A.T., *In the End God,* p.95. Fontana Books, London and Glasgow (1968)

9. Robinson, John A.T. *In the End God,* p.108

10. *The Oxford Dictionary of the Christian Church,* Ed. F.L. Cross. P.109. Oxford Press (1983)

11. Lewis, C.S. *The Problem of Pain*, pps..25,27.

Chapter 6

FIRST DAY LIGHT ON THE MOUNTAINS OF ISRAEL

Surely, a breakthrough in essential and covenant relations could be redeemed only by the grace of the Source of life. However, that would require the loving initiative of God Himself. Only God could repair and restore that which was lost. We should not be surprised to find that significant changes took place in the story of Adam's race. Yet, it would be foolish to fob off the redemption story as a primitive bedtime myth for children. *Moments of Light* will most certainly appear during this light sketch of the story of Israel. One thing will be very apparent: These moments mostly occur in the lives of significant individuals. Undoubtedly, and often, God reminded His appointed people that they were a *community chosen by Him*. He offered them various ways in which to live out their community identity. Nevertheless, in the Old Testament, the light of God's glory is to be most apparent in individual lives. However, these people, who can trace their origins to 'the sons of God,' are to be foundational in God's redemption story for the world.

Possibly inspired by a similar Mesopotamian account of a local flood, the story of Noah is one that is loaded with theological implications. "More than 500 deluge legends are known around the world and, in a survey of 86 of these (20 Asiatic, 3 European, 7 African, 46 American and 10 from Australia and the Pacific), the specialist researcher Dr. Richard Andree concluded that 62 were entirely independent of the Mesopotamian and Hebrew accounts.1 Ian Wilson adds, "Surely, a real-life Flood must lie behind these stories. The collective memory, scattered over wide geographical distances, is too prevalent, too deep-seated for this not to be the case..."2 By attempting to relate Noah's connection to Abraham, (and the Sons of God) he continues, "…the Turkish Ur is only 48 kilometers (30 miles) from Haran, which is the other main family location biblically associated with Abraham (Genesis 11:31)."3

Noah appears to have a natural connection with the sons of God (mentioned in Genesis Chapter 6); at least, he walks in the relationships intended for them (Gen. 6:8-9). The story speaks of the continuance of human rebellion, of judgment, of God's will to secure *a relational remnant,* and of a covenant hope that has its God-made sign in nature. Like the creation story, it is one which emerges from beyond the waters of chaos. The rainbow, *a colorful appearance of Fourth Day Light,* appeared to Noah as a sign that God had not given up on His creation or His purposes for it. This tiny, remnant community was helpless, and so God gave a sign of hope in the color of nature (Gen. 9:11-15). The story declares to us a principle that runs throughout the entire Bible:

> *On the basis of a faithful remnant, God is willing to maintain His purposes by saving the human race from extinction.*

But how could God, once more, sign His purposes through community? This was His purpose at the beginning, wasn't it?

THE RESTORATION OF COMMUNITY

The Tower of Babel (meaning, *confusion*; Genesis Chapter 11) speaks of the disintegration of community and of its essential unity of purpose. (It is not coincidental that this story is placed at the very point where the common language, used to proclaim God's purpose for a universal community, breaks down, and the children of God have lost the way, and desire, for such proclamation.) Yet, another lineage is found in this chapter; it is intended to connect the line of the *sons of God* from Adam to Noah, and then from his son Shem, and subsequently, through this branch, to the Mesopotamian family of Abraham (Gen. 11:10). Abraham seems to be well connected! Ironically, Abram traced his origins through a race that was on the leading edge of a form of natural religion. It is very popular today. Astrology is a religion that determines human destiny by the movement of *'lights in the sky.'* 4 (They are natural lights of Fourth Day!)

Once again, God did the choosing for such a special ministry. Clearly, He did not choose on the basis of merit (Deut. 7:7-8). Like the call of the reluctant Jeremiah (Jer. 1:4-5) this was *not an individual call to salvation*, but one of God's unique call to *leadership* of ministry within the community. But God's heart for an *individual response to become part of one universal community* is clearly echoed in 1 Tim. 2:4. Here, the writer, speaking of God, asserts:"…who desires everyone to be saved and to come to the knowledge of the truth."

It is no accident that the call of Abraham appears on the heels of the demise of community, as recorded in the story of Babel (Genesis Chapter 11) It was always in the sovereign plan of God for there to be a universal priesthood of creation. Maybe Cain had failed to understand why no blood was ever spilled in Eden. The offerings in Eden were of the first of innocence. Abel understood the fruit of nature was no longer one of innocence. Clearly, once beyond the gates of the Garden, humanity was in no condition to offer God the fruit of creation, i.e., *the fruit of innocence* (Gen. 4:4-5). *Everything that Adam and Eve had formerly done was an offering of worship.* There was no need for blood sacrifices; their entire life consisted of the priestly offerings of creation through lives of innocence.

The life is in the blood. "Only, you shall not eat flesh with its life, that is, its blood" (Gen. 9:4). A long story was to emerge signifying that reconciliation with God was going to be very costly. Once beyond Eden, a life had to be offered in a sacrifice of atonement. Much later in the story, we see that God, Himself, in loving grace stepped into the breach to pay such a price. Abraham, true to the natural religion of his culture, felt that God would be satisfied by the offering of Isaac, Abraham's only son. Even this costly gift could never be enough!

A substitute was found in the form of an innocent old ram that wished he had been on another mountain! *And, that concept of substitution was to become an integral part of the Jewish sacrificial system.* (See Lev. 16:15-19.) "The Lord will provide; as it is said to this day, 'on the mount of the Lord, it shall be provided'"(Gen. 22:11-14). Moriah is usually identified with the mountain in Jerusalem where the Temple was erected. 5 (And on that very mount, about 16-1700 years later, outside the city gates, God was to pay the costly provision of His own son)! Circumcision would soon become the sign of blood spilled in order to gain admission to the chosen community of God (Gen. 17:10-13).

Abraham's family (in the line of the sons of God) would become the community on earth charged with the apostolic commission of Eden.

"I will make you a great nation, and I will bless you, and make you name great, so that you will be a blessing. I will bless those who bless you, and the one who curses you I will curse; and in you all the families of the earth shall be blessed" (Gen. 12:2-3).

The Apostle Paul, many years later, was to offer an understanding of how this blessing of family was extended to all races upon earth:

"...for in Christ Jesus you are all children of God through faith...There is no longer Jew or Greek, there is no longer slave or free, there is no longer male and female; for all of you are one in Christ Jesus. And if you belong to Christ, then you are Abraham's offspring, heirs according to the promise" (Gal. 3:26-29).

The Pelagian idea that, individually, humans could pay the price of their own reconciliation has no place in the Big Story of God's redemption.[v]

Isaac became the father of Jacob who produced twelve sons. And, in line of the three patriarchs of promise, these twelve sons become heads of an ever burgeoning family. This family was to become the community of Israel. What the Bible reveals is that Israel was adopted to be the apostolic community of promise. Truly, by the grace and initiative of God, a community was born to bring light to the world! The story of redemption was now placed back into the life of community.

"For the creation waits with eager longing for the revealing of the children of God...the creation itself will be set free from its bondage to decay and will obtain the freedom of the glory of the children of God" (Rom. 8:19, 21).

The community of Israel was now on a journey far larger than one in which they were comfortable; and they didn't always remain true to their purpose. But, like the journey of their leading patriarch, Abraham, God would not provide them with a blueprint, but only a direction (Gen. 12:1). *Faith was to be the pivotal foundation of this relational covenant* (Heb. 11:1-2, 39; Jas. 2:23.) On this very vulnerable principle of faith, God foresaw that His purposes for Israel would succeed.

*It is their primary and essentially priestly purpose to be apostolic;*i.e. to invite the entire world into the community of God.

A very important principle of election appears to emerge from the calling of Abraham. Is it really about the call to a particular community, chosen to enable God's universal purposes?

> *In other words, is the question of their predestined purpose more in connection to the community, rather than to individuals; to the what, rather than to whom the call is extended?*

> **"It was not because you were more numerous than any other people that the Lord set his heart on you and chose you-for you were the fewest of all peoples. It was because the Lord loved you and kept the oath that he swore to your ancestors..." (Deut. 7:7-8)**

Thinking in individual terms, we have noted that the personal call of particular individuals was always associated with a community purpose residing in the heart of God. (For example, the reluctant Moses, and the equally reluctant Jeremiah were both fearful; not of a call to individual salvation, but a call to a very difficult ministry within God's community - Exodus Chapter 3 and Jeremiah Chapter 1.) From the very beginning, the community of Adam had a universal commission, but the apathy and disobedience of this community did not negate or destroy God's sovereign purposes. And so, in God's election, Abraham appears and receives a call. But, upon close examination, the call and the promises were not solely for Abraham, but for his community as it continued in obedience to its universal destiny (Gen. 12:3). Similarly, young Samuel's call was to be a prophet in order to enable the community of Israel in its original calling (1 Sam. 3:10-18). Hence, as with others, this call was a call to ministry and was associated with the original apostolic call of Adam (Jer. 1:5).

Thinking of those persons as individuals, we must hasten to note that all of them could have responded with a resounding "No" to the call of God. Indeed, Jeremiah, although he gave reasons to resist his call, replied with a "Yes." However, he paradoxically moved between bravery and fear throughout much of his ministry. But the point is that he moved! Similarly, Moses could have been the founding elder of a priestly tribe interceding between God and His people. It was because of his reluctance to say yes to God that the role was passed on to his brother Aaron (Ex. 4:13-17). Clearly, God remained sovereign in His purposes. He would even use the gluttonous power-seeking leaders of other nations to forward His purposes. King Nebuchadnezzar is a good example (Jer. 27:6).

Taking this principle into the New Testament, we see that Judas, whom Jesus knew to be His betrayer (John 13:21-26), most certainly could have resisted the lure of thirty pieces of silver. In the climate of that moment, a Judas could have appeared in any one of a whole range of people. God knew that! In the book of Ephesians we see a good example of the call of God being made to a community for the effecting of His universal purposes. For example, in Ephesians 1:5, 11, we note that Paul is speaking to a community of saints in Ephesus. He is speaking in the plural. In the sense of the illustrations we have considered above, we may say that the principle of election is not so much about a call to individual salvation, but a call to respond to God by ministering in His purposes for community.

With Christ as its Head and focus, the community is engaged in the universal task of bringing all creation into the essential relations of creation (1 Tim. 2:4). Again, in this creation context, predestination is seen to relate to the what of a community much more than the who of an individual. Predestination is all about the purpose of a chosen community, not the selective call of individual salvation.

So we speak of Israel as a community commissioned by God. The roots of this commission extend through the lineage of the sons of God, and all the way back to Adam. What we see emerging is that the identity, focus, and purpose of this community later becomes solidified by four supporting pillars. These four pillars are summarized in the words: Law, Prophets, Priests, and Monarchy. I am to suggest that Moments of Light appeared in the life of all four pillars. However, before the four pillars could emerge, the people of Israel needed a sign that they could trust Moses in his role of being their deliverer. Here, we see the beginnings of how the light of God's glory shone on all four pillars of Israel.

LIGHT UPON THE LAWGIVER

After Israel had resided in Egypt for about 430 years, Moses appears as a prince, a shepherd, and a deliverer. He is one of the individuals who, more than once, experienced the awesome light of God's glory. It was never natural fire! The fire is that of First Day Light! Such phenomenon occurred for Moses on Mount Horeb ("the mountain of God - Ex. 3:1). Later it was called Mount Sinai. No wonder he could only walk a little way into its blinding glory! No wonder he had to abandon his shoes in the awe of God's Shekina Presence! Was it possible to deny God's call to be a deliverer amid such awesome brilliance of Light? The answer is most certainly, "Yes." But God allowed for his feeble excuse not to be a public speaker (Ex. 4:10). The result was that his brother Aaron was given the mantle of Israel's priesthood. God's purposes prevail:

> *"... this is why I let you live: to show you my power, and to make my name resound through all the earth" (Ex. 9:16).*

They had become a raggedy group. After those 430 years in Egypt, they really didn't have an identity or a purpose as a community. The purpose of this tattered community was to cohere into a *sign* that would present to the world a relational life which once existed in the prototypical kingdom called Eden. Their function was to invite the fragmented world to join the dance! *This peculiar group needed deliverance from bondage, a focus in the God they could not name, and new values to bind them together into a distinct people and culture.*

Distinctive signs that God was blessing the leadership of Moses became tangible in the crossing of the Red Sea, the assurance of God's Presence in a cloud by day and fire by night, God's daily provision of manna and of water, the giving of the Ten Commandments, and the central focus of the Tabernacle. In these chronological events, the entire community also encountered distinct *Moments of Light!* (e.g., 1 Co.10:1-5) But the giving of the Torah is preeminently the prominent sign associated with Moses.

The Assurances of Presence:

Torah is the term often used to describe a variety of literary traditions (including the Pentateuch, or the entire Old Testament scriptures) but it is usually reserved to describe the Ten Commandments given to Moses on Mount

Sinai. *The idea that a deity would give a set of laws to enable relationships was something new to this people or to any people!* With God as their focus, they would learn how to live in relationship with Him and with each other. Not coincidentally, at the very moment the Commandments were being inscribed upon tablets of earth, the Israelites at the foot of Mount Sinai were worshipping a pagan god. (Maybe it was Apis, the bull, a god of provision for the Egyptians.) However, it was on Mount Sinai that Moses witnessed the most remarkable demonstrations of the light and fire of God's glory.

"Now the appearance of the glory of the Lord was like a devouring fire on the top of the mountain… " (Ex. 24:17).

On the same mountain, Moses had a remarkable experience of the power of God's awesome glory (Ex. 33:11-23). It was a powerful assurance of God's continued Presence for this person who was called to be leader of a holy nation and a kingdom of priests! (Ex. 19:5-6) Moses trusted this promise for the next forty years!

The Torah is therefore a set of laws, given by God, to enable a loving relationship with Him; and, as a result, a similar quality of relationships with others (Deut. 6:4-5; Lev. 19:18; Mark 12:29-31). But, like the idolaters at the foot of Sinai, we must never imagine that natural religion cannot re-assert itself in the community again. It does, even today, and it's getting stronger in the mainline churches! Matthew Fox, a Jesuit priest says:

"The creation-centered spiritual tradition is truly ecumenical…Teilhard de Chardin felt this way when he wrote that 'our consciousness, rising above the growing (but still much too limited) circles of family, country and race, shall finally discover that the only natural and real human unity is the spirit of the earth'…In ten years of lecturing and writing on creation spirituality I have seen how excited and amazed listeners get over how deeply this tradition cuts through religious differences and touches spiritual points of convergence." 6 Gia has returned! We are now facing the very same struggles with natural theology which the Israelites experienced of old! The Church of today surely needs to covet assurance of God's Presence in the revelation of both Word and Spirit.

Armed with God's assurances in the Law, the priesthood, the Tabernacle, and God's daily provision, *they should have entered the land of promise from the entry point of Kadesh Barnea* (Num. 14:22-23). However, it took more than thirty-eight years before Joshua, the anointed protégé of Moses, led God's people over the River Jordan. They were now in the land where they were called to establish God's reign. Like the Eden of old, Jerusalem was to be a focus and a city from which a universal mission would be launched. From now on the world was supposed to observe the implications of embracing the dance of Eden. How well was this task accomplished? In the New Testament, the Jerusalem that was intended to be an assurance of God's Presence, is seen to be a temporal and symbolic sign. It would be a sign that would give way to *a Jerusalem that is above and is free; a New Jerusalem that comes down from heaven - from above!* (Gal. 4:26; Rev. 21:1-2)

LIGHT UPON THE PRIESTHOOD

Aaron appears as the first priest from the family of Levi. His priesthood is centered round a sacrificial system of blood sacrifice. What we see in the Old Testament is that the continuing priesthood of Aaron had a primary purpose of reconciliation and atonement. Even in nations devoted to natural religion, a system of priesthood was devised as a means of mediation between the deity and his people. Subsequently, t*he priests of Yahweh uniquely offered sacrifices for the sin that caused estrangement from God and others.* The idea of estrangement from personal relationships with a deity was an original concept; unheard of in natural religion. This system is questioned in the New Testament where we note the fulfillment of blood sacrifice in Jesus, and a better covenant of creation is employed. The roots of this system are clearly already apparent in Old Testament thinking.

At the time of Abraham, we are introduced to Melchizedek, a mystical figure who continues to represent a priesthood of the innocence of creation. Melchizedek is *both priest and king* of Salem, which became known as Jerusalem (Gen.14:18-Salem means peace). Were not these the dual roles of Adam in Eden? We are immediately drawn to the idea that *Mount Zion is the central place for the ideal ministry of a priest and king of peace.*

By giving a blessing to Abraham, this priestly king offers him bread and wine - *an offering of the fruits of creation representing the fruits of innocence in Eden!* Surely, it is not coincidental that Jesus chose bread and wine as the creatures of offering at the Last Supper! What we see is that Melchizedek is prototypically a continuation of the royal priesthood of creation, that is, to *"The Most High God."* Blood sacrifice is not in the venue of his ministry. "Abraham, the 'friend of God' (Isa. 41:8), accepts the blessings of this Canaanite priest and recognizes this priest's God as his own. Yahweh, God of revelation, the God of Abraham, is also to be recognized as God Most High (Hebrew: El Elyon), God of the universe, the God of Melchizedek."7 Melchizedek, as a king and priest of the Most High God, merits Abraham's tithe of the spoils of war.

Nowhere else in the Old Testament, especially since the rejection of Cain's offering, do we see the hint of the elevation of creation's offerings over the blood sacrifice of substitution. The stage had been set for the hope that, one day, *a priest-king of creation*, will once more offer the *fruits of innocence* which could not be offered by Cain.

Under the headship of Aaron, this priestly tribe exercised a variety of rites and roles on behalf of the people (Num. 3:5-10). Clearly, the sacrificial system, necessitating the offering of blood, was of primary importance:

> *"For the life of the flesh is in the blood; and I have given it for you upon the altar to make atonement for your souls; for it is the blood that makes atonement, by reason of the life" (Lev. 17:11).*

We see that the very costly spilling of blood was a requisite and a means of securing the reconciliation of relationships. And so it was the priest's function to perform the initiation rites of circumcision.

> *"This is my covenant, which you shall keep, between me and you and your offspring after you: Every male among you shall be circumcised...when he is eight days old...So shall my covenant be in your flesh an everlasting covenant" (Gen. 17:9-13).*

Even Jesus was brought to the Temple in order for Him to enter the rite of covenant (Luke 2:21). Mary and Joseph may not have known that the spilling of *this* blood was but an initial sign of *a completed covenant Jesus would offer in the sacrifice of His own blood.* But did God shed His glorious Light on this priestly pillar of Israel? Would God's brilliance of glory ever show up on Mount Zion? Yes, it did!

We recall two examples. The first was at the dedication of the Temple. When Solomon's Temple was completed on Mount Zion (about 950 B.C.), we note:

> *"When Solomon had ended his prayer, fire came down from heaven and consumed the burnt offerings and the sacrifices; and the glory of the Lord filled the temple. The priests could not enter the house of the Lord, because the glory of the Lord filled the Lord's house"*
> *(2 Chron. 7:1-2).*

Many years later, around 740 B.C., Isaiah had a vision of the Temple which forever changed his vocation:

> *"In the year that King Uzziah died, I saw the Lord sitting on a throne, high and lofty; and the hem of his robe filled the temple"*
> *(Isa. 6:1).*

We see then, that the priesthood, focused in the high priesthood of Aaron (and his future descendant, Zadok) had a dual purpose - *not only to minister as mediator through whom sacrifices were offered, but also to be guarantors (signs) that God was faithful to His covenant promises with Israel.* Not surprisingly, therefore, Israel's priesthood is seen to be at the very heart of the nation's major feasts: Passover, Weeks, Tabernacles, Hanukkah and Purim.

LIGHT UPON THE MONARCHY

David stands out as the monarch par excellence. He brought the Ark of the Covenant from Hebron to Jerusalem. Clearly, *Jerusalem is the place from which the ideal king would reign as once he did in Eden.* (And that's the picture presented in the last book of the Bible - Rev. 21:1-6) Michal, David's wife, never understood the ecstatic joy of David as he led the joyous procession up the hill of Zion (2 Sam. 6:20-22). Dancing (apparently) naked before the Lord's presence, for one brief *moment, David was embracing the dance of Eden.* From the slow, measured speed of its deliberately-paced dance, he literally leaped into the joyous abandonment of a sensuous tango with God. Nakedly unashamed and transparent, He was innocently absorbed into the arms of God's glorious Presence.

For this one glorious moment, and bereft of all shame, the King of Zion embraced the ecstatic dance of Eden's innocence.

Samuel had been very uncertain concerning the desire of the people to have their own king. They wanted to be like the nations around them. But, as citizens of the kingdom, they were called to live under *theocratic rule*. To Samuel, God was their king!

Having settled in Canaan, they appeared to be a people developing a memory of whom they were called to be. But memory seemed to last for one generation alone. "...another generation grew up after them, who did not know the Lord or the work that he had done for Israel" (Judges 2:10).

Not surprisingly, at least twice in the book of Judges, we see words such as, "In those days there was no king in Israel, all the people did what was right in their own eyes." (Jud.17:6, 21:25.) For about two hundred years (some believe it to be about 400 years - 1 Kings 6:1) God raised up Judges from among them. Of particular note are Gideon and Deborah. Not surprisingly, the grumblers of Israel looked over the fence and wanted what all other nations possessed. They grumbled to Samuel who reluctantly heard from God that the people were not rejecting him as a judge, but *rejecting God as their king!* (1 Sam. 8:7)

Of the tribe of Benjamin, Saul was the first king. But, because of disobedience, and by resorting to the occult for advice (a return to natural religion), the anointing for kingship was taken from him (1 Sam. 16:13-14). Quite remarkably, and in fulfillment of prophecy, David, from the tribe of Judah, succeeded Saul. Predictive prophecy was on the side of the young man from Judah:

"Judah, your brothers shall praise you; your hand shall be on the neck of your enemies; your father's sons shall bow down before you...The scepter shall not depart from Judah, nor the ruler's staff from between his feet, until tribute comes to him; and obedience of the peoples is his" (Gen. 49:8, 10).

David was not to build the Temple (1 Chron. 28:3), but he supplied much of the foundational material for his son, Solomon. At the dedication of the Temple, the *fire from heaven* had a dual purpose. First, it was the awesome Light and Presence of God *to assure His people of a blessing on the monarchy*. Second, it was an assurance that *God's Presence could be found equally upon Mount Zion as it was on Mount Sinai*.

However, as is often the case, the promises of God are often *conditional* upon the responses of His people. The astounding and eternal promise, given to Solomon, was such a conditional promise:

> *"I will establish his kingdom forever if he continues resolute in keeping my commandments and ordinances, as he is today"* (*1Chron. 28:7; see also 1 Kings 9:4-7.*)

In 1 Kings Chapter 11, many reasons are given why this eternal promise was to be torn away from Solomon. (Interestingly, Solomon, the builder of the great Temple, isn't mentioned among the Old Testament saints in Hebrews Chapter 11. Like Adam, he seems to be omitted!) But God's purposes were not defeated. *How could the light of God shine, once more, upon a ruler from Judah? Actually, it took a long time, but it did!*

LIGHT UPON THE PROPHETS

The purpose of a prophet was to forth-tell the word of the Lord. However, it was also to foretell what was in the knowledge of God for His people. After all, the God who knows the beginning from the end (Isa. 46:10), in His Eternal Present, is able to reveal the future to His prophets (Isa. 9:6-7; Amos 3:7). Of course, there were times when the ancient prophets never lived long enough to see their own prophecies come true! (Jer. 31:31-34; Isa. 7:7-9, 14) And so, what we are to see in the life of this theocratic nation is a tension of prophet to king. It is intended to be a healthy tension in order to ensure the purposes of God for His community. A significant principle regarding a foretelling ministry may be summed up like this:

The word which is given in a particular context, for a particular time sometimes is seen to have far more significant meaning for the future. God's people have to trust in order to know.

Clearly, for the genuine prophet, God is the *Source* of visions. Conversely, prophets, such as Isaiah and Ezekiel, did see visions, and those visions were clearly part of the Big Story. For example, we note Isaiah's vision of the peace and harmony of a restored creation (chapter 11), or Ezekiel's vision of the river flowing from the Temple at Jerusalem feeding the nations of the world (chapter 47.) Does that remind us of the streams from Eden, and from the New Jerusalem of Zech. 14:8 and Rev. 22:1?

Broadly speaking, the prophetic ministry of God's community had a four-fold character:

First, to exercise an apostolic call; this involved the inviting of the entire world into a universal community of God (Gen. 1:28; 12:3; Isa. 26:18). As we shall see, *this primary apostolic call became a major problem in the life of Israel.*

Second, this invitation involved a specific call to Israel to live a prophetic life, which necessitated an attitude of *repentance*. But what did that mean? *Repentance was always in connection with the covenant they had received from God.* Syncretistically, they snuggled up to other cultures for their approval. Therefore, the prophets called the people to return to their peculiar roots in God.

Third, to call Israel to *demonstrate* for the world the character of life once lived under God in Eden. In other words, to *be a light to the nations* so that the world might respond to God's invitation to harmonious and essential relationships.

Fourth, the prophets continually reassured Israel that God sovereignly continued to involve Himself in their history. Their message was not simply a reminder of what God *had* done; it was an assurance of *what He will do in the future* (Isa. 48:3; Ezek.25; Jer. 32:37-41).

Clearly, therefore, the major role of Israel's prophets was to reveal the Word of God to His chosen community. Nevertheless, there are times when it is addressed specifically to an individual; especially to a monarch. One such example of this is the encounter that the prophet Nathan had with King David (2 Sam. 11:14-15). When directly confronted by God's prophet, the encounter resulted in David's *repentance* (Ps. 51). *Their standing in the community would always be of a charismatic nature. Genuine prophets of God could, or should not be institutionalized!* By acting as institutional chaplains, they would stoop to the level of the popular seer.

Amongst a people who supposedly came under theocratic rule, the history of the kings of Israel in the North, and Judah in the South, proved to be a litany of good news-bad news events. The good kings were those who listened to the prophet, and who worked to eradicate the enticing natural religions of their neighbors. God's intent was to raise a community, not only to *speak prophetically* to the world, but also *to live a prophetic life in demonstration of kingdom essentials.* Canaan was intended to be a land that would reflect, if not imperfectly, the character of life in Eden. Nevertheless, however well they rose or fell to the challenge, one prophet stood out as being representative of the entire prophetic ministry.

Elijah may not have been as busy as his successor, Elisha, nor may he have performed as many signs and wonders as his protégé, but one particular occasion stands out like a far-reaching beacon. The place was Mount Carmel in the Northwestern part of Israel. After a three-year drought, Elijah bravely challenged the natural prophets of Israel. Whose god, or gods, can save the people of the land? Mockingly, Elijah challenged the prophets of Baal. Those prophets prepared a sacrifice, but were challenged not to light a fire. After calling on their gods, nothing happened. Elijah did the same thing but poured water on his sacrifice. Calling on God, the *supernatural fire of the Lord* from above consumed the offering and everything around it (1 Kings 18:38). Soon, the rains appeared and the natural prophets of Baal were routed and put to shame. The event proved to be a watershed between those who followed natural religion (led by King Ahab) and those who turned to the God who revealed Himself. It was a magnificent *Moment of Light.* From that time on, Elijah became synonymous with the prophetic ministry of Israel. At the time of Jesus, many were still looking for his prophetic ministry to return.

The period between the return of the exiles (ca. 538 B.C.) and the heraldic mission of John the Baptist (ca. 30 A.D.) *could not be described as a return to the restoration of the four pillars of Israel.* Despite a growing hope, never again would the Jews have their *king* from the line of Judah; at least, not in the normal way they had anticipated! "The anticipation of a return of Davidic rule and national independence, held by a few people in the time of Haggai and Zechariah, had proved unfounded. The faith of the community survived, but it had all but lost hope for any significant future."8 Apart from the possibility of some parts of Daniel, the voice of *prophecy* had become relatively silent in the inter-testament period. However, the *Law* was honored, and a *priesthood* had returned to its ministry in the Temple.

A little later, post 70 A.D., the exiles of Diaspora, who were more likely to take their primary apostolic mission seriously, were literally forced into a ground-shaking ecclesial reform. There were no more kings and priests in their system, but through the genius of the recently emerged Pharisees, their emphasis on law, prophets, and prayer made Judaism accessible to the peoples of the world.

PROMISED LIGHT FOR A FUTURE REMNANT

Despite years of conflict, exile, assimilation, and loss of freedom, a hope remained that God would be a light shining upon their future:

> *"Arise, shine, for your light has come, and the glory of the Lord has risen upon you…nations shall come to your light, and kings to the brightness of your dawn" (Isa. 60:1, 3).*

Isaiah also looks to the day when the nation shall know peace and that First Day Light shall be their hope:

> *"Violence shall no more be heard in your land, devastation or destruction within your borders…The sun shall no longer be your light by day, nor for brightness shall the moon give light to you by night; but the Lord will be your everlasting light, and your God will be your glory" (Isa. 60:18-19).*

One day, on the eighth day of his life, a baby boy received the rite of circumcision. Standing nearby, Zechariah, the father of John the Baptist, "…was filled with the Holy Spirit and uttered this prophecy" (Luke 1:67-79). In that prophecy he said that God's messiah would be called, "the prophet of the Most High." His purpose would be to "prepare the way of the Lord," and that God would "give light to those who sit in darkness and in the shadow of death."

Similarly, and shortly after, there was a man in Jerusalem who constantly looked for deliverance for God's people; he prayed at the Temple for the Lord's Messiah to appear. One day, Mary and Joseph brought the baby Jesus to the Temple in order to be circumcised. When Simeon saw the Lord Jesus, his eyes lit up; he held the baby in his loving arms and prophetically breathed over the child. This child shall be:

> *"...a light for revelation to the Gentiles and for glory to your people Israel" (Luke 2:32).*

Thirty years later, John the Baptist pointed to his cousin and declared:

> *"Here is the Lamb of God who takes away the sin of the world" (John 1:29).*

> *"I baptize you with water for repentance, but one who is more powerful than I is coming after me; I am not worthy to carry his sandals. He will baptize you with the Holy Spirit and fire" (Matt. 3:11).*

> *'He must increase, but I must decrease" (John 3:30).*

Jesus appeared, and soon after John the Baptist exited from the stage of Israel's history.

> *"But you, O Bethlehem of Ephrathah, who are one of the little clans of Judah, from you shall come forth for me one who is to rule in Israel, whose origin is from of old, from ancient days" (Micah 5:2).*

Doesn't this text remind us, a little, of the nature of Melchizedek? It appears he also was something more than just a man (Heb. 7:1-3).

The apostolic hope for a universal community was alive in the remnant person of Jesus Christ. For the writer of Mathew's Gospel, Jesus was not only the Suffering Servant of Isaiah, but the anointed Messiah of Israel's future hope.

"This was to fulfill what had been spoken through the prophet Isaiah" (Matt. 12:17).

The famous passage from Isaiah Chapter 42 fills out the context.

Chapter 6 First Day Light Upon the Mountains of Israel

1. Hancock, Graham, *Fingerprints of the Gods,* p.208. Seal Books, McCelland Bantam, Toronto (1996)
2. Wilson, Ian, *Before the Flood,* p.25. Orion Books Ltd, London, 2001
3. Wilson, Ian, p.32
4. Kennedy, Richard. *The International Dictionary of Religion, p.22*
5. *The Bible Dictionary* p.794 (2nd edition) Tyndale, (IVF Press) Wheaton, Illinois 60187
6. Fox, Matthew. *Original Blessings*, Introduction, Bear & Company, Santa Fe, New Mexico, 1983.
7. *The Interpreter's One Volume Commentary of the Bible, Genesis,* Marks, John. H., p.14
8. Craigie, Peter C., *The Old Testament,* p.288

Chapter 7

THE REAL ADAM: THE LIGHT OF THE WORLD

THE STAGE WAS SET

In the apostolic charge to Adam, and later in the call of Abraham, we see clearly that this nation really *was intended to pioneer the creation of a redeemed and universal community.* We also observe that this nation would remain in a prominent place of honor to the very end. However, we are soon to see that God's ultimate rescue of His purposes is to be focused in a *One-Person Remnant.* Indeed, we are to see that *Jesus sacrificially spent His entire life, ministry, and death, embracing the dance of Eden's innocence.* As we have seen in the story of Eden, the dance included a charge to draw together a universal community under the lordship of Eden's rightful King. The time was drawing near for His appearance.

Four occurrences, *in chronological time,* had made the world a less provincially-minded place:

First of all, many of the Jews who had been taken into exile either remained in their new land, or chose to return to their homes in Judah. Maybe, for some of them, there was a glimmering sense that God's light could shine throughout the entire world!

Second, the *language and culture* of Alexander the Great was becoming commonplace throughout the Mediterranean and Near Eastern regions.

Third, the Romans, who adopted much of Greek culture, established *easy trade routes* throughout all the regions they had conquered. Clearly, there was now a common language of (koine) Greek. Because of this "common" language, international trade could be accomplished.

Fourth, there was an expectancy growing in Israel that God was going to send them a deliverer; a messiah may soon arrive. In Diaspora there was now a common language, and on every street corner, an opportunity for debate.

The entire world was becoming accessible! Never before, in the whole history of civilization, and particularly the life of Israel, was a universal and apostolic mission more possible. Talk about the timing of God! Obviously, in terms of *kairos*, the following verse makes a lot of sense:

> *"...when the fullness of time had come, God sent his Son, born of a woman, born under the law, in order to redeem those who were under the law, so that we might receive adoption as children"* *(Gal. 4:4-5).*

All creation, once more, would see the most extraordinary and powerful light reflected upon its face. This would be a *Moment of Light* that would *shed its light on the mountains of redemption and restoration.* In fact, the entire ministry of Jesus would be a Moment of Light. Jesus, the inbreathed and Real Adam, had entered the stage of history. Light was shining in the darkness once more! (John 1:15)

BUT, A VIRGIN BIRTH?

God most certainly chose the most common and unremarkable way to introduce Himself! But this was what He had planned even before time began. In the very moment God decided to create the universe, He also decided to pay an enormous price for its redemption (1 Pet. 1:20). He would clothe Himself with the same physical nature He had designed for Adam (Phil. 2:6-7). But His entry into the world would be *through the cursed birth pangs of a woman* (Gen. 3:16). This would be the way He would sign His kingdom character upon creation. *Suffering* was the pathway God chose to vindicate His sovereign purposes.

The virgin birth is clearly recorded in Matthew and Luke, but not as the pivotal event in Christ's appearing. (If people didn't believe in the fact of the resurrection, then the virgin birth would be very low in their priorities.) Nevertheless, most of the Christian world celebrates the birth of Jesus, *the Light of the world,* at a time of the year when much of the earth (i.e., the Northern Hemisphere) is at its darkest point. Without dwelling heavily on the birth narratives in Matthew and Luke, we must highlight the importance of the star that shone over Bethlehem.

In the account recorded in Matthew's Gospel, we realize that the writer was most certainly not honoring the ancient art of astrology. Indeed, he was using the story to underline the fact that the Gentile Magi, once having seen the "light for revelation to the Gentiles" (Luke 2:32), had to bow prostrate before the glory revealed in the baby Jesus. It was Jesus who was the real star of Bethlehem! But it's John's language that demands attention! He makes it very clear that the eternal identity, and the earthly work of the One who *is the Light,* must not be confused with the one who heralds it: i.e., John the Baptist (John 1:8). In fact, this verse shows clearly that no one else could ever shine as the Light of the world. The Message must not be confused with the messenger.

> *Guided by natural Light of the Fourth Day, Wise men bowed before the glorious Light of the First Day. They could never go back the same way again! (Matt. 2:12)*

But was this really a virgin birth? To many, it really sounds preposterous, doesn't it?

Then why did He come this way? It's all connected to the creation story. From that horrific *moment* when Adam began to devolve from his original nature, and from his heavenly possibilities, God posed the question, "Where are you?" *Nevertheless, in an awesome Moment of Light, God's incarnation in Christ answered the anguished cry of all humanity in the substance of, "Here I Am!"* The true Light was not ashamed of transparency! Indeed, the entire story of God's incarnation, is the story of Jesus' glorious dance of innocence.

Nowhere in the entire history of religious thought, do we observe anything that parallels the awesome incarnation of God in Jesus (Isa. 7:14). Nevertheless, the Jews were not given to the heroism and virginal birth stories of the superstars of Greek mythology. Mythology, of this sort, is better found amongst the Indians of New Mexico; the ancients of China; and the Hellenistic legends of Greek heroes like Hercules, Perseus and Ballerophon.1 A god-like hero, displaying the courage and vices associated with heroism, was not in the mind of Israel's prophets. *Jesus was no hero!* He was the *Suffering Servant,* (Isaiah Chapter 53) and the Anointed Savior spoken of in Isaiah. (See Isa. 42:1-4.) Matthew 12:17-21 That's why *Jesus can never, ever, be considered to be a superstar!*

Without laboring the point of virgin birth, we must consider its efficacy a little more. After all, two synoptic writers found it to be important! Clearly, it wasn't outlandish for them to accept that the God who created the universe, by the breath of His Word, could make possible a virgin birth. We are to see that *it is difficult to observe how the God of redemption could have achieved this miraculous work without considerable cost to Himself* (2 Co. 5:19).

A little girl once ran into the house on a cold and wintry day. She was crying. Her mom, a little disturbed by this, asked her what was the problem.

"I try very hard to feed the hungry sparrows, but every time I throw the bread crumbs, the sparrows fly away. I love them, mommy. What can I do to show it?

Her mom replied, "Maybe, in order to feed the sparrows, you have to become one."

And that's what God's Moment of Incarnation is all about!

No one knew the truth of Christ's birth more than Mary and Joseph! (Matt. 1:18, 25) But, in a dream, it took a miraculous appearing of an angel to Joseph before he was convinced. He proved to be a wonderful father; exactly the father figure needed for the formation of Jesus' humanity. Mary, chosen by God amongst all the women of the world, proved to be the perfect mother figure. She was overwhelmed because, amid all the excited gossip of an imminent messiah, she couldn't believe that she had been chosen. And especially without the aid of a man! Without doubt, the Hebrew, *"almah"* or the Greek, *"parthena"* meant "virgin" to Mary. "How can this be since I am a virgin?" (Luke 1:34) A literal rendering of *epei andra ou' ginosko* with its prefacing question would be, "How can this be since I do not know an adult male?" (In Hebrew thought, the verb, *to know* also speaks of physical intimacy - Gen. 4:1) Even more astoundingly, she was to bear God, Himself! (Theotikos) We see that it is Luke who traces the lineage of Jesus all the way back to "Adam, son of God." No wonder we are drawn to understand *why* Mary quietly "pondered these things in her heart" (Luke 2:19).

Who had ever spoken of the seed of a woman? Wasn't the seed of the man all that was required to make a baby? Of course, modern science has changed all that thinking. But the writer of Gen. 3:15 records that God had said to Satan that the seed (or the offspring) of a woman would bruise his head. After the baptism of Jesus, Luke continues with Christ's genealogy, showing that *Mary's offspring would be the one to cause the bruising of Satan.* He would be the *Son of the Most High,* the Son of God. (In terms of priesthood, similar metaphorical language is used of Melchizidek - Heb. 7:3.) Jesus was the Son who would reign on the throne of David in an everlasting kingdom. What an astounding lineage Luke records! (Luke 3:23-37)

> *The point is that the entire Big Story is now focused in One Person: Jesus Christ!*

It would seem obvious that Luke's record of the angelic annunciation revealed that the one who was to be born would be *both fully Human and fully God.* He would be the Son of the Most High who would be given the earthly throne of David, forever! (Luke 1:32-33) God would most certainly be in Christ, reconciling the world to Himself! (2 Co. 5:19) This notion of a miracle may not sound quite so outlandish to a *modern* scientist, but we must stress the theological point that,

> *God (Himself) has voluntarily entered into our dimension of life because we were no longer capable of reaching up to His.*

Such an act, from above, absolutely *requires a miracle!* When using the term, *Theosis,* Orthodox Eastern Churches were trying to explain deification, or union with God.2 Both Irenaeus and Athanasius put it this way, "God became man in order that man might become god."3 (Sometimes it is interpreted "divine" for "god.")Westerners sometimes become a little disturbed by this language. However, the small 'g' is used of deity because Eastern theologians are very eager to stress that God is ultimately unknowable.4 *We can never enter into complete union with God, because we will always be created beings who thirst everlastingly for the joy of knowing Him more and more.* There will always be a *distance* between the Creator and the created. Deification, therefore, is all about being *rescued in order to become what we once were - inbreathed, and living in the reflection of God's light and glory*. It's all about the fact that Christ has come to us in order to lead us back to God; to lead captivity captive (Eph. 4:8).

Rescue, therefore, *necessitates* a divinely appointed miracle! "...Christianity claims that in the extraordinary conception of Jesus we see the truth of which all those pagan stories are parodies. Of course this is shocking. Of course it is an affront to other worldviews. It only makes sense within the Judaeo-Christian worldview, specifically within the worldview that is opened up by the resurrection of Jesus."5

The entire incarnation of God in Christ was truly a Moment of Light.

"And the Word became flesh and lived among us, and we have seen his glory..." (John 1:14)

JESUS IN THE WILDERNESS

The ministry of Jesus begins at the very point at which Adam lost His inbreathed power. Jesus had just emerged from the waters of baptism (Luke 4:1) and the Spirit had fallen upon Him. In the wilderness, Satan attempts to attack Jesus in a similar manner as he did with Adam. What a contrast! From the paradise of a garden to the very wilderness of life, it was the only arena in which it really could take place. Clearly, his attempt to work on the ego of Jesus fell far too short. Jesus was very secure in His identity. He had nothing to prove. But we shall see that our *primary interest in this crafty encounter is in seeing how the entire story of redemption was under attack!* Jesus, the Son of God, is to undergo harassment *in His humanity and in His divinity*. We remember that Luke traces the genealogy of Jesus, beginning with Joseph, through David and back to God. Matthew proceeds backwards to Abraham. However, both authors agree on Christ's human and divine natures. Also, both agree that, unlike Adam, the Real Adam did not succumb to Satan's wiles (Heb. 5:15).

"If you are the Son of God, command this stone to become a loaf of bread" (Luke 4:3).

"If you are the Son of God…" is significant in that the definite article is used.

Probably, it was *the assurance of His divinity* which was under attack. And it began immediately after Christ's baptismal anointing. Had Jesus given in to the devil's taunt, then He would have secured for Satan a guaranteed following from then on! Jesus' mind was on eternal things of the kingdom, and not on short-term solutions!

The devil had offered Jesus a simple way to solve the problem of world hunger! Ironically, it was a problem of which Satan was diabolically the chief agent! How could a compassionate person resist such an offer? Jesus was not a sentimentalist! We note that He never denied that Satan had the power to give what he offered. Had He given in to this easy solution, what would it mean concerning His compromised kingdom? *Did Satan really believe he had the power to change, or take hold of the ultimate nature of God's kingdom on earth?* The kingdom principle in Eden was that God provided, but His children would cultivate fruit in a life of worship. Satan wanted nothing less than worship. If he could only get Jesus, right now? We remember that everything which was performed in the Adam community was in accordance with God's purposes; *at least while Adam kept his focus on the kingdom of God!*

The second temptation bears out the point of Christ's dual nature. The devil offered Jesus the kingdoms of the world (Luke 4:5-7). Had not this been previously offered to Adam by God? (Gen. 1:28) What an arrogant usurper! Who had allowed Satan to roam the earth in the first place? (Job 1:7) And then, who was it that had to win back the kingdom by the price of His own blood? *A successful attack on Christ's mission, exercised in humility, would have meant that Jesus had sold out God's entire redemptive purposes (Phil. 2:5-10.) The short-term goal would certainly have relieved Jesus of the cost of dying for the sake of humanity's redemption!*

In the third temptation, it would appear that Jesus could have been enticed. After all, He still possessed what Adam had lost. Had Jesus acquiesced, it would have meant that humanity possibly could have secured for itself the control, or the restoration of all time. Humanity could live forever, after all! (Satan was using the original tactic once again.) The *consequences* of detracting the worship focus from God's kingdom authority would have been disastrous. *No longer would faith in God be needed!* "Do not put the Lord your God to the test" (Luke 4:12). Putting the wilderness temptations in their kingdom perspectives, we realize that it was Jesus, *both Man and God,* who said, *"No"* to Satan. Like us, He had the perfect freedom to say, *"Yes"* to the devil, but He didn't! He made decisions from bigger perspectives than those of His own ego. *He made His decisions according to His obedience to every word proceeding from the mouth of God.*

The point that will be made later is that Jesus, as a man, really did calm the storm; He really did walk on the water. *But He did so as the Real Adam!* The Big Story requires that sort of identification of God to humanity through God's inbreathing. This was the reality that was reflected upon the world. Pondering Peter's brief, pre-Pentecost encounter with Christ on the water makes us wonder how much of Adam's original nature still resided in Enoch. And how, from time to time, have we marveled at such glimpses (or signs) in Elijah and others to this very day? "Do not put the Lord your God to the test."

WHO DO THEY THINK HE IS?

It's not surprising that the people of Israel didn't pounce on this notion very quickly. (In fact, as a nation, they rejected Him - John 1:11.) They could deal with ideas of God speaking through creation, through history, and through the prophets (Heb. 1:1), but they found it very difficult to embrace the thought that God had become human. Emmanuel - God Himself is with us! Not surprisingly, the Apostle Paul found it necessary to give an explanation of the need for *divine rescue* when he wrote to his Greek-thinking converts at Philippi. He said,

> *"...who, though he was in the form of God, did not regard equality with God as something to be exploited, but emptied himself, taking the form of a slave, being born in human likeness" (Phil. 2:6-7).*

> *It's not that the Gospel of Jesus Christ was more sophisticated than humanity had ever known, but that the Trinitarian God of Jesus was much more complex than rational thinking could ever comprehend.*

The god of Babel will always be too small. Truly, the nature of the Trinitarian God defies adequate description. It won't be explained fully by the story of a community on a journey, or by the theoretical logistics of a faith borne in rationalism. Examples of two different persons presenting two different Christs are found in the persons of Albert Schweitzer and Rudolph Bultman. Are these two persons at the root of the strange, modern expression, *"the Christ in you"*? It's as if Christ were a different person in everyone!

The truth is the reverse: We are all different persons in Christ (Gal. 4:19, 2Cor. 3:18).

In the early part of the 20th century Albert Schweitzer made a genuine attempt to find the Christ of faith in the historical *events of His life,* particularly as the events related to His Jewish context. Schweitzer was on a *quest for the historical Jesus.* It was in this context, as a Jewish man that, "…the self-consciousness of Jesus underwent a development during the course of his public ministry."6 In his quest to uncover the historical context in which Jesus ministered, and of the perceptions His followers had of Him, Schweitzer determined, "Our conclusions can only be considered valid so long as they are not found incompatible with the recorded facts as a whole."7 It sounds all right, but will the *facts do all the talking; are they enough?*

Quite differently, Rudolph Bultman felt that there was another way to uncover the Christ for all people. His approach to *the Christ of faith* was really quite simple: Reinterpret the so-called miracles of Jesus, and you finish up with someone you can believe in. Miracles are not needed to give credence to Christian belief! *Bultman was far less interested in facts, if the Christ of faith could be discovered beneath the mythology ascribed to Him.* He believed his purpose could be achieved by *de-mythologizing* Christ's so-called miracles. For him, the miraculous intervention of God was an anachronistic notion. As such, it was no longer needed in a more sophisticated understanding of the Christian story. The resurrection of Jesus is sometimes thought of this way.

Bultman believed that miracles were equated with simplistic mythologies inherent in primitive religion. They could be abandoned by Christians in favor of the system he called *"de-mythology."* The intent of his schema was to recover deeper meanings behind mythological concepts. 8 "….de-mythologizing makes clear the true meaning of God's mystery."9 But will faith without the facts of history be enough? The reality is this: The Christ of faith can only be discovered through *fact and faith*; that is if we want authentic Christian experience.

> *When we tread the way of revelation, we walk the pathway of faith as it is paved with the well-worn stones of history.*

The intentions of both Schweitzer and Bultman were admirable. However, in some sense, both attempted to transfix the image of Christ into a papier-mache′ of their own making. They were not alone in forging paths in such directions. Indeed, the 1960's and 70's saw a huge surge in *existential thinking.* However, we cannot point back to pioneering atheists, such as Jean Paul Sartre or the biblically-minded Paul Tillich as the primary voices exalting individual experience as a major arbiter of truth. Subsequently, some Christian thinkers believed in the idea that *my present reality is the way which determines the process of truth.* Indeed, the very idea that subjective, individual human experience becomes the focus of truth's integrity has been relished in the Post-Modern mind. And the notion may have roots in Heisenberg's "uncertainly theory." (circa 1926)

Jesus once asked His own disciples the ultimate question: "But who do you say that I am?" Actually, He would not have asked them that question earlier in His ministry. As a matter of fact, He was more likely, in those early days, to have said, "See that you say nothing to anyone." (Matt.8:4) Jesus wanted the effects of His kingdom life, and the faith which He exercised, to do all the talking. His dual nature had to emerge before them. But now, the twelve were faced with the most awesome question of decision. Peter wasn't very shy! He seemed to be their spokesman anyway. "You are the Messiah, the Son of the living God" (Matt. 16:17). In the Matthew account, Jesus gives a much longer reply than we see recorded in Mark and Luke.

For over 1700 years, this difference has been a major point in deciding the place of Peter in the universal Christian community. However, never, ever did Jesus appear to exalt one person to a place of headship in His community. The mother of James and John certainly discovered that! (Mark 10:43) Let the scholars continue this debate concerning the Matthew addition. (The real problem here was that Christ's disciples had not yet begun to understand the nature of His kingdom. Subsequently, when Jesus washed the feet of His disciples, the event blew their minds. The Kingdom is all about serving one another!)

The Apostle Paul simply addresses the question of Christ's uniqueness in the following way:

"For in him all the fullness of God was pleased to dwell" (Col. 1:19).

"For in him the whole fullness of deity dwells bodily" (Col. 2:9).

His use of the Greek phrase, "pan to plaeroma" means that *absolutely nothing of the fullness of God's deity was left behind!*

WHO DOES HE THINK HE IS?

Until the latter part of His ministry, Jesus downplayed His own divinity by preferring to *let it appear*. In describing Himself, He used the term *Son of Man* with some frequency. In choosing this approach, He was showing that He was truly a real *son of God*; that is, in terms of the relationship associated between God and the family of Adam; i.e., His humanity (Gen. 6:2; Luke 3:23,38). It was also the terminology often used by the prophet Ezekiel when speaking of the ideal prophet and watchman of Israel. Later, He began to assert the nature of His divinity.[10]

For 2000 years the Church has well acknowledged the dual nature of Christ. Suffice it to say that many of the theological problems we encounter in the contemporary mainline Church are usually connected to a poor appreciation, or experience, of the Trinity. Biblical writers were wise in avoiding long theological explanations of an incomprehensible mystery. However, they did not back away from the reality that, *once Christ had appeared on the stage of history, an entirely new apologetic for the nature of God had to be acknowledged.*

And, in the baptism of Jesus, we see both the fullness of God and the perfection of humanity! God was well pleased:

"...the Holy Spirit descended upon him in bodily form like a dove. And a voice came from heaven, 'You are my Son, the Beloved; with you I am well pleased' " (Luke 3:22).

Doesn't that sound like, "It was very good," after Adam had appeared on the scene?

We will also see that the life offered by Jesus (John 10:10) is a reversal of the consequences inherited from the Adam of Eden. It is precisely what God intended for His creation. Secure in His identity, He could say:

> *"And this is eternal life, that they may know you, the only true God, and Jesus Christ whom you have sent...So now, Father, glorify me in your own presence with the glory I had in your presence before the world existed" (John 17:3, 5).*

We remember that the reason why Jesus died was precisely because He claimed to be the Son of God; i.e., in His divinity and humanity! To the leaders of the religious establishment He declared it (Mark 14:61-63; John 19:7). The High Priest was angry! To the representative of the world's secular power, Jesus answered affirmatively that he was the King of the Jews (John 19:33). Pilate caved in to the crowd! *Then, what had Jesus said and done in order to elicit a reply to that astounding and ultimate question?* In the process of discovery, we are to see that Jesus maintained the Spirit-filled ability to do what Adam once did, but lost. He was truly the Charismatic Christ. Secure in this identity, He could face further taunts of Satan, as the man of Eden most certainly did not.

THE REAL ADAM BRINGING CREATION UNDER CONTROL

Wouldn't it be true to ask, if Jesus was *more than a prophet or a guru*, He would have to show He was capable of doing the things that Adam had failed to do? Of course, we are here thinking about the power of Jesus as a human being. Signs and wonders of the Spirit had been evident in some of Israel's Old Testament individuals. Moses, Elijah and Elisha are good examples. But could there be a remnant Person who would actually be the model for an entire *reborn community?* Language is important. Instead of making use of the more spectacular word *miracle*, both John and Luke prefer to use the word *sign* (saemeon). *The call to kingdom life is a call to live in anticipation of the power and obedience of the Real Adam.*

Throughout His ministry we are to see that *Jesus never did say that His kingdom was complete by virtue of His arrival;* hence His teaching on The Lord's Prayer (maybe more aptly named, The Kingdom Prayer - Luke 11:2-4). Rather, as God had given Adam the task of working on nature, so Jesus, and His community, would *demonstrate* what God had intended at the beginning. It was *from the House of Israel, the new community of Eden focused in Jerusalem,* that Jesus would create an apostolic community for His universal mission to the world.

Jesus was not given a new mandate from God. Indeed, after His baptismal inbreathing, Jesus returned to His home town of Nazareth. In the synagogue, He astonished His familiar neighbors with the words of Isaiah:

> *"The Spirit of the Lord is upon me, because he has anointed me to bring good news to the poor. He has sent me to proclaim release to the captives and recovery of sight to the blind, to let the oppressed go free, to proclaim the year of the Lord's favor. Today this scripture has been fulfilled in your hearing" (Luke 4:18-19, 21).*

We note from this mandate that Jesus' mission was summed up in the words: *Proclamation* and *Service.* Clearly, service to others included the justice mission of a hoped-for Jubilee, which never appeared to have happened in the Hebrew community. Jesus subsequently signaled the apostolic character of His mission when speaking to the diminutive Zacchaeus:

> *"I came to seek and to save the lost" (Luke 19:10).*

D.M. Baillie comments on the words of Claude Montefiore, an Anglican bishop who was formerly of the Jewish faith. Montefiore saw a striking difference between the Old and New Testaments. The God of Jesus was, "....a seeking God, whose very nature it is to go the whole way into the wilderness in quest of man." Commenting on this observation, Baillie adds, "Now that does not consent well with a theology which speaks only of the human quest of the Divine, and which will say no more even about the climax of the quest than that it is the supreme discovery by the supreme pathfinder."11 "Where are you?"

Soon after the baptism of Jesus, John the Baptist found himself in prison. He was now questioning if he had been right in taking the role of Jesus' forerunner. No wonder he sent his disciples to Jesus for an assuring clarification. In reply, Jesus quoted a familiar messianic scripture:

"...the blind receive their sight, the lame walk, the lepers are cleansed, the deaf hear, the dead are raised, the poor have good news brought to them" (Luke 7:22-23).

Wasn't this precisely the ministry that Isaiah had foretold of the Anointed Messiah? (Isa. 61:1-2) Let the facts speak for themselves.

Jesus is the healer of nature gone wrong. Mark begins his Gospel with breathtaking alacrity. In a matter of three chapters Jesus had: Exorcised an unclean spirit, healed Peter's mother-in-law of a fever; cured several sick people, and cast out more demons; He healed a leper and a paralyzed cripple, and He also healed a man with a withered hand. Much of this He did in order to show people of the religious establishment, "...that you may know that the Son of Man has authority on earth to forgive sins" (Mark 2:10). His authority did not reside in the religious structures; however, the powers of darkness most certainly feared it. This was clearly an authority of a charismatic nature. Mark Chapter 4 is very significant:

In this chapter Jesus demonstrates His authority over nature itself. Miracles are a significant and essential part of that story.

The miracles of Jesus demonstrate the wholeness that God would have continued to exercise through the inbreathed Adam!

Jesus, the Real Adam declares this in bringing together the meaning of authority (exousia Matt. 28:19) with power (dunamis - Acts 1:8)! All authority in heaven and in earth was given to Him, as was the power to perform it (Matt. 28:18; Luke 3:22). Was not this the same authority and power that was given to Adam?

Here Mark introduces us to a remarkable event. He is with His disciples in a boat under dangerous conditions. The boisterous winds were battering their vessel with merciless violence. Jesus rebuked the winds and waves *by the power of His Word*: "Peace! Be still! Then the wind ceased and there was a dead calm" (Mark 4:39). Does not this remind us of disordered beginnings in the creation process? Similarly, on another occasion, Jesus shows His mastery of chaos, and of the barriers to God's purposes; *He walked on the unruly sea!*

I have a profound admiration for Dr. Hugh Ross and his scientific contributions to contemporary Christian thinking. However, I am not always happy with his theological interpretations. In chapter ten of his book on the Cosmos, Dr. Ross explains how Jesus, *in His divinity*, is able to transcend the limitations of a four-dimensional universe.12 As a physicist, when he explains it to a layperson, such as myself, he makes a wonderful case. Ross explains how it is possible *(when not confined to four-dimensional limitations)* for Jesus to walk on water. Having shown in *mathematical terms* how this is possible, Ross then makes an enormous *theological leap*. He attributes the miracle to the unfettered *divinity of Christ*.

My major problem with this leap of interpretation is that the incarnational identification of God with humanity becomes very weak. In this instance, Jesus can simply don His divinity hat when encountering natural difficulties. As human beings, we are all faced with situations of chaos and disorder. Unfortunately, there is hardly any consolation for us when, in similar situations, we see that Jesus overcame difficulties by donning His divinity mantle. Wasn't He tempted in all points as we are? (Heb. 4:15)

The first Adam did possess this ability to overcome such difficulties - as a human being! (Gen. 1:28) In point of fact, we recall that, in this particular incident, *Jesus invited Peter to walk on the water!* What a cruel invitation if the challenge were not possible. Surely, the invitation was given to Peter precisely because the problem could be overcome *in his humanity!* (I refuse to spiritualize this event when, as an historical event, it is of such significant theological importance.) For one brief Moment of Light in the human experience, *Peter really did walk in creation authority*. Well, he did so until he took his focus off Jesus, and surrendered to the limitations of his fallen nature (Matt. 14:22-33). But, *for one glorious moment, like Jesus, Peter was a breathtaking sign* of what was once possible through the Spirit's inbreathing. And that situation is very similar to the believing Church of today; at least, when it moves in Spirit power. Such signs can happen today, but not in a measure that would signify that the Kingdom has arrived in its fullness. We need to take heart that God can surprise us with such signs.

By taking a large swath to show Christ as the Word of creation, and as the Real Adam of its perfection, John writes his Gospel around seven major signs. Chapters 2-11 are wonderful examples of how this theological schema is presented. These chapters *present Jesus in relation to the seven signs of the kingdom (*and seven days of creation, including the Sabbath). *Clearly, for John, the finished work of Jesus culminates in the resurrection of First Day Light.* In mentioning these seven signs, we see that Jesus stands as the *true cosmic Christ. He straddles the apex of all time as the heart and focus of new creation* (Eph. 1:10; Col. 1:17):

1. Chapter 2:1-11. Changing water to wine: Jesus had come to recreate new wine *(the vibrancy of new creation)* from the impotence of the old order.
2. Chapter 4:46-54. Healing of the nobleman's son: Jesus is the focus of faith and the source of healing and restoration. As in the beginning, we see signs that *there is no sickness or death in the new creation.*
3. Chapter 5. Healing of the crippled man on the Sabbath: *Jesus is Lord of the Sabbath; He is the pioneer of restoration's advent.* First Day Light was made for humanity, not the other way around.
4. Chapter 6:1-59. Feeding of the 5,000: *Jesus is the Living Bread, the Word of Life for God's people, and for all time,* including the ancient wilderness people. (vss.58-59) The twelve baskets remaining supplied Life for the entire apostolic witness to the world.
5. Chapter 6:16-21. Jesus walks on the water: Not bound by the waters of chaos, *the Real Adam has complete authority over all creation, as He does in the new creation.*
6. Chapter 9. Jesus heals the blind man: *As in the beginning, He is the Light of the world illuminating the world's darkness and gloom by the power of the Word. "I am the light of the world"* (John 9:5).
7. Chapter 11:1-44. Jesus raises Lazarus from death: *He is the essential sign of resurrection to new life - the Alpha and Omega of new creation and restoration.* (And, unlike Lazarus, who experienced a *resuscitation* of the old life, Jesus was the "first fruits from the dead" (1 Co. 15:20). When Lazarus died, again, his remains were eventually buried at the Church of St. Lazarus, Lanarka, Cyprus. But Jesus rose with a *restored* body (i.e., the one *essential sign* of the body fitted for the new creation).

In Jesus, God has given us a glimpse of what creation was intended to be, and what it will be at the restoration! In a much better way, through Jesus, humanity reigns in a new creation. Jesus is the head of this restored community. But it is one fashioned from, and through, the old community of Abraham (Gal. 3:29). It will be through this apostolic priesthood that a Spirit-enabled community will continue to sign kingdom life until *the day of the Lord is fulfilled.*

Interspersed in the signs of who Jesus is, John *connects word and action* by recording the astounding claims Jesus makes of Himself. Clearly, for John, verbose claims of Jesus meant very little unless they had been demonstrated by signs of authentic kingdom life:

> *"I am the way, and the truth, and the life. No one comes to the Father except through me" (John 14:6).*

> *"I am the bread of life" (John 6:46).*

> *"I am the light of the world" (John 8:12).*

> *"...before Abraham was, I am" (John 8:58).*

> *"I am the gate" (John 10:9).*

> *"I am the resurrection and the life" (John 11:25).*

Not surprisingly, for some, the notion that John did not write this Gospel is very attractive. The above statements are so incredibly profound they leave little room for the kind of inclusivity such people desire. Indeed the case for authorship ranges between the single writing of John (the brother of James) to a dual authorship. In Raymond Brown's commentary, he also makes note of a German scholar who postulates that there may have been six authors of John's Gospel.13 Further, for many of a more liberal persuasion, John's Gospel usually represents the reflections of a mid-second century community in Ephesus. The Gospel summarizes for them what they feel *Jesus has become* to them as a community. (Is this not a truly existential basis for biblical theology?) If this claim were true, what does it say about the historical integrity of the book, or the honesty of first person language?

Scholars, such as Robert M. Grant, are convinced that John's Gospel was written around the time of Rome's invasion of Jerusalem (70 A.D.) 14 D. Moody Smith notes the distinctive nature of John's Gospel and relates one theory of its origins. "Nevertheless there has been a wide consensus on such things as the likelihood that the Gospel of John represents a distinct form of early Christianity arising out of a Johannine circle or community and that this community possessed traditions about Jesus independent of, if not related to, the synoptic."15 John Robinson may have pressed his case too far. However, in his view, the teaching of Jesus clearly points to Himself as the new Temple of Israel.[vi] Robinson cannot see how the fact of the Temple's desecration and destruction would not have been noted in a later dated Gospel of John. He therefore concludes that John's Gospel was written prior to 70 A.D., and at a time when the claims of the fledgling community could be challenged! 16

The Eastern Orthodox Church is adamant in asserting that John brought Mary (the mother of Jesus) to her new home in Ephesus. From the time of the Ascension to the period of the Temple's destruction, at least thirty-five years had transpired. Clearly, the young John had a considerable amount of time to reflect on the life and ministry of Jesus! He didn't need another fifty years!

Quite regardless of an early or late first century dating, the final content of John's Gospel relays a further tradition that historically supports and broadens the Gospel focused in the *historical Jesus*. Clearly, important historical facts of Jesus' life are there, and especially as they focus on the resurrection! Therefore we simply note that, if the first of the New Testament writings were penned somewhere between 55-60 A.D., then the common apostolic teaching and experience was understood *at least twenty to twenty five years before any writings were being penned or circulated.* And the vast majority of so-called Christian-related Gnostic writings, which later challenged the Church, *did not begin to be written until after the second century was well under way!* Whatever challenges they may or may not hold up to the Church, the Gnostic gospels cannot be considered as possessing any apostolic authority.

We will resist the temptation to linger with these astounding statements in John. However, one thing must be said. *Those statements shock people today equally as much as they did in the time of Jesus.* The fact is that what is often described as a Gospel summary, i.e., John 3:16, is also a summary of the dignity of free choice offered in God's creation. *Therefore, the Gospel is both inclusive and exclusive.* Eternal life is for the *whosoever* that believes. But the corollary to this statement is that eternal life is *not* for those who disbelieve!

But, what about Jesus' connection to the four pillars of Israel? Surely, if Jesus is the fulfillment of Israel's history, then He must be significantly connected to its four pillars. What we are to see is that *the entire Bible, as one Big Story, becomes one story in the person of Jesus Christ.* But we will not begin with Christ's relation to David, the great king. We will begin with the king in Eden.

THE REAL ADAM, KING OF ISRAEL

Jesus saw himself as king, but what sort of king? First of all, He was the Real Adam, *the king of creation.* Mark sees Jesus as the Adam who was not subject to anything in nature at all. Adam had been given authority over all creation; he failed, but the Real Adam didn't. No wonder Christ's disciples were in awe, "Who then is this, that even the wind and sea obey him?" (Mark 4:41) "In the Old Testament the sea is hostile to God, and God's victory over the primordial ocean is celebrated in song. So too in the New Testament, Christ's kingship is seen in his calming of the sea..."17 We also note in Matthew's Gospel that Jesus claimed astounding authority, *from above - not from His followers!*

> *"All authority in heaven and on earth has been given to me"*
> *(Matt 28:18).*

When Christ comes again, He is to return as the Real Adam, King and Master of God's new creation! (Mark 13:24-26; Rev.11:15)

However, Jesus does have a connection with David, the great king of Israel. In Luke's genealogy, Jesus' lineage goes all the way back to "...Adam, son of God" (Luke 3:23-38). However, Matthew dates the lineage back to Abraham (Matt. 1:1). But both make the connection to David. There is no doubt that Jesus saw Himself to be the Lord of King David. Therefore, His ministry showed Him to be the promised ruler of a New Israel:

> *"David himself, by the Holy Spirit, declared, 'The Lord said to my Lord, Sit at my right hand, until I put your enemies under your feet.' David calls him Lord; so how can he be his son?" (Mark 12:36)*

"My kingdom is not from this world" (John 18:36).

Jesus perceived His position to be greater than that of King David. In Jewish eyes, David was the ideal king, but nevertheless David was subject to Him (Mark 12:35-37). Speaking of a *future, eternal reign,* He taught about His own place in this restored community of God (Matt. 13:41, 16:28; Luke 22:30). On other occasions, He also spoke of Himself as *judge and ruler* in God's kingdom (Matt. 25:31-35). Secure in the authority given to Him, He consistently challenged others to grow in the essential characteristics of the kingdom.

From Old Testament perspectives, Jesus saw Himself to be the centre of a predicted messianic reign in the new creation (Zech. 9:9). On the occasion when he rode on a donkey into Jerusalem He did nothing to dispel the jubilation of the crowd:

> **"Hosanna! Blessed is the one who comes in the name of the Lord! Blessed is the coming kingdom of our ancestor David. Hosanna in the highest heaven" (Mark 11:9-10).**

The entry into Jerusalem (the present sign of a new Eden) was an eschatological sign of the coming kingdom! If this meaning is not understood, then the occasion stands as a pathetic parody of a pretended authority. The Holy City of Jesus was to be a *New Jerusalem; a Jerusalem above; a Jerusalem that is free!* (Gal. 4:26) A prophet, much later than David, saw the picture:

> **"My servant David shall be king over them: and they shall have one shepherd...and my servant David shall be their prince forever. I will make a covenant of peace with them; it shall be an everlasting covenant with them; and I will bless them and multiply them, and will set my sanctuary among them for evermore" (Ezek. 37:24-26).**

> **"For here we have no lasting city, but we are looking for the city that is to come" (Heb. 13:14).**

And, therefore, Jesus saw His universal commission to begin from Israel's old city:

> *"All authority in heaven and earth has been given to me. Go therefore and make disciples of all nations..." (Matt. 28:18-19; Luke 24:49; Acts 1:4, 8)*

Without a shadow of doubt, the apostles of Jesus began to see a little more clearly that He was to be the king of a new creation. Although this kingdom would appear in a *moment of restoration,* it is very real. In some way, it is *connected to this present world.* It is, in fact, the kingdom that God has prepared from the foundation of the world. Jesus is to occupy centre stage in it. He was fully aware of the fact! Unabashedly, He asserted that *He has the authority to judge and rule in this kingdom, which He, Himself, will bring to consummation* (Matt. 7:21-23, 25:31-46, 28:17-20; Luke 21:27, 22:28-30, 23:42-43; Rev. 5:9-10).

THE REAL ADAM IS OUR HIGH PRIEST

In all major versions of the Greek New Testament, the word for priest, *'hieros'* is used in three ways only. *But never, in the New Testament, is the word ever associated with a specific order of Christian ministry!* However, New Testament mention of priesthood is clearly related to:

> *The priesthood of the Temple, the finished, High-Priesthood of Jesus (Hebrews Chapter 7), The priesthood of all believers (1Pet. 2:9).*

In this sense, as it was in the beginning, it followed the original pattern of Adam and Eve. *The entire Body of Christ is the appointed priesthood of creation.* And, in Christ's connection with the priesthood of Melchizedek, the entire priesthood of believers is also a priesthood of creation - but *not of blood sacrifice!* The connection of priesthood with Jesus is, to the writer of Hebrews (now that Jesus has completed the Aaronic blood sacrifice), associated with Melchizedek, and not now a lingering shadow of the blood sacrifice of Aaron. If this is not true, then the finished work of Jesus is really not finished at all! It *is* finished, and is always efficacious as an offering of creation's innocent fruit in the community of the redeemed.

Both Peter and Paul agree that *the primary function of the present New Testament priesthood is* kerigmatic; it is one of universal proclamation of the gospel of reconciliation. (2 Co. 5:19-20; Rom. 15:16; Acts 2:38-40, Acts 4:18-20) In the Book of Revelation, the writer looks to a picture of *consummation* with a kingdom of priests reigning on earth, and in priestly service to God (Rev. 5:10). Isn't that the way it was in the beginning? However, *in the completed work of Christ, it is Jesus, as High Priest and victim,* who offers the grace of God to a needy and penitent world. He is the Abraham (priest) and Isaac (victim) that never really happened!

Moses believed the *whole nation of Israel* was called to be a priesthood (Ex. 19:6). But, in the ministry of Jesus, we see Him as the *Great High Priest of a nation of priests,* existing *on behalf of all nations* (Matt. 28:19-20). Clearly, it is only in seeing Jesus as the High Priest (in the *finished* offering of Himself, Lev. 7:6) and the perfect victim (which was slain, Lev. 1:3) that we understand His New Covenant work as High Priest. Also, we see Him to be the focus and Head of a new and universal priesthood. *It is a restored priesthood of creation.* It is a priesthood consisting of both male and female. As in the beginning, it is a priesthood with a mission. It is called to "proclaim the mighty acts of him who called you out of darkness into his marvelous light" (1 Pet. 2:9). Clearly, this was the apostolic mission to which Abraham's race had previously been called (Gen. 12:3). And the priest holding greatest significance for him was Melchizedek! In Jesus, we see *God's priesthood* of love reaching to all the nations of the earth. "For God so loved the world...." (John 3:16)

The New Testament plainly points to the priesthood of Jesus as the one Mediator who completes the blood sacrifice of the Aaronic priesthood. But the Old Testament, recognizing the genealogical mystery surrounding Melchizedek, does not appear to connect the sacrificial priesthood of the future Aaron with the eternal priesthood of Melchizedek (Heb. 7:6). However, the writer to the Hebrews does speak of the *completion of this Aaronic priesthood in terms of the finished work of Christ* (Heb. 7:11-24, 9:12, 24). Now, the original priesthood of the Adam community is figured again in the *eternal priesthood* of Melchizidek. *It is the rightful, New Covenant priesthood of Jesus. The New Covenant (Luke 22:20) is celebrated in the offering of the fruit of new creation innocence (bread and wine)*. Of course, once beyond the gates of Eden, Cain couldn't do it. And, ultimately, neither could Abel (Heb. 12:24). Surely, Abraham, the father of Israel, prefigured this by offering a tenth to Mechizedek and by *receiving the fruit of creation from his hand - bread and wine*. In His own body and blood, Jesus offered the *innocent sacrifice of creation*. Jesus was the innocent, and perfect, Paschal Lamb. In other words, it was not simply and exclusively a priest, on behalf of the people, offering the sacrifice of substitution, but Jesus the High Priest, like Melchizedek, gracefully offering to the priesthood of all believers, the restored offerings of Eden's innocence.

It is now, in Christ, that His entire priestly community is graced to enter into the celebration of the *fruits of His innocence!* It is a New Covenant, which connects and *completes* the Aaronic work of redemption in *Christ's own body and blood* (Heb. 5:5:6). It is the celebration of a priesthood no longer limited to gender, but consisting of the entire redeemed priesthood of a new Eden. Therefore, at every service of Holy Communion, the duly appointed celebrant, *on behalf of the entire priestly community*, is graced to present the *worshipful fruits of innocence*. In some orthodox language, this offering is described as the "sacrifice of praise and thanksgiving." (Like David, should not the participants literally dance to the banqueting table of God?) But this terminology should now be seen as an act of innocent worship. Praise and thanksgiving can now, through Jesus, be *offered in a state of innocence*. (Heb. 13:15-16 is then best understood in the light of Rom. 12:1.) Jesus, alone, is our Mediator, who stands between God and His people. He does so for all time by offering to God's people the fruits of Eden's innocence! Who wants to join the dance? The Lord's Presence is actually with those who do!

"For this reason he is the mediator of a new covenant, so that those who are called may receive the promised eternal inheritance, because a death has occurred that redeems them from the transgressions under the first covenant" (Heb. 9:15).

> *"You are a priest forever according to the order of Melchizedek...accordingly Jesus has also become the guarantee of a better covenant" (Heb. 7:17,22).*

The eternal banquet of a New Covenant, alluded to by Jeremiah, is now focused upon an intimate and eternal *relationship* with God through Jesus Christ

(Jer. 31:31-34; Heb. 8:8-13). Further, it is brought, as Jesus implies, to fullness of meaning in the *priestly sacrifice* of His own body and blood. And so, on Calvary's cross, Jesus incorporated the now *completed ministry* of the Aaronic priesthood with the eternal priesthood of Melchizedek. Therefore, at every communion service, *the entire priestly community is accounted as the innocents of Eden* when they, in penitence and worship, are graced to enjoy the benefits of creation's fruit of innocence.

JESUS OFFERS A MYSTERY

As the High Priest of New Creation, *there was an awesome sense of mystery when Jesus touched the ordinary stuff of the earth.* At the last supper, He astounded His disciples by offering the daily, common elements of bread and wine. The first of two wine cups (in Luke) may have represented the Chaburah fellowship of a teacher with his disciples. Typically, such a community, comprising a synagogue, met weekly for a meal and spiritual sharing. By the awesome consecration of the second cup, *Jesus brought together (in a new covenant) the sacrifice of Passover. (i.e., the Aaronic Passover of the blood, a passing over of God's judgment) with that of the Melchizedek offerings of innocence.* These are the creation offerings of innocence in bread and wine. Like David, the priesthood in celebration embraces the dance of Eden's innocence. And the very Word, which spoke creation into being, also said:

> *"This is my body which is given for you" (Luke 22:19).*

The saving manna of Moses was the life-giving body of Christ (Ex. 16:4; John 6:30-35). Then, He took the second cup with the words,

> *"This cup which is poured out for you is the new covenant in my blood" (Luke 22:19-20).*

This is precisely the language of a new covenant, which Jeremiah predicted! It would be a covenant of a *heart-relationship* (Jer. 31:31-34).

Most certainly, it is at this Eucharistic feast that the *most incomprehensible mystery* is presented to Christ's followers. Gloriously, this offering represents both a new covenant of heart relationship with God, and also the mystery of sacrificial worship; a sacrifice offered and completed in the body and blood of Christ. *It is a mystery connecting, in the body of Jesus, the offering of the fruit of innocence (dating back to Adam's innocent offering of creation) with the fruit of Christ's completed sacrifice. Obviously, we can't be invited to enter into the life of an unfinished sacrifice.* The Aaronic priesthood is over, and its completeness is celebrated at every celebration! (Heb. 7:11) Very clearly, the writer to Hebrews sees the Aaronic priesthood (now completed in Jesus) to be one, now completed in the light of Melchizedek's eternal priesthood of innocence. It is *eternally* ministered in Jesus (Heb. 7:17).

Apart from the priesthood of *all* believers (1 Pet. 2:9), surely it is not accidental that the New Testament *never* refers to a priestly order of ministry in the new covenant community. We do observe a structure advocated in Corinthians when *elders* are instructed to conduct worship decently and in order (1 Co. 14:40). Surely, the Catholic-Protestant tensions concerning Eucharistic theology must both be challenged with the question: Why did the ministry of elders (presbuteroi), not priests (hiereoi) not evolve in the first century i.e., to an order of priests? (Some, condescendingly, describe this era as belonging to the Primitive Church. What was primitive about its remarkably diverse structures? Please note the author's book, There Must Be Another Way.) There is no etymological connection between hieros and presbuteros; except by its subsequent, continuous usage. Further, *in asking this question, considerably more questions will be applied to our present ecclesiology.* However, whatever the tradition, the astounding *mystery* of the Eucharist must be maintained.

We can't get away from it! In fulfillment of the Aaronic priesthood, Jesus, vicariously offered bread and wine in the words, "This *is* my body" (Luke 22:19). "This cup...*is* the new covenant in my blood" (Luke 22:20; Lev. 17:11; italics mine). Jesus never said that the bread and wine *represented or symbolized* His body and blood anymore than a sign post in the sky represented the universe under construction. "Do this" may also be translated as, "Celebrate this"-poieo. The Word, which once said, "Let there be," also said, "This *is*." Jesus said it, and we believe it! (Luke 22:20) Here, we are speaking of spiritual realities which *no amount of theology may explain, or explain away!* We can't explain the mystery of Christ's Presence, any more than we can explain its so-called absence. Whatever disagreements exist in denominational thinking, we should at least agree that the connection of the Last Supper with the promised new covenant of Jeremiah is all about the recovery of the eternal and *essential relationships of Eden's innocence.* And these covenantal signatures, offered at considerable cost to God, are the lively assurances that the penitential recipients are now accounted as innocents of the new Eden. It's all about Presence! "Where are you?" is a question *never asked* at this celebration.

Quite possibly, much of the theological disagreement concerning the Eucharist, which has often occurred since the sixteenth century, may have been avoided, had there been an equal consideration of a *Melchizedek-creation theology centered on Eden's fruit of innocence.* At the Last Supper, Jesus was about to make possible precisely what Jeremiah had predicted (Jer. 31:31). He offered to His disciples, the *fruits of His own innocence.* "This cup…is the new covenant in my blood" (Luke 22:20).

The New Covenant, anticipated by Jeremiah, took flesh in that astounding Moment of Light. Jesus, the Bread of Life, said so! (John 6:35) The final steps on the path of redemption began from a banqueting table. From the moment of Christ's resurrection and ascension, a restored priesthood of creation would continue to invite the world to a lavish *celebration* that would last forever!

> *The Last Supper was an anticipatory moment of an eternal banquet, celebrated at a table of everlasting abundance. And those who participate in this banquet feed eternally without the sweat of their own labor, or by the signature of their own effort.*

Jesus, as priest and victim, has offered the sacrifice of Himself, once and for all! Through this offering, Jesus drew into Himself a universal priesthood; *a priesthood of proclamation.* "…be a minister of Christ Jesus to the Gentiles in the priestly service of God, so that the offering of the Gentiles may be acceptable…" (Rom. 15:16) This eternally graced priesthood, as in Eden, is now declared to be:

> ***"…a royal priesthood…God's own people, in order that you may proclaim the mighty acts of him who called you out of darkness into his marvelous light" (1 Peter 2:9;.italics mine).***

THE REAL ADAM IS BOTH PROPHET
AND LAW-GIVER

So was Moses, by the way! (Deut. 34:10) In His dissertation, sometimes called, the Sermon on the Mount, Jesus once said that He had not come to abolish the law, but to fulfill it (Matt. 5:17). What did He mean by that? Surely, He could not have meant that He would demand strict obedience to the old covenant! Surely, He wasn't asking His followers to obey every Levitical law, and the myriads of tedious laws that were added on by the Pharisees! Of course not! In His wonderfully perceptive way of explaining God's principles for creation, Jesus reinterpreted how the essence and purpose of law was simply to enable God's people to live in the personal embracing of *essential relationships of Eden's dance.* Jesus' view of kingdom character goes all the way back to a harmonious Eden. Jesus, in obedience to the Father, was able to fulfill those impossibly high standards where Adam had failed.

His view of law was a matter of heart relationships. "I will put my law within them, and I will write it on their hearts; and I will be their God, and they will be my people" (Jer. 31:33). A good example of how Jesus got to the heart of relationships is gleaned when we make a quick comparison of the character difference between The Decalogue (Ex. 20:1-17) and The Beatitudes (Matt. 5:1-12).

Almost consistently, each of the Ten Commandments is prefaced with a *negative tone of admonition.* These commandments, as a call for changed behavior, are prefaced by the words, "You shall not..." No doubt Jesus preached the principles of the Beatitudes many times, and in a variety of places. Clearly, He felt no need for restraint in times when He was challenged on matters of law. "You have heard that it was said...But I say to you..." (Matt. 5:27) *It was Jesus who could delve into the very heart of the Law!*

We observe in Jesus *an approach emanating from a heart condition* (Jer. 31:33). It is clearly His pattern of life. Behavior would proceed from the basis of heart relationships; just as they once were in Eden. "Blessed are those..." In Him there is a call to certain types of behavior representing a quality of joyful relationships. Jesus taught His listeners that their primary focus was to be one of living out the principles of the kingdom of God. "But strive first for the kingdom of God *and his righteousness...*" (Italics mine; Matt. 6:33)

Jesus used this famous Sermon on the Mount to encourage His listeners to live by such motivation and standards. Actually, much of the Sermon on the

Mount appears to be addressed to His disciples, not the crowd. He was not casting pearls before swine. The call of Jesus was to one of total commitment to life in the kingdom of God (See Matt. 5:1-2; Luke 6:20). Sometimes, in the same context, as Jesus intimated, we may cast pearls where they are not appreciated (Matt. 7:6). In other words, the character of a life with Jesus at the centre is a kingdom-focused life.

As such, Jesus positively attributes happiness (makarios- also translated, *blessed*) to those who *are* living with a covenant focus and a kingdom motivation. It is incomprehensible to imagine how anyone can live up to the teachings of the Sermon on the Mount. *But these standards, which are impossible to attain to perfection, point to the fact that, in order to live the kingdom life, God's community has to rely on His grace alone.* After the seemingly impossible standards He had set, the exasperating admonition to be perfect, as is our heavenly Father (Matt. 5:48; 2 Co. 13:9), is a call to a quality of discipleship that reaches to *kingdom standards of relationships.* They are not lowered to levels of sentimental individualism, or to the petulance of a fickle culture. Nor were they lowered to an easily attainable level of a Barabbas crowd. Clearly, all of humanity stands in the need of grace. The Apostle Paul didn't invent the idea of justification by faith (Rom. 1:17, 5:1). He did not initiate the idea of living joyfully in the grace of God (Eph. 2:8). Habakkuk had already caught a glimpse of this (Hab. 2:4). Jesus clearly intimated it in everything He said and did.

> *God, by grace, accounts us as worthy to receive the full status of adopted children (i.e., sons of God; John 1:12) even though our individual efforts will never match His standards of "essential relationships."*

This prophetic tone of hope may be observed in many places throughout the New Testament. In 2 Pet. 1:19 the prophetic message is also likened to a *lamp shining in a dark place.* The Word is truly a lamp to our feet and a light to our path (Ps. 139:105). All the Synoptic writers show Peter, James and John witnessing the Transfiguration of Jesus (e.g., Mark 9:2-8). Before their very eyes, Jesus is bathed in glistening light. The event was a signature prelude to the victory of the Resurrection and Ascension. Reflecting on this astounding *Moment of Light,* Peter, like John, sees an *inextricable connection between Light and Word*

(2 Pet. 1:16-19; John 1:5). The three apostles are privileged to gaze upon the same glory that shone upon the First Day of creation, and also on the proto-typical mountains of Israel. Standing with Jesus were Moses and Elijah. They represented the *only two* foundational pillars that were to *remain* in the future life of Israel: the Law and the Prophets. After the sacking of Jerusalem in 70 A.D. there was no longer a priesthood, and neither was there a monarchy!

The entire event is prophetic. *It is symbolic of a Judaism that is to continue without a city and a temple; at least, not as they had known it!* To this very day (apart from orthodox Jews and others who continue to hope for a king and priest in Zion) *Judaism reveals itself in the light of Law and Prophets.* The Pharisaic vision of a Judaism existing through synagogue worship had succeeded. But, on this mountain of transfiguration, the brilliance of dazzling light was given to Jesus, not Moses or Elijah! Jesus is the very Shekina Glory that illuminates the mountains of those pivotal figures. Clearly, the Mountain of Transfiguration appears to signify a dazzling pinnacle of revelation declaring completion. This teleological event completely focuses the story of Israel in the light of Christ. Not coincidentally, the account ends with the following words. As the images of Moses and Elijah fade away, the three followers of Jesus heard a voice from above:

> ***"This is my Son, the Beloved; listen to him. Suddenly when they looked around, they saw no one with them any more, but only Jesus" (Mark 9:7-8).***

Greek texts clearly denote the use of the passive voice when referring to Christ's change of appearance. *It was made possible by an act from above!* Christ is acted upon by the Father, whose desire, through the Spirit, is to reveal the Son, the Light of the world! (John 16:13-14) It is no accident of the pen that Moses and Elijah are then seen to fade right out of the scene.

> *The entire story of Israel is now summed up in the One*
> *Who is its Adam and Eve, its Light, its Word, and its Glory.*

And the Law of relationships in the community is now summed up in the words:

"You shall love the Lord your God with all your heart, and with all your soul, and with all your mind…And a second is like it: You shall love your neighbor as yourself. On these two commandments hang all the law and the prophets" (Matt. 22:39-40).

"I give you a new commandment, that you love one another. Just as I have loved you, you also should love one another" (John 13:34).

Does this mean that the story of redemption is now over? Surely, such consummation could not possibly occur until at least Jesus had assumed the full role of the obedient servant of Isaiah (e.g., Isa. Chapter 53). Wasn't Jesus born in order to die? The sacrifice of Christ could not be simply a sentimental myth or a beautiful theological story. *It had to be an indisputable fact of history.*

Chapter 7   The Real Adam and the Light of the World

1. Day, Gardiner. *The Apostles Creed*, p.58. Scribners, New York 1963
2. Meyendorff, J., *St. Gregory Palamas and Orthodox Spirituality*, p.38. St. Vladimir's Press N.Y (1974)
3. Lossky, Vladimir., *The Mystical Theology of the Eastern Church*, p.134. St. Vladimir's Press (1976)
4. Meyendorff, J. *St. Gregory Palamas and Orthodox Spirituality,* p.40
5. Wright N.T., *Who Was Jesus?* P.84 Wm. B. Eerdmans, Grand Rapids, Michigan (1992)
6. Schweitzer, Albert. *The Quest Of The Historical Jesus*, p7 MacMillan Publishing Co., 866, Third Av., New York, N.Y. 10022. 1968.
7. Schweitzer, Alfred, Ibid. p7
8. Bultman, Rudolph. *Jesus Christ and Mythology*, p.18. The Scribner Library, Charles Scribner's Sons,New York, 1958
9. Bultman, Rudolph, Ibid. p.43
10. Meyendorff, John *St. Gregory Palamas and Orthodox Spirituality*, p.123
11. Baillie, D.M. *God Was In Christ*, pp.63-64, Faber and Faber Ltd. London, 1961
12. Ross, Hugh. *Beyond the Cosmos*, p.119
13. Brown, Raymond E, (Editor: Francis J. Maloney) *An Introduction to the Gospel of John*, p.47, Doubleday of Random House, 1745 Broadway, New York, NY, 10019. 2003
14. Grant, Robert M. *Historical Introduction to the New Testament,* p.160 Harper and Rowe Publishers, 49, East 33rd St., New York 16, N.Y. 1963.

15. Moody Smith, D, *John Among The Gospels,* p.75. Fortress Press, Minneapolis, 1992

16. Robinson, John A.T. *Redating the New Testament,* p.275, SCM Press. London, 5th impression 1984

17. Leach, Kenneth. *True Prayer*, p.6. Anglican Book Centre, Toronto, 1980.

Chapter 8

WHEN IS REDEMPTION'S STORY COMPLETE?

Jesus was the perfect icon of kingdom life. Yet, although He fed the multitudes, He went to bed each night surrounded by throngs of starving people. Although He healed the sick, He went to bed each night surrounded by all manner of disease and disorder. Although He raised a few people from the dead, He went to bed each night as thousands faced a dark night of death. Although He preached about new birth, He went to bed each night with millions living in ignorance and darkness. Although He taught and lived the meaning of peace and justice, He slept in a world gripped in the vice of horrendous conflict and injustice. His entire ministry had been one of signature. His works proved to be signs of the kingdom yet to be fulfilled in His completed work.

In Jesus, God gave us a glimpse of what creation was intended to be, and what it will be at the restoration! But now, the time had come for an earth-shaking sacrifice; it would be one that would change the course of sacrificial history forever. And where would this sacrifice take place? On Mount Zion, of course! As we follow the Easter events from Friday to Sunday, we shall be privy to momentous *Moments of Light* summarizing the entire meaning of creation, redemption and restoration.

CALVARY WAS A DECISION

The question is, *whose decision?* Jesus didn't have to go to Jerusalem - at least, not unless the will of the Father was of the first order in His life (John 8:28-29). As a matter of fact, Jesus had already told His disciples that it was necessary for Him to die in order to rise again (Matt. 16:21-23). At that time, they didn't have a clue what He was talking about and, as usual, it was Peter who spoke up with a naïve, though well-meaning attempt to protect Jesus. In Luke's Gospel, Jesus, knowing what was before Him, deliberately trod the path to the Holy City because, "no prophet can die outside of Jerusalem" (Luke 13:22, 33). *But Jesus didn't see Himself as a heroic martyr.* He knew He was to be the Savior and Suffering Servant for the world. Having said this, Jesus must have known the theological tension that would arise by accepting this role.

Jewish scholars have always been perfectly correct in identifying the Suffering Servant as the community of Israel. Even Jesus declared to the Samaritan woman that, "...salvation is from the Jews" (John 4:22). However, we must also acknowledge that, to the time of Jesus, the suffering of the Jewish nation had come largely through their *disobedience* to God. "And many nations...will say one to another, 'Why has the Lord dealt in this way with that great city?' And they will answer, 'Because they abandoned the covenant of the Lord their God, and worshiped other gods and served them'" (Jer. 22:8-9). On the other hand, we see the opposite occurring in the life of Jesus. It really was upon a single and Remnant Person that suffering was inflicted through the fruits of *obedience.* "...we do see Jesus...now crowned with glory and honor because of the suffering of death, so that by the grace of God he might taste death for everyone" (Heb. 2:9). Subsequently, the *new community of Israel, the offspring of Abraham, through faith in Christ* (Gal. 3:29), was, in the same way, called to tread the path of suffering in obedience to God. "If we have died with him, we will also live with him; if we endure, we will also reign with him" (2 Tim. 2:11-12). This is really one Big, and continuing Story!

It was only after Calvary, and in subsequent *moments of Easter,* that Peter began to see this *Big Story* clearly:

> **"He was destined before the foundation of the world, but was revealed at the end of the ages for your sake. Through him you have come to trust in God, who raised him from the dead and gave him glory..." (1 Pet. 1:20-21)**

For some, the fickle crowd acclaiming Christ's entry into Jerusalem parodied the reality of Jesus' sense of mission. One theologian believes that Jesus saw in His limited success in Galilee, His betrayal, His rejection, and, in the whimsical nature of the crowd, *the ultimate failure of His past ministry.*[1] Edward

Shillibeeckx goes on to describe this *second phase* as no less of a failure. The ministry in Jerusalem is, "...an attempt to salvage the 'fiasco' in Galilee."2 Quite regardless of that rather weak theory, it is important for us to stress that, if we don't believe Jesus saw Calvary to be the necessary climax of *His redemptive ministry* then, what was to follow in Jerusalem would surely be a continuation of this *fiasco*.

> *The crucifixion, in the mind of Jesus, was to be the highlight, and the climactic Moment of Light in the entire story of redemption.*

The idea that suffering would figure prominently at the heart of faith goes against the grain of our stoic, me-centered, wanton, and feely culture. Suffering, not triumphalism, is the norm of the Christian journey! (Rom. 8:18; 2 Co. 1:7-8) *We see the identification of God with humanity more profoundly in the suffering of Jesus than in any other part of the human experience.* The cross was the will of the Father (Matt. 16:21). Jesus knew this before He entered Jerusalem! Fully cognizant of the role prophetically laid before Him, Jesus walked the way of Zion in active obedience to the Father's will, and also in the knowledge that He was to be:

> *"...delivered up, according to the definite plan and foreknowledge of God..." (Acts 2:23)*

Even though the Father didn't offer it, Jesus might have easily justified to Himself another course of action! In another Garden, called, Gethsemane, Jesus refused the desirable fruit of self-centered survival. Satan was in this garden too! Silently, without argument, He accepted God's cup of redemptive sacrifice.

> *"...I always do what is pleasing to Him" (John 8:29).*

> *"...remove this cup from me; yet, not what I want, but what you want." (Mark 14:36)*

THE BARABBAS SYNDROME

Why did Jesus choose the cross? Because it was God's idea! Some may desire to blame the Jewish establishment, or Pontius Pilate, or Judas. Or they may want to blame the crowd for its fickleness in choosing Barabbas. All of these factors are somewhat responsible agents in the death of Jesus! Here, we see what we may call, *The Barabbas Syndrome* appearing in stark and ugly form. What does this term mean?

The crowd will always choose a Barabbas over Jesus.

The crowd is much more easily manipulated than are thoughtful and deliberate-minded individuals (1 Pet. 3:15). It's interesting that, when it suited their own agenda, *the religious establishment* incited the crowd on the basis of *an appeal to its lowest instincts.*

Isn't this still happening? Imagine: it was members of the religious establishment who enticed the crowd to respond to Pilate at the level of *eros.* Eros, a Greek word denoting sensual love, speaks a lot of making choices at the level of the emotions, or of self-centered sentiment. It is never used in the New Testament to describe a way of discipleship.

Jesus, at the post-resurrection appearance to Peter, challenged him at the level of *agape* - total and uncompromising commitment. (Used in John 3:16.) Agape denotes the way of the cross. Peter wanted to settle for *philia* - a more middle ground word denoting friendship, or being a good pal (John 22:15-17). Taking the Sermon of the Mount as another example (Matt. 5-7), we see that Jesus calls for the *very highest in humankind* in order to live a kingdom life. It can be lived out by God's grace alone. And so, what we see here is that members of the religious establishment set the tone for a *Church becoming more willing to be chaplains to the culture than to be prophets within it.*

In the contemporary Western world, the media has become the most powerful tool to entice the crowds with the agendas of a new social establishment. The Barabbas Syndrome really works for the media! And, in equally subtle ways, the syndrome also continues in most mainline churches of today. The crowd, allowing biblical ignorance and their sentiments to reside at the very easy level of a Barabbas, *appears to be very tolerant* during the expectation of higher standards. In contrast, people who love enough to call for the highest in us challenge us in empathetic love, but may appear to the crowd as being very intolerant.

Jesus stood before the crowd, the religious establishment, and also the Roman authority, prepared to go the way of the cross. As God's ultimate icon, He appeals to our highest impulses! Here, we sentimentalize a Barabbas while we fashion a Jesus into a plastic image of our own making. For a crowd, sentiment easily triumphs over truth and righteousness. For this crowd, Barabbas *never* poses a challenge to their chosen life-styles. He appeals to the lowest in all of us. *It would appear that Barabbas theology is appearing in many of our mainline churches today.* If the best of Roman justice and ideals had prevailed on that day, Barabbas would have taken the place of Jesus! His name means, "son of father." But what father?

THE PASSIVE CHRIST

"The story of the death of Jesus and of what led up to it and flowed from it, which occupies such disproportionate space in the Gospel (a third of Mark and nearly half of John), reflects the decisive importance for the early Christian preaching of the death and resurrection of Christ."3 This period proved to be the most significant turning point in the earthly ministry of Jesus. It is the period in which *He allowed* the powers of destruction to go unimpeded in their ravenous desire to secure His death.

To the point of His betrayal, *Jesus had been actively in control* of His life and ministry. Verbs associated with Jesus are usually in the active mood. He initiated the course of events; *He is at the centre of activity; Jesus is always in control;* when He is around, something is always happening! He is fully in charge of the outcome of each event. "It is the activity of Jesus which maintains the momentum. He is constantly moving from place to place, from situation to situation; and always it is His intervention in word or deed which changes the situation."4

Once Jesus is handed over in the Garden of Gethsemane, a change in grammatical mood, particularly in Mark, is plainly evident. "The change of manner consists in this - that from this point to the moment of Jesus' death on the cross, a period which occupies, in Souter's text, one hundred lines of narrative, Jesus is the grammatical subject of just nine verbs. And the reason for the change is not, of course, that Mark has now gone on to a different story and that Jesus is no longer there. Jesus is there all the time, at the very center of the story. But now, He is no longer there as the active and initiating subject of what is done. He is there as the recipient, the object of what is done."5 The Suffering Servant of Isaiah Chapter 53 was:

"...oppressed and he was afflicted, yet he did not open his mouth; like a lamb that is led to the slaughter, and like a sheep that before its shearers is silent, so he did not open his mouth."

In spite of opposition in Jerusalem, and particularly from the time of His cleansing the Temple, Jesus had not shied away from public ministry. But the *nature of the Paschal Lamb* had to become apparent to worldly powers before it was offered in sacrifice. *He was to be led* like a lamb in a passive manner. By walking the way of Old Testament prophecy, it is here that some commentators don't want to be too hard on Judas Iscariot. They have a point. John Vanstone makes some interesting observations about the language used to describe Christ's betrayal.

In the gospels the verb, *to betray-* prodidomi, is used only once, while the verb, *to hand over* - paradidomi, is used on thirty-one occasions. This is a relatively colorless word; but it is this word which describes the act of Judas, "...and the word is by no means the kind of derogatory or offensive word which we should expect from writers who thought so very ill of Judas."6 Quite possibly, Vanstone is reminding us that, in the selection of this particular word, we all understand what it means to *hand over* Jesus. *Peter did!*

Upon His arrest and confrontation with Pontius Pilate, Jesus was faced with the question of whether or not He was the king of the Jews. The Romans had been forced to put down a few guerrilla skirmishes in the recent past. Pilate needed an answer. In one of the few words Jesus spoke, He replied:

"My kingdom is not from this world. If my kingdom were from this world, my followers would be fighting to keep me from being handed over to the Jews" (John 18:36).

Pilate didn't have a clue what Jesus was talking about! What on earth is a *spiritual kingdom* in a polytheistic world?

There's every possibility that Jesus could have avoided being crucified. The Jews had a fair number of sects among them; one more wouldn't have been a problem. However, this Jesus seemed to be saying something more than any sectarian leader. At His trial, the High Priest asked Him:

> *"Are you the Messiah, the Son of the Blessed One? Jesus said, 'I am; and you will see the Son of Man seated at the right hand of the Power, and coming with clouds of heaven'" (Mark 14:61-62).*

Now, that really did seal His fate! *Surely this response, and the angry tirade from the High Priest, could only be understood if Jesus' messianic claim were also a claim to His Deity.* In Christ, God became vulnerable; God was silent.

WHY SHOULD GOD PAY A COST ON CALVARY?

The thought of God paying a cost for our redemption has often been downplayed. Not all people intentionally try to diminish the finished work of Christ, but Peter Abailard (1079-1142) maybe unwittingly fell into this trap. Consequently, his *opinion* on the meaning of the cross is proving to be an easy way out for many present-day revisionists. The idea of exemplarism has become popular.

Abailard leaned "...towards an exemplarist theory of the Atonement according to which the suffering of Christ was our supreme example, though little more."[7] So it is not at all uncommon, or surprising, to hear eloquent and passionate cries to follow the supreme example of Jesus. But then, if this sacrifice was merely to be of the caliber of selfless sacrifice, doesn't Gandhi fit in there too? But, even here, when confronted with his assassin, Ghandi shouted, "No!" As a comparison, Jesus then becomes the *Christian example* of sacrifice. We don't hear from those revisionist pulpits that Peter Abailard's opinion was rejected by the Council of Soissons (1121 A.D.). When notions of exemplarism are held up, solely, we shouldn't be surprised that *the connection is missed between the empty cross and the finished work of redemption.* To make such a correlation would be to admit that all persons needed to be rescued from a situation they could not achieve on their own! Archbishop William Temple pondered the meaning of the *nice man* of his generation. "Why anyone should have troubled to crucify the

Christ of Liberal Protestantism has always been a mystery."8 In preferring to think that basically, everyone is good, we miss the point:

> *God, in His holiness, could no longer bear our company!And yet, in*
> *Jesus, He paid the utmost price in order to secure it!*

In consequence of this estrangement, *we can hardly bear our own company!* At its best, the Church will never minimize the substantial cost paid by God for our redemption. But what does all this talk about cost really mean?

DOES GOD OWE EVIL A DEBT?

It all sounds very legalistic and forensic, doesn't it? At least, it sounds a bit like a kidnapper demanding a huge ransom so that a rich man may get his kid back! Is it really possible that God owes something, or that He has to pay a price to the powers of evil? Well, that's precisely the language of people like Irenaeus. That notion has remained in the minds of many to this day.

Actually, the idea of *ransom* does have a place in New Testament thinking (Matt. 20:28; 1 Tim. 2:6). However, it's over-elaborated when interpreted by theologians such as Irenaeus, Origen and Gregory the Great. They use the word in the context of the slavery of their own day. Their use of the word gives the impression that God, somehow, got the better of a deal between Him and Satan. And, in spite of that fact, Satan did secure some satisfaction! But here we must stress that the primary point in using the word *ransom is that God paid a price for our redemption*. The whole point of ransom, ".... is our rescue from a perilous predicament through the very costly self-giving of Jesus. Rescue and costliness are the point."9 "…it is something infinitely costly, a giving up by God of His only Son in the process of dealing with our sins."10 Here, the rescue we speak of is one of *deliverance from the penalty of fracturing our relationship with the holy God and His creation!* We must not elevate the forensic approach over the relational recovery.

Earlier, we thought of the impossibility of aspiring to the standards that God, Himself, has set. A sentimentalist view of the problem might go something like this:

God is all-loving; His love for us is unconditional. Therefore, a loving Father would simply look at His errant child and say, "It's all right, don't worry about it; it really doesn't matter." A simple example here may be the story Jesus told of the Prodigal Son. (This is really the story of Israel, Luke 15:11-31.) The loving father, waiting for the return of his errant son, didn't need to hear the penitent words of this son, *but the son needed to say them!*

What does this say about God's standards for relationships? On the other side of the question, what does it say concerning *the awesome holiness of God being insulted by a casual or deliberate view of sin?* What does it say about Him leaving us to suffer the consequences of our own choices?

> *It says that His requirements for living the "essential relationships"*
> *of creation are not worth the paper (or the tablets) they are written on!*

They don't have any worth at all.11 There are really no standards or requirements for us to meet in engaging with the awesome and holy God. The law breaker "...cannot simply be let off. The law must be upheld, its dignity defended and its penalties paid."12 It would say that, ultimately, God's standards don't require a cost to meet them. There is no point in redemption. We really don't have to accept personal responsibility, because a loving Father would simply say that everything will be OK, anyway!

> *The fact is: God's laws declare that they do matter; everything is not OK,*
> *and that we really do matter to Him.*

The standards of the kingdom are not lowered because we cannot measure up to them. Jesus demonstrated this with His Sermon of the Mount. And then, He blasts all our sense of self-righteousness with: "Be perfect, therefore, as you heavenly father is perfect" (Matt. 5:48). God, in Christ, pays the impossible price for us because we are of ultimate worth to Him. *But to whom is the price paid?* God owes Satan absolutely nothing! Satan doesn't have any bargaining power when God enters the arena of satisfaction.

> *God pays the price to Himself in order to satisfy His own standards of*
> *relationships!*

"Satisfaction is an appropriate word, providing that we realize that it is he himself in his inner being who needs to be satisfied, and not something external to himself. Talk of law, honor, justice and the moral order is true only in so far as these are seen as expressions of God's own character. Atonement is a necessity because it 'arises from within God himself.'"13 God is satisfied that the price was commensurate with the standards He set. *Humanly speaking, the price is impossibly high because the standards of relationships are of immeasurable worth.* And the price was fully met in and through His beloved Son! We see that the Paschal Lamb, which was offered at every Passover feast, had to be perfect, without any blemish. Now, this is a lot more than a forensic transaction; it is a costly restoration of relationships made possible by God alone. That's what justification by faith is all about (Rom. 5:1). Yes, God really was in Christ reconciling the world to Himself (2 Co. 5:19).

THE CROSS AND CULTURE

Near the end of this book, we shall make mention of the horrendous breakdown of all *essential relationships* in latter days. A well-known mega church in the USA recently publicly admitted that they had produced many thousands of converts; but have now realized that they have made very few disciples. What has this got to do with the cross of Calvary?

There is a Stoic denial of suffering which pervades our culture in the West. Such an idea runs counter-culture to the demands of walking the way of the cross. Will the Church of latter days have the stomach for the suffering and pain which has already started? Will it petulantly deny that suffering is of the very essence of the Gospel, or will it produce another, much more palatable gospel? (Gal. 1:7) Maybe, if we briefly identify some of the dominant marks of our *Post-Modern culture*, we may be shocked to find just how much of it has invaded the present life of the Church.

What does it mean when Jesus tells us to take up our cross today? "...you will be hated by all because of my name...and whoever does not take up the cross and follow me is not worthy of me" (Matt. 10:22, 38). The NIV refers to "his cross." No one else can take up the cross of Jesus!

Many Christians of the Third World and the Southern Globe would be able to answer these questions. The Apostle Paul tells us that we are children of God and joint heirs with Christ,

"…if, in fact, we suffer with him so that we may also be glorified with him" (Rom. 8:17).

We will make a very brief examination of some of these values dominating our present globalized and Post-Modern culture. This is not a blanket portrayal of modern values. Clearly, we do observe in a younger fringe of the population a ready willingness to embrace both morality and absolutes arising from their growing sense of mystery. Nevertheless, this examination will challenge us to examine them in the light of why Christ's death is meaningful for the Church's witness today.

CONSUMERISM

God loves the world; He doesn't hate it! (John 3:16-17) We aren't Docetists who hate physical things! God really did make a material world, and He put us in it. The prophetic role of the Church is not adequately exercised in a Church that studiously avoids the reality of the material. Biblical prophets never displayed a Gnostic revulsion to material things. However, they did remind the community of God how to be responsible stewards of the things He had given.

When Christians devote equal time and effort to acquisitiveness as do others, what message does it give to the world?

Christians may often fall prey to media images that obscure the distinction between need and greed. How then are we seen to be different from the world? Are we really so different when we place higher value on those who are best able to consume? (James 2:1-4) Does the Church rise above the superficiality of consumer values by investing its own life in sharing with the needy and those suffering injustice? Can the Church minister this way with no thought for gain? e.g., some Western aid actually results in further wealth to the givers; interest rates on loans are one example (Luke 14:12-14). When we read of the Post-Pentecost community sharing in order to meet the needs of others, we are not reading a manifesto for Communism. *What we read is that there is a cost in loving one another* (1 John 3:16-18).

What sign do we present to the world when we will not sacrifice the gluttonous life-style so common to our own goals in life? There is a price to be paid for change. Our ethical priorities seem out of place, and *our leaning to a prosperity gospel sounds obscene.* Can you imagine the enormous difference which would be made if churches of the West made the problems of AIDS and of poverty the *priority* of stewardship? When new carpets and better sound systems are sacrificed for such priorities, what message does that give to the world? Given the choice, do we plant churches where people can afford them, or where people *cannot afford* them?

The values of the world tell us that our *sense of worth is related to our ability to consume.* We acquire the advertised product, *because we are worth it!* The cross speaks of our infinite worth in the sight of God. God, who knows the very number of the hairs on our head, considers each individual life to be deserving of His sacrificial love. There is a verse in Romans which could strike terror into our hearts, if not properly understood,

"So then, each of us will be accountable to God" (Rom. 14:12).

Some years ago, in Snow Lake, a little mining town in northern Manitoba, I was conducting a teenage Bible study on one of their favorite topics, "Obey your parents in the Lord!" (Eph. 6:1) I let them rattle on about their *rotten parents* who made them come home early, who made them do chores, who made them study, who made them...! To most of the teenagers in the town, one fifteen year-old girl was a hero. She could do anything she wanted. She could come home when she wanted; she could drink booze and play around with young men. She was there and said nothing!

After about half an hour, she threw up her hands and screamed, "You guys are so lucky!" Silence descended with a thunderous crash! "Why do you say that?" I asked. With tears in her eyes, she replied, *"If once, just once, my mother or father told me to get home by eleven, then I would know that they love me."* About fifteen years later, I happened to see her again holding the hand of a little girl. She looked beautiful. "Are you married?" I asked her. Quickly, she retorted, "No! Who would have me?" Time didn't prove to be a healer for her. After all those years, she had not acquired a confidence in her own self worth. As years had progressed, she simply became more and more crippled. And it all started when not even her very busy parents had loved her enough to call her to account.

Accountability means worth!

For those in Christ, accountability to God will not be an occasion for cringing before an angry judge for the hope of salvation, but an honest facing of how they have used, or misused, the gifts which the Father had given them (Matt. 25:19). If God calls for an account of our life, then He cares about it, and it holds enormous worth to Him! *The cross speaks of a love that credits our life with value. It credits the world with value!* God loves us so much that He came down to us when we could no longer reach up to Him. Christ bridged the gap when we were incapable of crossing sin's barrier. He saved us when we had failed to save ourselves. He redeemed us when we had lost the power of purchase. He accepted us when we could no longer accept ourselves.

INDIVIDUALSIM

Ever since the Garden of Eden, the wants of *"me"* have become more important than the needs of the community. The Trinitarian God created community from the pattern of His own relational nature. In the primal sense of community, we cannot conceive of identity in terms of individuality. We are created with a sense of dependence upon God and others. God's very nature is one of otherness. In this fashion, the Church exists primarily for the benefit of others. But the prevailing attitude of society is one of *meism*. What is good for me? How do I live in a system of values which is dominated by the needs of others?

> *In congregations where most of the time, energy, money and resources are spent on their own needs, how is the Christian community seen to be different?*

Individualistic arrogance prevails everywhere (including the Church) and it is the primary reason for the breakdown of community. Some congregations are told to live like *king's kids*. Children of the King deserve the very best! Miracles come on demand, provided you have enough faith! And if you can't name it and claim it, then it's a problem of *your* faith! *This prosperity gospel looks obscene* when we think of committed Christians in developing nations whose basic struggle is one of *survival!* Is their faith, to some degree, inferior to that of the gluttonous and waist-bulging Christians of the West? Nowadays, the sense of the universe, with *me* at the centre, sometimes begins from very early days.

Many years ago, a very bright and caring friend once suggested that we are now living in a child-centered world. My questions were:

"How are we helping our children face the realities of this cruel world? When they grow up, how will they cope with the truth that they are *not* the centre of the universe? They are not, and they're destined for a rude awakening. Are we helping them when they feel they have a right to whatever they want? Are they not destined for a grinding and hurtful time ahead? Will they become a petulant and demanding generation of adolescent adults, resentful of annoying inconveniences of life?"

Now, I think we wonder if the children of our generation have learned what it means to live a life of sacrifice for others. It seems to be a refreshing change when we see these children expending themselves in sacrificial love for others. Is it any wonder that, in order to attract this generation into the life of the Church, we fall for the ploy of enticing them with a gospel of comfort? The reverse may be more of a truism. A great many people of this generation need and desire a challenge!

The cost of discipleship seems to be remarkably elusive in a me-centered and feely Church. No wonder efforts in evangelism may be couched in accepting a syrupy Jesus; or of being enticed to attend a comfortable church; or of joining our particular community because we can help solve your problems. We must wonder how this Jesus can ever be resisted! How often do we hear that reigning with Christ is always preceded by suffering with Him? (2 Tim. 2:12) In recognizing their own very serious problems, Third World Christians have much to teach us regarding their suffering for the Gospel of Jesus. They also have much to teach us about joy!

How much is the Church of the West seen to be in the forefront of ministering in the gap between rich and poor? *How much are its leaders actually seen to be sacrificial in their life-style* in order that others may have more? Where is there a genuine apostolic focus? How do the words of Jesus strike us when we pride ourselves on our *born again* experience but *sacrifice* little or nothing for the poor, the lonely and the sick? "Truly I tell you, just as you did not do it to one of the least of these, you did not do it to me" (Matt. 25:45).

We have seen, all too clearly, that creation theology lauds community (not individualism) as a reflection of the nature of God. However, our present culture has learned only too well the lyrics of the song, "I did it my way." Our arrogance and prideful individualism is offensive to a holy and righteous God.

A perversion has occurred when the wants of the individual become more important than the needs of the community.

Clearly, when individualism runs rampant, what we observe in all societies is: a loss of identity; contempt for values from a higher source; sexual inequality; racial discrimination; the despair of loneliness; a lessening of commitment to relationships; and the frenetic seeking of status measured in wealth.

We hear it from the pulpits too! Both the Old and New Testaments speak of values, promises and challenges that are primarily addressed to *the community of God*. The Old Testament is replete with conditional promises of God to a community called to observe His criteria for signing a life of justice, righteousness and peace. However, time and time again, preachers speak on these scriptures as if they are addressed to individuals alone. Consequently, when preaching becomes absorbed by the need to be relevant to people's perceived needs, *such preachers contribute to a very individualized spirituality*. Often, it is a spirituality lacking in a social context. No wonder biblical revisionists, even when their Christology is weak, have been given enormous energy in demonstrating compassion and justice. It's the only gospel they have left!

"The vocation of Christians is to be builders of communities that join with them what is highest in themselves within another and within the whole human race. The most basic thing that Jesus does when he liberates us is to make us caring people who then have the commission to build communities in the place where we live and play and work."14 Quite apart from its evangelistic potential, it is for reasons such as these that *the Church needs to rediscover the immense value of structures that are based around the small home group. The basics of Christian community are learned and practiced in these foundational organisms.* We are not here speaking of churches that simply run home groups, but churches whose very *structures emanate from* the relational insights discovered in those smaller communities. [vii]

APATHY

In many ways we have become a passive and impatient society. We want things done for us, and we want them now! The idea of *commitment* is not always easy to see. Yet the very life of the gospel demands it! (Matt. 10:38-39) Commitment in the human psyche hasn't completely gone out of the window. Some years ago we were impressed by Chinese students who gave up their lives for the cause of freedom and democracy. When perseverance and commitment, such as theirs, is not apparent, often *apathy, disillusionment, and despair set in to the psyche of the culture.* This despairing syndrome often resolves itself into self-destruction. It is presently happening amongst young native people of Canada. One newspaper journalist describes the native population of this country as "Canada's Tibet."15

The late David Watson once wrote this: "A Communist once threw out this challenge to a Christian: The gospel is a much more powerful weapon for the renewal of society than is our Marxist philosophy...How can anyone believe in the supreme value of this gospel if you do not practice it, if you do not spread it and if you sacrifice neither time nor money for it...? We believe in our Communist message and we are ready to sacrifice everything, even our life...But, you people are afraid to soil your hands."16

In many of the Western churches, we have a serious problem with the developing of basic discipleship in our membership. In point of fact, *all too many churches have very little idea of how to make disciples,* even from among their present membership (Matt. 28:19-20). The making of disciples is a *process requiring classroom theory and marketplace application.* An ongoing process such as this is all too uncommon in churches where institutional success is measured by money and attendance.

RELATIVISM

In a globalized economy, absolute values are thrown out, but the freedom of politically-correct religion is heralded.

While lauding individual values, society has been encouraged to become intolerant towards any suggestion of absolutes. Truth is therefore relative to each individual and culture. There are no absolutes, except those being lauded in a globalized world economy. *When the Church displays insecurity before such intolerance, it also begins to espouse the same attitudes; it begins to lose its distinctive and prophetic identity.* The Church exists *prophetically* to inform the world, and to *demonstrate* that all meaning consists in Jesus Christ. Jesus is not *a* truth; Jesus is *The Truth.* The Christian faith rises and falls on this fact. There really are Christian statements of an absolute nature, although not as many as some would think. Nevertheless, they are absolutes because they don't exist in relation to anything else.

The Church has never been called to act as a chaplain to the world; *it is called to speak prophetically, and to live prophetically before the world.* We are called to show the world that a sign of Eden still exists. The world has every right to reject what it sees and hears. *But it has to see and hear first!* In doing precisely that, the Church itself has to be prepared for crucifixion. It has to be prepared for rejection and death. It is not in the business of survival! It adopts the mindset of crucifixion because it believes in the power of Christ's resurrection!

A subtle form of relativism today is in the area of spirituality itself. We are called, by incessant pressures from the media, education systems, social institutions, business etc., to hold spirituality as an individualistic and private enterprise. (This is one example of how well-meaning institutions, including the Church, may become perverted and may act as cultural chaplains.) The Post-Modern era has produced a vast amount of people who are spiritually hungry. Yet *cultural spirituality* not only denies claims to absolute truth, but forbids the appearance of such values before the public and in the social arena. The above influences and institutions will tell us what is *politically correct*; for now, at least!

In a western culture changing about every twenty years, we can't be dogmatic about our present belief!

Relativism quite clearly has its bases in the popular *pluralism* that dominates our western thinking. It really may not be too outlandish to postulate that a major influence in these attitudes is fostered by the proponents of a globalized economy. Possibly, too much blame is pointed in this direction, but it is abundantly clear that the major values of a world economy and those of Christ are at odds. However, let me repeat: one such analogy that arises in this spiritual vacuum of absolutes is that of a God (in whatever form) who waits at the top of a mountain to welcome all who come to the top. It really doesn't matter which pathway is taken. For the thinking Christian, this kind of approach is not only intellectually insulting, but also insultingly sloppy! Which God will be there? There will be unbelievable contradictions. The fact is: God has chosen the pathway. It's a *reversal* of this pathetic analogy. God has already decided to meet us. But, where? *At the bottom* of the mountain! (2 Co. 5:19) *It is Jesus who leads us to the top - to the one and only God whom He has revealed to all humanity!*

Entering the waters of baptism, Jesus signified a death to self. In His death on the cross, all the idols of culture come under severe scrutiny, and that's because the cross not only has the power to expose, but also to redeem them.

> *The message of the cross challenges people of all cultures, and it challenges the entire life-style of the Church.*

The Church may, or may not, be successful in demonstrating to the world the way of the cross. However, in throwing out the challenge of The Way, in relation to culture, I must add that there are many wonderful signs emerging in the West. For example a form of Neo-Evangelicalism is emerging and forging superb inroads into social areas of depravity and injustice. This movement combines the personal spiritual gospel with that of the real-felt needs of society (James 2:17; 1John 3:16-18). As with the example of Jesus, success or failure is not its motivation. Kingdom imperatives require faithfulness in living out the implications of this Jesus Gospel. A radical renewal of the meaning of the cross, and of its required lifestyle, is therefore imperative; that is, if our primary desire is to be an anointed, and authentic, sign of the kingdom. This most certainly means that the Church will often operate in counter-cultural directions.

FEELINGS

If it feels good, do it! This is a really *big one* for today. It's all about eros! Not only has a feely-based culture created an extraordinary me-centered therapeutic industry, but it has also bolstered a never-flagging consumerism. And this equates the power of purchase with the perceptions of self-worth. Rightness is all too often determined by the criterion, "How do you feel?" From a counseling perspective, that is usually a good question, and it often leads to positive and healing responses. However, in our culture, the question is often posed in order *to eliminate personal feelings of guilt or responsibility.* Consequently, people are usually *not led to grow and learn through their difficulties, but are affirmed in them!* It doesn't take an Einstein to realize that, when values are based on individual feelings, the contradictions that ensue in a community will most certainly devolve in socially disastrous directions.

Quite remarkably, modern church synods have often been profoundly influenced in debate, not on the basis of substance, but individual feelings, e.g. "I am deeply hurt by your position." Having the privilege of speaking in many churches, I find that pastors often share a common complaint. After all their sermons, they find it more difficult than ever to get people committed to areas of ministry. "I can't commit myself for more than a short time." "I didn't feel like coming last week," etc., etc. The fact is, all too often, feelings, and the will, are accepted as a basis for doing ministries. Of course, on that basis, there is no reliability.

One of the greatest tragedies of putting feelings before commitment is that of marriage. The breakdown of the basic unit of society is raising enormous problems. Children often grow up with insecurities because feelings dominate the lives of their parents. Social problems occur with much more frequency in the children of parents who have put feelings before commitment. Of course, this is not to say that there really are no disastrous marriages; some times emotional health and physical abuse cannot be dealt with so long as the couple stays together.

From biblical perspectives, the pathway of growth in mature Christian discipleship is never equated with feelings, but with the power of decision in walking the way of the cross.

CHRISTIAN COMMITMENT AND CULTURE

A culture may live with diversity, but not with contradiction. The result will be cultural suicide. Similarly, that is precisely true for the contemporary Church. We see this dilemma in the revisionists of our day. As prophets to the world, their voice has been rendered silent. The main reason is because their voice is no longer needed. It sounds the same as that of the world! While we have suggested that, from a theological point of view, most revisionists are aligned with old-fashioned Modernism, from a sociological point of view, they are clearly Post-Modern in their attitudes. It is a perfect combination for the rise of a brand new form of religion (Gal. 1:7). The religion is inevitably one of chaplaincy to the culture - at least, for a while! Obviously, a glaring question needs to be asked:

How do we live in the world but not of it?

Surely, we are not to abandon the culture in which we live. How can we dialogue if we are apart? Commenting on the question: *Of, but not In,* Don Posterski notes: "Many contemporary Christians have abdicated from the world. Often out of good intentions to be 'godly,' we have confused the biblical injunction to 'be separate' with social segregation...Clarity comes when 'not of the world' while being 'in the world' is understood to mean 'different from the world.' "17

George Hunsberger offers a way to witness by going into and through the culture's pluralistic assumptions. He believes it to be a more effective stance than one formed out of resistance and opposition to those dynamics. He encourages a style that moves alongside 'the principles that govern a pluralistic society: acceptance of diversity...appreciation of options..., and interaction with alternatives.' He judges that the tolerance factor in pluralism is an open opportunity for evangelism, not a barrier that stymies it.'18

Clearly the meaning of the Cross starkly confronts the values with the awesome realities of sacrifice. Also, we have strongly suggested here, that Jesus really did sign the meaning of all the four pillars of Israel. In Christ, we see that there cannot be a biblical distinction between two stories. In Christ, there is but one Big Story. But also, from God's perspective, i.e., of viewing the entire story *in God's Eternal Present*, there can only be one Big Story. Having considered something of the procession of this story, laden in facts of history, it cannot reveal its meaning unless it is highlighted in the way of the cross.

> **"He was destined before the foundation of the world, but was revealed at the end of the ages for your sake" (1 Pet. 1:20). "...this man, handed over to you according to the definite plan and foreknowledge of God, you crucified and killed by the hands of those outside the law" (Acts 2:23).**

Chapter 8 When is Redemption's Story Complete?

1. Shillibeeckx, E. *Jesus*, p.296. The Crossroad Publishing Co., New York, N.Y. 10017, 1986.

2. Shillibeeckx, E. pps. 297-298

3. Robinson, John A.T. *Can We Trust The New Testament?*, p.114. A.R. Mowbray, Oxford, 1977.

4. Vanstone, W.H., *The Stature of Waiting*, p17 Seabury Press, New York, N.Y. 10017, 1983.

5. Vanstone, W.H. p.21

6. Vanstone, W.H. pps. 5,7,9

7. *The Oxford Dictionary of the Christian Church,* Second Edition, op.cit. p.3

8. Temple, William. *Readings in John*, Introduction Morehouse-Barlow Co. Inc., Conn. 06897, Reprint 1985.

9. Green, Michael. *The Empty Cross of Jesus,* p.62. Inter-Varsity Press, Illinois 60515, 1984.

10. Baillie, D.M. *God Was In Christ*, pp.185-186. Faber & Faber Ltd. London, 1961

11. Stott, J.W. *The Cross of Christ*, p.101. Inter-Varsity Prss, Illinois 60515, 1986.

12. Stott, J.W. *The Cross of Christ,* p. 114

13. Stott, J.W. *The Cross of Christ,* p.123

14. O'Connor, Elizabeth. *The New Community*, p.58. Harper & Row Publishers, New York, N.Y. 10022, 1976.

15. Bill Kaufmann, *The Calgary Sun,* p.15 February 7th 2005

16. Watson, David. *I Believe In Evangelism,* pps.12-13.Wm. B. Eerdmans Publishing Co. Grand Rapids, Michigan 49503, 1977.

17. Posterski, Donald C, *Reinventing Evangelism,* pps.27-28. Inter-Varsity Press, Illinois, 1989

18. Hunsberger, George R and Craig Van Gelder, *Church Between Gospel and Culture,*p.23, William B. Eerdmans, Grand Rapids, Michigan, 1996

Charles Alexander

Chapter 9

THE ROAD OF TIME FROM CALVARY TO HELL

On a dark hill called Calvary, the inevitable clash between the kingdoms of the world and the kingdom of God was mercilessly played out. The cross of Jesus Christ shows up the counter-nature of our contemporary culture. When Pilate raised the question of truth to Jesus, he couldn't see The Truth before his own eyes! *The Truth lay in a Person, not in ideas!* (John 14:6; Heb. 13:8) But, in order to consider the bedazzling questions that are needed in this chapter, we will have to reflect on some of the words Jesus spoke from the cross.

WHY HAVE YOU FORSAKEN ME?

The scene at Calvary hardly appeared to be one of triumph. In spite of His powerful and compassionate healings, His teachings, and His miracles, there was hardly anyone to say good-bye. Possibly a few women remained, but where were His apostles? Where were those whom He had healed and delivered? Jesus was alone! Hell had begun!

Humanly speaking, the scene was one of abject failure. Jesus, who was now dying, was surrounded by indifferent executors of state law, and of a religious establishment rubbing its hands in awkward self-justification. It was truly a scenario not simply highlighting the bigotry of the intolerance of religion. Here was an establishment convinced it had stamped out the challenge to its own view of truth. But also we see a detached and dispassionate establishment of Roman secularism. For them, compassion or vindictiveness had actually given way to an easy political solution. It's not surprising that Good Friday is sometimes viewed in the religious as simply an historical sign of exemplary sacrifice! But Jesus knew that the path of Calvary was clearly and indisputably *the sign* of abject failure.

The cross of Jesus stood starkly in signature of the wretched failure of all humanity. Jesus was intended to walk the path of human failure.

How may the shallow theories of exemplarism possibly account for Jesus' kenotic and desperate cry of loneliness? In a *moment* of despairing abandonment, He cried, "My God, my God, why have you forsaken me?" (Ps. 22:1; Matt. 27:46) *What an astounding reversal!* We have heard throughout this entire redemption story that, throughout the portals of all time, the longing voice of God has cried, "Where are you?" And now, in this awesome moment of pain and of Eden's reversal, the Real Adam cried, *"Where are YOU?"* The sinless and innocent Christ (Heb. 4:15), on behalf of despairing humanity, began to experience the hell of separation from God. *For the first time in His experience, darkness blanketed the Light of God's glory.*

Angry and despairing humanity, not knowing the meaning of this astounding reversal, often reiterates the question. However, it is often not shouted amidst the pain of separation, but in the anger at a God not being there when required. But a genuine sympathy does exist for those in pain and anger. For example, six million Jews suffered horrendous injustice and death in the great Holocaust. Many of their surviving relatives in frustration and pain became atheists. How could God desert them in such an hour? But God did understand. In Christ, God also suffered separation from the beloved crown of His creation. But God, in His *Eternal Present,* already knew the pain. He knew it from the beginning of time (1 Pet. 1:19-20). However, in His humanity, this was Christ's moment of inglorious darkness. And that meant, *for all humanity,* hope, or even the very meaning of life, could exist no longer.

They had witnessed the cruelty of crucifixion before, but when the disciples from afar witnessed the death of Jesus, "… it was also their own death because Life had been taken away from them; they could no longer live but merely exist."1 "If it were possible for Christ, with all that he represented, to die upon the cross, this meant that human hatred was stronger than Divine Love; human hatred had managed to repulse Divine Love, to banish him from the habitations of man, had rejected and killed him at Calvary."2

FORGIVE THEM

"Father, forgive them; for they do not know what they are doing" (Luke 23:34). Amazingly, and deserted by all those who loved Him, the closing thoughts of Jesus was for their redemption. How many people who were there even heard those astounding words of reconciliation? How many even cared? For most people, this was just an ordinary day. Probably, they passed by with scarcely a glance. The soldiers were professionals. The only difference between this day and all others was that these executions had to be over before four o'clock. The disciples of Jesus, and the women in waiting, could have hardly heard what He said. However, they knew that these words were for them. It would take a little time for them to realize that those very words were for the whole world!

Normally, the entire scene would have been a recipe for disaster. The blame game of Eden was bound to emerge amongst them. Quite possibly, in attitudes of self -justification, everyone would have gone their own way; gone back to the way they were before they had met Jesus. The purpose of the Twelve, as the foundations of a New Israel, may well have evaporated forever. But He forgave them! *In forgiveness, all was not lost.* Forgiveness is the way of reconciliation!

With those words, Jesus made possible a new humanity which, as the Real Adam, He could present to the Father in a priesthood of offering and victimization:

> *"From one ancestor he made all nations to inhabit the whole earth..." (Acts 17:26)* [viii]

> *"He has abolished the law with its commandments and ordinances, that he might create in himself one new humanity in place of the two, thus making peace, and might reconcile both groups to God in one body through the cross, thus putting to death that hostility through it" (Eph. 2:15-16).*

In Christ, our Real Adam, we have *the Leader of the procession,* marching together from Calvary to the New Jerusalem (Isa. 35:8-10; Eph. 4:8).

WITH ME IN PARADISE

There are some very important clues here regarding our condition after death. The two thieves who died beside Jesus clearly *represent the condition of all humanity* in relation to Christ's work of atonement. Both of them died on crosses, and both agreed they got what they deserved. One died by himself, and sealed his eternal fate. The other died with Jesus with a hope for God's kingdom on his lips. Jesus promised him a place in Paradise. It was a *place* where life could be lived forever. (It's quite possible that this person had seen or heard Jesus during the time of His ministry.) Jesus responded:

"Truly I tell you, today you will be with me in Paradise" (Luke 23:43).

Before we consider Jesus' astounding statement, we must make note of three things:

First, the promise was not extended to the other thief.

Of course, we are not allowed to make judgments on the eternal destiny of anyone (Matt. 7:1-2), but this passage provides little or no support for those who say that entry into heaven is simply a matter of time. In other words, even if it takes a million years, everyone will get there! Universalism finds no support here. *Time* has ended at death's advent of unconsciousness. Therefore, *without some miracle of restoration,* time's dimensional constituents of *place and space* are clearly absent! With the absence of these constituents, all that might remain would be a purely spiritual existence. Although Gnostics believed in such an existence, Jesus did not. His post-resurrection appearances prove the point.

Second, the passage lends support to the principle that, for the most part, and within the context of closing time, we cannot know who has decided for a relationship with God in Christ.

The dying thoughts of that one thief were towards the lordship of Christ and His kingdom. Of course, this man perfectly epitomizes the teaching that Jesus had formerly given regarding the master who hired laborers to work for a daily wage. In the *final hour* of the day, he hired people who received the same reward (Matt. 20:1-16). God's fairness is His business! Anyway, it is really all about God Who will never resist anyone desiring a genuine relationship with Him. And that principle applies *no matter how late in the day the response to God's invitation is received. Salvation has absolutely nothing to do with deserving; it has everything to do with the grace of God!* Clearly, it's beyond our knowledge to know how Christ may, or may not encounter persons in the closing moments of their earthly existence. However, it may well be that such an encounter with Jesus will be at a cross!

Third, "today" is the Lord's way of saying that time had been restored to the penitent thief. He was already in eternal life! (1 John 5:12; John 11:25-26) He had already entered into the day, or the moment, of Calvary's finished work. We would lose the meaning of this *Easter moment* if we insisted that "today" should be defined within a particular chronological parameter. "Today" is part of the entire meaning of Easter - of this astounding *Moment of Light*. For that particular thief, it would be a *Moment* with Jesus which would last forever. This encounter is so important we will have to visit it later.

"IT IS FINISHED"

It was at Calvary that Christ's final shout may have sounded like a whimper of defeat, "It is finished" (John 19:30). The history of the Church has proven otherwise. This was truly a shout of victory! With these three words, the Real Adam, our Great High Priest, King, Prophet, and Law-giver declared the completion of the Redemption Story (Matt. 3:15). *But at that particular Moment, no one really understood the triumph of the cross. And, wherever the cross is memorialized in sentimentalist terms, the same holds true today.*

Why would Jesus utter this agonizing cry of finality in the closing moments of His ministry? In spite of living in signature of kingdom life, the problems surrounding the cross were massive. There was overwhelming evidence all around Him that the problems of *essential relationships* were not lessening. In our present and wonderful age of instant communication, thoughtful and compassionate people understand that they, with increasing frustration and despair, exist at despairing levels of fractured relationships. Jesus had not *consigned the poor* to a hopeless future of poverty (Mark 14:7). He simply spoke realistically of the nature of a self-centered humanity continually living in spiritual poverty. In fact, *social conditions were destined to get worse!* I want to venture three reasons why the cry of Jesus was absolutely correct in its biblical context; and for all other moments of time.

FINISHED: ITS RELATION TO LAW

It must be done to fulfill all righteousness (Matt. 3:15).Those were the sentiments Jesus relayed to the reluctant baptizer. John the Baptist knew that the One standing before him was to take away the sins of the world (John 1:29). Jesus was fully aware of His own relation to the legal requirements of the Law. In fact, near the beginning of His ministry, He told His eager listeners that nothing would depart from the Law *until all things were fulfilled.* This was the moment! All of the Law was summarized in Jesus. It is quite possible that the specific law of which He spoke was the Decalogue. Ever since that moment, neither Jews nor Christians have felt that the Ten Commandments have become obsolete.

The Decalogue and the Sermon on the Mount still serve, in very practical ways, to show the ethical behavior required to remain in relationship with God and with others. What we particularly observe in the *laws* of Jesus is the motivation to enable the keeping of the Law. *It is the compelling force of love. It often eludes all of us, because we allow feelings, not will, to dominate our motivation.* What Jesus was speaking of here is the *consequence* of not meeting the requirements of the Law. Paul was later to put it this way:

> *"There is therefore now no condemnation to those who are in Christ Jesus. For the law of the Spirit of life in Christ Jesus has set you free from the law of sin and death. For God has done what the law, weakened by the flesh, could not do: by sending his own Son in the likeness of sinful flesh, and to deal with sin, he condemned sin in the flesh" (Rom. 8:1-3).*

The work of Jesus could not possibly be finished had He not come alongside the human situation:

First of all, by identifying with the *condition of sin* that was deeply embedded in all human nature,

Secondly, by identifying with the *consequences of choice* arising from that condition.

The failure of humanity to rise above both of those situations necessitated, not only *rescue from* its perilous condition, but *grace to move on* without the binding curse of condemnation. In relation to the former covenant, *the cross is God's perfect icon* by signing His own demands that reconciliation be fulfilled for all time. Just to cite one example: *There is no longer any need for a peculiar order of priesthood* within the community of God. Jesus, alone, continues as the Mediator of God to humanity and humanity to God (Heb. 7:25-27). Jesus is the High Priest of a royal priesthood. Having offered the sacrifice for all time, He continually mediates the intercession of His priesthood back to God.

FINISHED: ITS RELATION TO SIGN

The cross is the icon and the tangible means whereby *reconciliation is conveyed.* Although Paul had a good understanding of the world's pluralistic thinking (we didn't invent it in the twentieth century), he realized that its natural philosophy and the redeeming message of the cross were not compatible (1 Co. 1:18). Not surprisingly, this was to be the determining factor that represented the hallmark and sign of his entire ministry, "For I decided to know nothing among you except Jesus Christ and him crucified" (1 Co. 2:2). *The cross was the perfect icon of Christ's kenosis,* i.e., the total outpouring of Himself for the sake of others. Clearly, for Paul, Jesus understood that His baptism would lead nowhere except to death (Rom. 6:3-4). But, as the cross was the redemptive signature from death it also signaled the gateway to resurrection life.

Two beams, one perpendicular and one horizontal, represent the perfect icon of reconciliation.

One beam stretched perpendicularly, with *one end rooted firmly into the earth,* and the *other end stretching fully towards the heavens.* Possibly scores of criminals had been pinned to that very beam where it remained solidly fixed into the ground. But this beam meant nothing to the dispassionate Romans and spectators. The body of Jesus hung upon the well-used wood, and in one awesome *Moment of Light,* this body *connected earth to heaven and heaven to earth.* In that *Moment,* oblivious to the indifferent soldiers and gaping bystanders, *the hope for the salvation from the human predicament was emblazoned upon the entire pages of human history.* The healing blood of Jesus seeped into the soil of a groaning creation, and through His outstretched body the awesome chasm between God and His creation was closed.

The other beam stretched horizontally across the perpendicular. Thinking of the essential nature of humanity we see that humans are *directly related to God, and also to the earth.* The iconic representatives of all humanity (Jew and Gentile) stood on either side of the cross. *The Greeks* (representing the rational, natural, and narcissistic philosophy of the world) were on one side, and *the Jews* (representing a faith played out in the medium of story through the Law) were on the other side. *In terms of human hope, both systems had not achieved the reconciliation of essential relationships.* The entire human condition was impotent in securing fellowship of *essential relationships!*

The Pillars of Israel represent a hope of what was to come. In themselves, they had not guaranteed the promises of God to an unfaithful and apathetic people. All the promises were wonderful, but the responses were not. On the other side, all the wisdom of an Aristotelian world had not unlocked the mysteries that were intended to bring the informed into union with the holy and righteous God. The arrogant results, and the failure emanating from the Enlightenment period, force us to realize that the wisdom of all ages has miserably aborted human hope (1 Co. 1:18-19). *Both elements of hostility, Jew and Gentile, could not touch each other! Humanity was lonely!* With arms outstretched, Jesus embraced in His own body both Jew and Greek. In this final ministry of *theosis* the great High Priest raised both Jew and Gentile into the arms of a waiting Father. *The cross is truly our shame, but it is also God's awesome glory.*

We are not stretching the words of the writer to the Ephesians: Here; he really is saying that *all nations are invited* to become one race through the redeeming blood of Jesus Christ:

> **"For he is our peace; in his flesh he has made both groups into one and has broken down the dividing wall, that is, the hostility between us" (Eph. 2:14-16).**

In Christ, our Real Adam, we have *the Leader of the human procession* that marches together to Zion (Isa. 35:8-10; Eph. 4:8).

Earlier in this book we asked questions about the origin and nature of evil. We concluded that the loving God, in making a world free to be itself, had deliberately allowed for the possibility of evil to be present in His creation. The omniscient God, in His *Eternal Present,* would surely know of the horrendous suffering that was to follow. We also concluded that a loving God would also have to allow for the possibility of evil; the very nature of love demands it.

God has faced up to His responsibilities for that decision.

But is it enough that Jesus was dispatched to a relatively quick death (which was often much longer for most criminals)? When reading the daily newspaper, we don't take long to realize that hell's fury is not yet spent! Violence and hatred still persist.

But the cost of evil's furious rage was absorbed completely, and for all time, by Jesus on the cross!

At Calvary, the Savior of the world suffered the fierce lashings of hatred, fear, lies, rejection, bigotry and the suffering *of all time! There was no period in all chronological counting that was not covered by the sacrifice of Jesus on Calvary!* Finally, as is the destiny of the entire human condition, the Life of the world suffered the awful insult of death. The holy and awesome God could not bear to look upon the face of His own Son.

The despairing cry of Jesus, "My God, my God, why have you forsaken me?" (Matt. 27:46) was a piercing wail of abandonment. Hell began for Jesus in that *Moment* of desolation; it continued until the *Moment* He was raised to lead captivity captive (Eph. 4:8). But when was that? The Man, Christ Jesus, suffered excruciating separation from the life-long and intimate relationship He had with the Father. *His suffering was that which was experienced by all those who share an eternal separation from God.* He uttered those words on our behalf. Paradoxically, His understanding of the cry, *"Where are you?"* must have grown immensely in that dreadful moment of time. He had never experienced anything like this in His entire life! This was truly to be indicative of the tormenting pain to be experienced by all who reject God's free and loving offer of reconciliation. On the cross, the Real Adam traversed the time-long procession of *all those who dejectedly looked back to the gates of Paradise, now closed to them forever.*

Charles Alexander

THE CROSS: ITS RELATION TO TIME

The cross speaks of the efficacious suffering of God for all time.

In our introductory discussion on the nature of time, we concluded that *all of it exists in God*. He sees and experiences all of it in the *eternal now*. What this means, in redemptive terms, is that, *in one Moment of Light, Jesus drew into Himself the entire pain and the sin of all ages. All time (past, present, and future) met together in that one Moment in God.* To see this in any other way would mean that God, even after heaven and earth had passed away, would still be dealing with the consequences of humanity's sinful nature. It would mean that if God continues to suffer, then (for God and Man) the *consequences* of Christ's sacrifice on the cross have not been fully met. Clearly, in that *Moment* of which we speak, God also experienced all the fullness, and all the effects of creation's brokenness. It's astonishing! How could the writer of the book of Revelation, with his limited knowledge of time, speak of Christ suffering from the foundation of the world? (Rev. 13:8) Theology makes powerful sense when it is revealed by God! The cross of Jesus Christ proves to be the astounding *Moment when all time is redeemed!* Maybe the reality of this revelation can be illustrated in the following way:

In that "moment," and on that historic cross, God, in Christ, suffered the agony of humanity's departure from Eden; He suffered the anguish of His despairing children in exile; He suffered the agony of His Son's abandonment at Calvary; He suffered the death of all those martyred for the sake of His Gospel; He suffered the pain of His dying people at Auschwitz; He suffered the dying cries of starving children in barren Ethiopia; He suffered the anguish of desperate mothers brutalized by sadistic rapists; He heard the despairing cry of the vagrant in the lonely city; He suffered the murderous vengeance of Rwandan Christians in conflict; He felt for the Ugandan baby dying of AIDS; He suffered with the poor watching food being destroyed for the profit of a futures market; He felt the despair of a gasping creation choking in the pollution of death; He was pained to see it repeated again, and again, and again.

> *Amazingly, in that apparent moment of defeat, and for all time, the entire redemption story was gloriously won in a magnificent Moment of Light.*

Paradoxically, at the very end of the sixth day, that one *hour* of darkness is, for all time, the ultimate sign that the Light in humanity and all nature had been fully extinguished. If the Light and Life of the world had died in the Real Adam, *then it had died in all humanity.* On the sixth day, God completed His work of creation and rested on the Sabbath. The ugly, yet paradoxical sign of the Real Adam's obedience was that *Jesus finished His work of redemption* on Friday. In time for the Sabbath, His body was laid to rest in a dark tomb of hopelessness. If this was the final destiny of the Real Adam, then how could life ever hold meaning for anyone else?

> *A defunct meaning of time now loomed its largest; its very elusiveness would signal enmity to all humanity!*

Yet, in that incredulous and paradoxical moment of *apparent defeat,* the obedient Christ, in triumphant cry, shouted: "It is finished." In hope, and faith, He saw Himself leading a procession of the redeemed as they sang their way to Zion. *Jesus believed it, but He had to die in order to know it!* In that moment of atonement, Christ's redemption crossed the awesome barriers of time in rescue of the saints of old, *and at the very point of their extinction.*

Is it just fanciful philosophical thinking (devoid of any solid bases) to think that the pain of all time could be encapsulated by Jesus in that awesome *Moment?* What we are saying here is that the astounding accomplishment of Christ's victory is that, in one *Moment of Light, Jesus took upon Himself the pain and insult of all time.* To some, this is not just a fanciful theology without firm foundations. From mathematical perspectives, Hugh Ross postulates how God, who exists in infinitely-dimensional ways, can do this!

"A significant part of what transpired in Christ's payment of all that our death warrants took place in God's extra-dimensional realm....With a second time dimension, God could move along, that is, experience, these twenty billion lines. He would possess a plane of time that could encompass all of them. Thus, while Jesus suffered on the cross for six hours on our time line, He could have experienced the suffering of twenty billion infinite timelines in two other dimensions of time."3

God has no further need to experience the pain of past, present, and future. "*It is finished!*" He doesn't grow with *future* experiences; *He has experienced them in all their fullness, and for all time!* He doesn't continue to be the suffering God. We understand how God, in Christ, completed His work, once and for all. We realize that:

> *The fullness of time itself was redeemed in that awesome moment of abandonment!*

When Jesus died, He was surrounded by a world bearing the cruel marks of despair, oppression, and injustice. But the victory was won; it was finally signed on a hill called Calvary! The ravages of chronological time would yet make their gluttonous demands on a battered world, but it is now a world possessing an ever-enduring icon of hope. Humanly impotent, and upon two wooden staves, Jesus won the victory for all time! With total abandonment and confidence in God, Jesus, the priest and victim, shouted, "It is finished." And, in that awesome *Moment,* the veil of the Temple was torn in two (Matt. 27:51).

> *The Great High Priest had made it possible for an entire priesthood of believers to enter into the Light of First Day glory. The story of redemption was now complete!*

"Father, into your hands I commend my spirit" (Luke 23:46). It was another glorious *Moment of Light!* Christ, the Light of the world, had begun His descent into the nihilistic darkness of hell, while His body was still bound to the cross. We should never minimize the astounding force of Christ's final statement. He had voluntarily turned His face towards Jerusalem. He did so, in total and absolute confidence in the Father's plan for redemption. Making way for His own death required an enormous capacity for trust and faith in God's plan of redemption.

> *Jesus believed in the resurrection, but He had to die in order to experience it. He had to trust in order to know it!*

HOW DID JESUS DESCEND INTO HELL?

It was Saturday; God's Sabbath rest from the work of creation! The body of Jesus was laid in a hollow and stone-cold tomb, and sealed into the darkness of nothingness. Ironically, this cruel condition was guarded and kept intact by the forces of the religious establishment (Matt. 27:62-66). The *rest* of Sabbath was now a homonym for death of the human condition; the very crown of God's completed creation was lifeless. And so, *the tomb of Jesus becomes a hollow sign that all natural hope of meaning in immortality is firmly and absolutely dead.* Its covering stone, sealed shut, is an immoveable sign reminding us that nothing less than a miracle *from above* is able to change that reality.

Doesn't it stretch the credulity of believers to ask them to believe that Jesus actually descended into hell? What can this possibly mean? We have pondered the meaning of the cross in that, at the moment of Christ's finished work, *all time had been redeemed.* What this meant was that the hopeless condition of humanity, for all time, had been claimed back. And its benefits are promised to all those who *responded to Christ's invitation.* Well, that sounds good for us, but *what about all those people who died before the time of Jesus?* The Apostle Peter seems to ponder the same question when he asserts:

> *"For this is the reason the gospel was proclaimed even to the dead, so that, though they had been judged in the flesh as everyone is judged, they might live in the spirit as God does" (1 Pet. 4:6).*

Recognizing the importance of time, we note here that that the Gospel was proclaimed to the dead. In other words: *these people, at some point in their dying, earthly existence, still had a consciousness of life, and therefore, of time.* So, was it possible for God to snatch them back from the fire? (Jude 23) After Jesus died on the cross, a stone-cold body was laid in a borrowed tomb. Does this mean that the eternal Second Person of the Trinity was dead? Of course not! *While a dead body lay in the tomb,* Jesus, in His *divine and Eternal Present,* encountered people, *of all time (past, present, and future),* at the very point at which, for each individual, death was to take its natural course. Therefore, His descent into hell speaks of Christ's meeting point with all those who face extinction during the moment of *complete* separation from consciousness. In the finished work of Christ, redemption was intended to be possible for all. It is for this reason we are to view Saturday, not so much in chronological terms, but as the necessary connection in the entire story of Easter. After all, *in the playing out of this Moment, the dawn of First Day beginnings was to emerge.*

Connected with Christ's resurrection, many saints of old became incorporated into the God-graced fellowship of restoration. In Hebrews Chapter 11, the writer speaks of the great saints of old who walked the path of faith. There are many others, of course. If they could not be invited apart from the finished work of Jesus, then how could they be invited at all? *Jesus, in His Eternal Present, met each person at the point of their extinction*; the very point at which hell exacted its fullest toll. *It is no great feat for God to meet anyone at any point in time.*

The activity of God is not confined to chronological time, as we see it. Abraham, Sarah, Moses, Rahab, and David, et al, were met by Christ in His divinity. They had to be invited in this way because Jesus really is the pioneer and perfecter of faith! (Heb. 11:40, 12:2) Apart from Him, there is no restoration at all! But what about the little Hindu lady from rural India who died last night? *Will the saints of Hebrews Chapter 11 share an eternal home with people whose God is not the god of Jesus? After all, this little old lady never even heard of Jesus!* Then, if Jesus really is the Way, Truth, and Life, how may this lady see or hear Christ's invitation?

Clearly, without resorting to sentimentality, the same principles are in place here. God, as the sovereign Lord of all time does make an opportunity for all people (at the point of the extinction of consciousness) to receive the invitation to share restoration life with Jesus. Jesus really is the Alpha and Omega of life, the Way, the Truth and the Life. And so, to the very last moment, our loving God presents Himself and reaches out to all who seek Him and desire Him. But clearly, all who encounter Christ and His salvation, also encounter His cross.

> **"I love those who love me, and those who seek me diligently find me" (Prov. 8:17).**

A chronology of thousands of years (both sides of the cross) is *embraced in that one moment.* No one, from any age, will be able to accuse God of not presenting an opportunity to meet the inviting Christ; the One who is the Light of the world. That is why the thief on the cross, and those working for but one hour (Matt. 20:10-16), and those who are on the ebb of life, and those who have died previously, and all those yet to be born, *are all embraced in that one Moment of hope and final decision.* In other words, as we have previously intimated:

> *In the mystery of time's restoration, people like Cain, King Saul, Jezebel, along with King David, Rahab, Mary, Martin Luther, and Mother Teresa, met the inviting Jesus at the Moment of death's eternal unconsciousness.*

But, as we see in the parable of the rich man and Lazarus, we cannot presume that all people respond positively to Christ's invitation. Some may be concerned that a ruthless and murderous dictator may jump to the opportunity of a cheap confession at the moment of meeting Christ. However, we remember that only one thief, when dying with Jesus, asked for eternal life. And, in the parable of the Rich Man and Lazarus, the rich man was too self-possessed to ask for forgiveness. How dare we cheapen the judgment of God! Isn't He the God who knows the secrets of all hearts? (Rom. 2:16) He will not be mocked (Gal. 6:7).

We are now getting back to questions of time. Saturday represents a period bearing witness to the fact that Christ's body was now stone-cold dead in an empty tomb; it is the ultimate fate of all humanity, i.e., apart from the finished work of Christ. But it also represents a *connection of all the Easter events.* The connection is the redemption of time between the point of death, and the restoration of time, to new and everlasting beginnings.

There isn't much point in trying to work out a precise chronology of events to describe this awesome, history-changing, *Moment of Easter.* So we won't even try. To trace the moment-by-moment events of how Jesus was restored, descended to hell, and then appeared to His followers, would be to miss the wholeness of the entire events. (Although, we are certainly not disputing that, at some point, on the first day of the week, the physical body of Jesus was raised.) Maybe, in terms of the entire Easter Moment, an exact chronological approach is not the way to go! However, the third day of new beginnings is vitally important. What we do know is that, while the lifeless body of the Man, Christ Jesus, lay in the darkness of death, God was busy!

Chapter 9. The Road of Time from Calvary to Hell

1.   Bloom, Anthony. *Meditations on A Theme*, p.118. Mowbrays, London and Oxford, 1972.
2.   Bloom, Anthony. *Meditations on A Theme*, p.116
3.   Ross, Hugh, *Beyond the Cosmos,* p.126

RESTORATION

Chapter 10

ETERNAL LIFE:
IS IT FOR EVERYONE?

In this Easter moment of restoration, the Light of First Day once more burst upon the darkness of creation's chaos. There are many people, some through ignorance or tradition, and others who are still in denial of the penalty of sin, who somehow believe that restoration to eternal life can be gained through natural means. Some say that we all live forever. If that is true, then what's the point of the resurrection? If they were right, then the most important event in the Christian calendar would be rendered meaningless. After all, we began our theological journey understanding that, by grace, it was always God's purpose for us to live forever. If natural means are not enough to secure that life, then we really must consider why resurrection and miracle are both connected.

Miraculously, the Day of Resurrection ushers in the restored time of First Day Light.

NATURAL IMMORTALITY

Almost all the natural religions of the world hold a belief that we naturally move from this life to another. Many in the Christian faith believe the same thing. But is that true? We are aware that the impressive pyramids of Giza in Egypt housed the remains of pharaohs and other important dignitaries of the land. Graham Hancock suggests this wasn't the sole reason for their existence.1 Here, we see examples of a common hope that resided in many of the natural religions. The Egyptians spoke of the soul going to Amenti, Babylonians to Aralla, and Ethiopians to Si,ol.2 In Egypt, a pharaoh was laid in a sarcophagus and surrounded by food and various symbols of wealth. Sometimes, servants were walled up in attendance, and then left to die. (Few people volunteered to be servants of an aged pharaoh!) All of these trappings *symbolized the hope of a continuance, or even an improvement on the state of life the pharaoh had left behind.* Unfortunately, his servants were destined to spend an eternity serving their former master. For them, immortality wasn't much to look forward to!

The Egyptian Book of the Dead holds a view *that life continues in roughly the same way as that which was left behind.* It is simply a matter of *continuation of what went before.* In primitive and natural ways, Egypt had conceived of some form of resurrection. The idea didn't develop very far. "...Osiris, on the other hand, did come back. Although he was murdered by Set, soon after the completion of his worldwide mission to make men 'give up their savagery,' he won eternal life through his resurrection in the constellation of Orion as the all-powerful god of the dead."3 Similarly, North American Indians speak of happy hunting grounds in the life beyond. Caribou may have volunteered a second opinion! What seems to be common in all natural religions is the wish for continuation of life, or holding the disbelief that this magnificent human creature could ever die. Didn't we notice something like this previously? (Gen. 3:4)

A HEBREW VIEW OF DEATH

Historically, in spite of the fact that the ancient Hebrews were surrounded by natural beliefs in immortality (and they had spent 430 years with the Egyptians), they most certainly did not emerge from Egypt with a natural view of an afterlife. Maybe in the recesses of their collective memory they recalled, "...you are dust, and to dust you shall return" (Gen. 3:19). During the larger part of their history, resurrection to eternal life was not considered. Therefore, we are not surprised to read of a very hazy Hebrew view of *Sheol.* It was sometimes described as the Pit. As a form of existence it was all ambiguously foggy and shadowy. (Nevertheless, we must add that however vague may have been the belief in the nature of Sheol, some hazy and undefined form of consciousness seemed to remain in order to experience it).

Sheol represented a condition where, after death, all the physical senses are gone. Nothing is clear; and maybe not the clear awareness of self-consciousness! There is no ability to see, feel, smell, touch, or relate to anything. *There is no light!* (Job 10:21) Try proving your existence in total isolation from all other people! It's particularly hard to do so *without senses* that offer some sort of connection to other things or people! To all intents and purposes, every person is dead in Sheol! The existentialist philosopher Descartes, in considering proof of existence, concluded, "I think, therefore I am." That philosophy cannot easily lend itself to a belief in the continuation of life beyond the grave. Of course, for the Hebrews, there was no ability even to think in Sheol! Even God would not be able to find them!

"For I will soon lie down in the dust; you will search for me, but I will be no more" (Job 7:21). "For in death there is no remembrance of you; in Sheol who can give you praise? (Ps. 6:5) "I am counted among those who go down to the Pit; I am like those who have no help, like those forsaken among the dead, like the slain that lie in the grave, like those who remember no more, for they are cut off from your hand. You have put me in the depths of the Pit, in the regions dark and deep...Do you work wonders for the dead? Do the shades rise up to praise you?" (Ps. 88:5,10) See also Ps. 7:5, 22:15, 28:1, 103:14-16, 115:17; Eccles.2:14-16, 3:19-21, 9:5). "By the sweat of your face you shall eat bread until you return to the ground, for out of it you were taken; you are dust, and to dust you shall return" (Gen. 3:19).

While most of us may consider that King David's celebrated psalm of the Lord as Shepherd (Ps. 23:6 - NIV), suggests eternal life, most Hebrew scholars interpret *forever* (NIV) as being *long life* (NRSV). Indeed, this view may well be reinforced by the psalmist who writes:

> *"With long life I will satisfy them and show them my salvation" (Ps. 91:16, i.e., salvation from long-lasting problems).*

This sense of hopelessness in Sheol isn't restricted to Wisdom literature because Isaiah continues to use similar imagery (Isa. 38:18-19). Quite possibly, the ambiguity of belief in immortality may account for the philosophy we see emerging in the book of Job. This skeptical approach to eternal life may also explain the idea of a prosperity gospel emerging in some areas of Christian fundamentalism. It's very easy to see that Job, in being faithful to God through all his horrendous troubles, was rewarded with more wealth than he had at the beginning (Job 42:10). When there is no view of eternal life, *it is easy to see why material wealth becomes the reward for righteousness. What else is there?*

The verses above may be contrasted with Ps.139:8 where, in the later life of Israel (possibly including a part of Daniel e.g., 12:2) and nearer the time of Jesus, *the Pharisees believed in some sort of hope beyond the grave.* (But the Pharisees came into existence hundreds of years after most of the psalms were written!)The point is: a theology of eternal life emerged very, very slowly in the life of Israel.

LIFE AFTER LIFE EXPERIENCES

There have been a plethora of books in recent years that speak of life after *near death experiences (NDEs).* They are often cited as experiences which offer natural proof of life beyond this present existence. By the way, I am not denying the fact that people have such experiences. Some of them are good, and some of them are very bad. In fact, as a result of them, some have lost their fear of death; others are totally terrified, while others see them as life-changing encounters with God. Common testimonials of such brushes with death include rushing through a long tunnel and being enveloped in a soothing white light, or crossing over a bridge and meeting an inviting white-clad figure. In contrast, others speak of a horrible blackness, or even a terrifying abyss of nothingness. (Sounds a bit Jewish, doesn't it?)For three reasons I want to suggest that *none* of these experiences demonstrate that life continues after death:

> *First, the experiences, as relayed, come from people who have lost consciousness and have stopped breathing - for a relatively short time.*

Apart from death in frigid, watery conditions, none of the reports come from people who have lost total consciousness, and who have stopped breathing for a length of time, such as a day or two. At some point, significant *brain deterioration begins to take place.* (Brain deterioration begins to set in after about four minutes when breathing has ceased.)

Neurologists tell us that, when brain cells are deprived of nutrients and oxygen, hallucinations may occur that are triggered by endorphins. At such a point, the person concerned would not be considered to be clinically dead. The brain is still in an active state. At this point, the person may still be revived! It's during this state, when consciousness is suspended, that the person seems able to experience what is often called, *life after life experiences.*7 Obviously, at some level, the brain is still functioning, *but within the context of time!* Natural time has not yet ceased to exist.

> *Second, the spiritual experiences relayed are normally consistent with the religious (or non-religious) memory of the individual.*

For example, a Buddhist rarely speaks of an encounter with Jesus Christ any more than a Muslim may speak of an encounter with the Buddha. Apart from the possibility of a miraculous kind of encounter, *past memory seems to determine the nature of the religious experience.* In moments of stress, it is understandable that a person, raised in a Christian culture, crosses a bridge and is met by a *Christ-like figure.* Similarly, another person may recall an encounter with a figure representing the religion in which he or she was raised. The point is: *the religious experience takes place in the context of time, as we know it.* Brain cells are still alive and producing a religious experience consistent with a person's normal religious memory.

> *Third, neurologists are able to produce identical or similar experiences in volunteer patients.*

Under controlled conditions, a person may enter a hallucinatory state. Encounters that are recalled are often shown to be of the same nature spoken of by people in their supposed *life after life state, or their near death experience.* Hallucinatory drugs have also been known to produce comparable effects.4

Some *researches are now questioning whether all consciousness really does reside exclusively within the brain.* "…consciousness could exist in the absence of a functioning brain….If that is so, then those cells still alive when someone is declared brain dead may perceive events that are otherwise inexplicable. This hypothesis may lead us away from the interpretation of NDEs as evidence of an afterlife."5 This recent area of research lends a measure of scientific credence to the hypothesis that, because some measure of *consciousness* is still present, then *revelations and decisions of some sort may continue to exist.*

Wilder Penfield, a renowned pioneer of modern neurosurgery, is one who is now convinced that mind and brain are distinct from each other. In that realization, he has concluded that human beings consist of both body and spirit.6

Dr. J.P. Moreland, a nuclear chemist with a master's degree in theology, agrees that consciousness and the brain are distinct entities.

When questioned concerning the case that *consciousness and the soul are immaterial entities,* and speaking as a scientist, Moreland agrees with Penfield's conclusion. Nevertheless, he leaves us with a theological *assumption that immaterial* must also mean *immortal.* For him, the soul is made in the image of God, so it is *immaterial* "…while the human soul survives the death of its body, I don't think the animal soul outlives its body. I could be wrong…" 7 (Isaiah may have something to say about that; he has a vast array of animals in the new creation! Isa. 11:6-7)

I may also be wrong! But there is another way of thinking concerning the nature of humanity as a whole. John Polkinghorne, a British physicist, who is also a Christian, speaks of a certain complimentarity residing in the distinctions of the human condition. This is particularly evident when comparing the distinct nature of both mind and matter. "One could summarize this as dual-aspect monism. There is only one stuff in the world (not two – the material and the mental) but it can occur in two contrasting states (material and mental phases, a physicist would say) which explain our perception of the difference between mind and matter." 8 He continues by quoting Thomas Nagel's dismissal of a dual aspect theory: "The strange truth seems to be that certain, complex, biologically generated physical systems, of which each of us is an example, have rich nonphysical properties. An integrated theory of reality must account for this, and I believe that if and when it arrives, probably not for centuries, it will alter our conception of the universe as radically as anything has to date," 9 Now this idea of non-duality is truly amazing; it has profound implications for the validity of the bodily resurrection of Jesus Christ. We'll get to that later.

Getting back to so-called proofs of natural immortality, no one wants to deny the extraordinary power, or the reality of near death experiences. They have had profound effects upon many of the persons concerned, and mostly for the good! But what we see here is that all the experiences mentioned occur within the context of *natural time.* As such, they are not proof, whatsoever, of life beyond the grave. However, we may say that these experiences do show that *there may still be awareness, a consciousness of life; but always in the context of time that somehow still exists for the person.*

WHAT ABOUT PURGATORY?

For our purposes, and theological directions, we may lump together the notion of *purgatory* with that of *universalism*. Purgatory is "According to Roman Catholic teaching the place or state of temporal punishment, where those who have died in the grace of God expiate their unforgiven venial sins and undergo such punishment as is still due to forgiven sins, before being admitted to the Beatific vision."10 Universalism is the doctrine "…that hell is in essence purgative and therefore temporary and that all intelligent beings will therefore in the end be saved." 11 I want to suggest here that notions of purgatory are, ultimately, a denial of the dignity of humanity; especially in the area of free will.

For both of these situations there is an assumption that, beyond the grave there is a consistent procession of chronological time. (Of course, if eternal life is of a spirit nature, then there is no reason for time.)However, this procession of time raises a serious problem. Presumably, from the moment of death, a spirit would depart to this state in order to wait, and prepare for the judgment or some point of acceptance to heaven. Apart from the fact that there is absolutely no biblical evidence to support this notion, (1 John 5:16-17 is the attempt to justify it), *we must remember that time, as a distinct entity, requires its material dimensions to be in place.* For those selling indulgences in the sixteenth century, time was certainly an important factor.

Once we consider the question of time, then we must, of necessity, *consider the physical dimensions which make it possible.* We see, from basic creation principles, that a condition for both purgatory and universalism requires such dimensions, but not for spirits. So where is there a physical place we may call purgatory? What we are suggesting in this thesis is that body, soul, and spirit (the constituents of a human being) all die at the point of death. Is it just a spirit undergoing expiation? So somewhere in purgatorial thinking, essential elements of humanity are missing. But somehow, if a spirit can exist in isolation, the parts must surely come together again. Now, what would all this say concerning the ability of Jesus, at the point of extinction, to embrace the penitent of all time into the fullness of His finished work of redemption? The difficulties of this thesis should become clearer!

A CHRISTIAN VIEW OF DEATH

To the question: Is there life beyond the grave? the Christian answer is, Yes, and No! The fact is that, in a chronological sense, everyone who had ever lived was now dead and buried! As far as biblical revelation has taken us, to this point, there is nothing more; *Dust to dust.*

When the Apostle Paul speaks of all being dead in Adam, he is not simply speaking analogously about some sort of spiritual darkness. As Polkinghorne has suggested, we can't really separate the spirit from the physical anyway. Wasn't it the *inbreathing* of God that separated humanity from all other creatures? Speaking to the Romans, Paul offers a simple polarity of existence versus non-existence (Rom. 6:23). Let me repeat, *everything that constitutes the human condition died on the day of Christ's death.* And, in spite of attempts to explain away a real death, the fact remains that the death of Jesus is a matter of historical record. There are two vitally important factors implied in this effort to emphasize the complete death of Jesus.[ix]

> *There was absolutely nothing remaining in Jesus that gave Him the ability to raise Himself from the dead. Humanity was totally impotent!*

On that Good Friday, it didn't take long for His body to become as cold as the tomb in which it was laid. Nicodemus and Joseph of Arimathaea had placed His dead body to rest, and it was wrapped in linen cloths, which were soaked in precious spices (John 19:38-40).

If the most wonderful and obedient Person who ever lived, had died and was then buried, what possible hope can there be for anyone else? This fact alone doesn't really offer much to support the claims of other religions in their claims to secure natural immortality.

"...as all die in Adam..." (1 Co.15:22)

"For the wages of sin is death..." (Rom. 6:23)

The logical consequence we arrive at is that there really isn't any hope for humanity beyond the grave. *And that's it, folks!*

But what about the promise Jesus gave to the thief on his cross? What can it possibly mean for him to be in Paradise with Jesus?

I cannot overstate the importance of returning to the statement which Jesus made on the cross. *Nothing less than the sovereign purposes of God for creation are at stake here* (1 Pet. 1:20). Let me put my concern in the form of a question:

> *If God's purposes are really sovereign, would they be defeated, or even need modification, had His original plan for creation proved to stand in need of revision?*

Put very briefly, we have simply noted that God made a material world: He placed in it physical, inbreathed, people who were intended to live in it *forever in blissful intimacy with God, and in an apostolic life of stewardship.* If, at the end of the Big Story, all those elements are not in place, how can God's purposes be sovereign?

Before His crucifixion, Jesus had confused His disciples with a statement they failed to understand. (At least, they didn't understand it until after the Resurrection!)

> *"In my Father's house there are many places (Greek: menai-places remaining, or to settle). If it were not so, would I have told you that I go to prepare a place for you? (topos-dwelling). And if I go and prepare a place for you, I will come again and will take you to myself, so that where I am, there you may be also" (Parentheses and Italics mine; John 14:2-3).*

We have to get back to that statement Jesus made on the cross. In the *Moment* of His identification with all who had lived outside of the Calvary experience, Jesus led the procession of all the saints, including the penitent thief. He took them to *the Paradise of God.* It was a *real place* accomplished by God in Christ's victory through the *entire Easter events.* "…today you will be with me in Paradise."

The Greek word, *paradeisos* has its derivation in an oriental word meaning, *park, or garden.* In the Greek version of the Old Testament (the Septuagint), the same word is also used to describe the *Garden of Eden* (Gen. 2:8). In the New

Testament, the word is used when referring to a celestial paradise.12 It is also the word used by Paul when describing his heavenly vision (2 Co. 12:3). The same word is used again in the apocalyptic vision of John:

> **"I will give permission to eat from the tree of life that is in the paradise of God" (Rev. 2:7).**

With Jesus at the Head, the new creation is, therefore, a *better place* than that which fell into decay. *But it is a real place!* (John 14:2) Not all scholars agree that Paradise is the ultimate destiny for those in Christ. The renowned English scholar, Bishop N.T. Wright of Durham is certainly one of them. "Paradise, in Jewish thought, wasn't necessarily the final resting place, but the place of rest and refreshment before the gift of life in the resurrection." 13 No doubt, such a possibility must remain at the back of our heads. But, here, we must also remind ourselves of four biblical realities:

First: There is no biblical evidence that the Man, Christ Jesus, with the repentant thief, entered into a state of rest and refreshment after death. It was in His resurrected condition that He appeared to many in the fullness of humanity (1 Co.15:3-8). Life never ends to those in Christ (Rom. 8:38; John 11:25). Connection to Christ's resurrection means connection to the *fullness of Easter*, which includes His ascension into heaven. We remember that the great saints of the Old Testament are *already* participating in Christ's resurrected life (Heb. 12:1).

Second: God's original purpose for humanity was for them to be stewards of the earth, forever! (Gen. 2:15-17) This means that *material people were intended to live in a material world forever.* They were fashioned from clay. Spirits were not hanging around a temporary, celestial existence. God did not say, Spirit you are and to spirit you shall return." Are God's purposes not sovereign after all? Have His purposes failed; have they been modified? But, as Isaiah says, God really does know the beginning from the end, and His purposes will not fail! (Isa. 46:10)

Third: The paradise about which Tom Wright speaks is solely postulated to be possible within the confines of chronological time. It is a way of explaining a sequence of events in time as we know it. But God draws *all time into Himself.* Only in this way was the Transfiguration made a reality. Moses and Elijah really did appear with Jesus. To inhabit, with Jesus, the Paradise which God intended, is to enter into the fullness of the *Easter Moment.*

Fourth: We enter into a difficult area when we introduce any condition which speaks of existence in an intermediary state. That is also how the problems of purgatory and universalism may appear.

We will stop here, but the above four points lay sufficient weight for us to think literally of the promise given to that thief who, near his last breath, met the Christ who was able to offer entrance to the eternal banquet in Paradise.

We are back to our original thoughts about *time being related to space and place.* In other words:

> *Because of the resurrection of Jesus, time itself has been restored forever; as it was in the beginning! Time really is related to place and space!*

The most unnatural implication is that this paradise is *unearned.* In the Christian Big Story, it has been given by grace *from above,* and through the finished work of Jesus. Isn't that an astounding miracle? Also, God's sovereign purposes are intact. Paradise or the *place* Jesus prepares is still a four-dimensional creation which, as at the beginning, has time that never ends. Quite possibly, with Jesus as the Head, the new community may well, once again, be capable of exercising stewardship with enormous Spirit-filled possibilities. At the heart of the new creation is the Holy City, the New Jerusalem which *comes down from heaven* (Rev. 21:1-2). This place is a brand new creation, *but is somehow connected to that which fell into decay. Of course, the same principle exists when we look for recognizable connections between the old and the resurrected body of Jesus.* As we shall see, the connection is real, but is nevertheless a mystery. The apocalyptic writer records, "See, I am making all things new" (Rev. 21:5).

IS THERE A POSSIBILITY OF TOTAL ANNIHILATION?

This is a very important question which has divided scholarly and godly people throughout the ages. I am suggesting here that, apart from a miracle:

> *Our final lack of self-awareness, somewhere beyond consciousness is also the point of our annihilation.*

It happened to Jesus! Nothing can change that *unless, at this point of helplessness, God takes the initiative to offer some sort of miraculous intervention; something which could not be offered by nature itself!* It is also important that we avoid notions of sentimentalism. We remember that, in honoring the creation principle of free choice, the *Gospel is always offered by way of invitation.* We are free to embrace or renounce it. The Gospel order is very clear: God issues the invitation; we are called to respond. The process does not begin with our decision. *Hence, the question of eternal punishment in hell is raised.* However, at this point we are also forced to ask the question of whether there really is a *place* called hell.

According to Jesus, we are certain that *Paradise is a place.* If hell is really a place, it means that people are raised from the dead, but for what?[x] Is it to spend eternity in the everlasting torment of a *place* that has physical dimension? The existence of an eternal hell would necessitate one, or both of two images:

First, unless it is spirit alone that continues after death (which we have discounted) the *possibility* remains that time, with its dimensional constituents, has been restored for *all people in Christ.* If there is time, then there is place and space!

We have posed the theology that *time is definitely restored in the power of the resurrection and, if there is time, then there must also be place and space.* What evidence do we have that the restoration of time is for those outside of Christ? We did not observe a thesis of restored time in the Old Testament, except for the remote possibility that a place called hell existed in the mind of a very late writer of a single Daniel text. (Even this text has given rise to a variety of explanations - Dan. 12:2.) In the wonderful vision of Isaiah concerning a new creation (or a new created order) we note the language of length of days, not everlasting days (Isa. 65:17-20). In this passage there are infants and those considered to be accursed because they did not reach a hundred. Does not the resurrection promise of restored time extend *forever* to the redeemed only? Did God raise Jesus in order to create a place called hell? *Are there really two entirely different forms of existence beyond the grave?* (This would mean that there is a spiritual existence, while the second is one of a material order.) If hell is not a physical place, would that, of necessity mean that a *spiritual existence* is reserved for those in hell while there is a *physical existence* for those in Paradise?

Second, if an eternal, *spiritual place* called hell really does exist, would it not mean that *all persons* possess a natural, spiritual state of immortality - regardless of where and how eternity is spent? (This latter point takes no account of creatures that are created as spirit-beings.)

Such a postulation means, unquestionably, that a *spiritual existence* takes place for all people. But this existence is of a spiritual nature, not one that is physical! But, once again, we are back to considering *the nature of humanity*. In this schema of thought, the creation theme of humanity's wholeness of body, soul, and spirit is clearly changed. We continue to be left with questions regarding God's sovereignty; particularly one of settling for a different life situation than that which was designed at the beginning. *Human beings were never intended to be spirit-beings!* We are all people with a nature consisting of body, soul, and spirit. Therefore, we would have to be recreated as spirit-beings in order to experience an eternal fire of hell. Meanwhile, because of the finished work of Christ, the redeemed are already whole people who are enjoying life in a new creation.

If, as is strongly postulated here, we cannot accept the latter thesis that all people become spirit-beings after death, then we are left with one alternative: Like the fate of the unrepentant thief, and for all those choosing to live outside of the finished work of Christ, their destiny is one of *total annihilation*. Humanly, they cannot possibly fit into the purposes for which God intended in creation. *Can they humanly exist for any other purpose?*

There are many who are horrified by the thought that a loving God could consign people to everlasting torment simply because they rejected the choice God had given them. (Maybe such people should consider the possibility that it is humans who consign themselves to their future condition.) Clark Pinnock offers a view of total annihilation, but it may not be for the best reasons! He says that a loving God wouldn't torture people forever for sins done in the context of finite life. For him, it doesn't make any sense to suppose that a lake of fire exists with souls burning in it forever.14 Pinnock may not have ventured into the arena of sentimentality but:

> *This question should not be debated on the basis of sentimentality,*
> *but on biblical substance.*

We're speaking of *free choices*, all of which have their consequences. God's love is clearly unconditional, but it does not interfere with the natural *consequences* (for good or ill) which flow from our decisions. Hence, God's plan of salvation is to rescue us from natural consequences; not to accept, without any consequences, the decisions that are offensive to His awesome holiness.

Hugh Ross offers another theological view which, I believe, may also be flawed. He feels that the traditional approach of an eternal hell can still speak of a loving God. This God can consign people to hell because they are *spirit-beings* and so *they cannot be eradicated*. Therefore, for spirit-beings, "Hell is a place people choose. While the people in hell will despise their torment, they have demonstrated their preference for it over eternal fellowship with God and with all who love the Light."15

Obviously, I cannot concur with both of his assumptions, i.e. that future life is one of purely spiritual existence, nor can I hold the view that hell is a place. It seems strange that a scientist would speak of a *spiritual existence* in, what seems to be a *physical place*. Quite apart from this very serious difficulty, we see that Ross preserves God's character of love because, "...those who inhabit the lake of fire occupy the best possible realm for them. God expresses his love and compassion for hell's inhabitants by afflicting them with sufficient torment to prevent the place from being as bad as its inhabitants have the capacity to make it."16 Where is there biblical evidence for this thought?

Hell becomes, therefore, *an everlasting degree of torment, relative to the present state of the individual!* Unless Ross is prepared to define *the lake of fire* as simply a spiritual metaphor suggesting an eternal torment, then he is clearly speaking of a *place* called hell. *Hell, as a metaphor, therefore becomes a condition, not a place.* We know that we can speak of a condition of hell while we continue to live on earth, but our thoughts are on the question of whether there can be a *material hell.* Wouldn't this eternal continuance mean that God is continually involved in such a place of torment? Where do we find any evidence to support such a claim? It can't be that bad, because God seems to continue taking a hand in it! Fire, as we know it, is a form of energy. Then, who supplies this material substance of energy? Does, or can, Satan produce the energy for his own eternal torment? (Rev. 20:10) *On the other hand, if hell really is a place, then it must possess dimension in order for eternal time to be experienced.*

Who created this hell with dimensions? Revelation 20:1-4, 10-11 (see also 2 Pet. 2:4 and Jude 6) may allude to the possibility that God has reserved this condition *for spirit-beings called the devil, his angels, the beast, and the false prophet.* (Who can possibly know what eternal torment these spirit beings will experience at their judgment?) But this raises further questions concerning the nature of life existing in such an ethereal state of hell. So we ask; *Where do we find solid evidence that the physical bodies we possess (as originally intended by God) suddenly become spiritual bodies with no connection to the physical?*

We must face the fact that the notion of an eternal punishment, in a place called hell, *can find some sort of biblical justification!* e.g. "They serve as an example of those who suffer the punishment of eternal fire" (Jude 7). This literal position can be found as far back as the fourth century. In the middle of the fourth century, Cyril of Jerusalem described the death of Jesus in this way, "For upon Christ death came in reality, for His soul was truly separated from His body, and His burial was true."17 A century earlier, even Origen may have said the same thing. We must emphasize again the power of revelation. The Old Testament text does *not* say, "Spirit you are, and to spirit you shall return," but "...you are dust..." (Gen. 3:19)

The position taken by Cyril of Jerusalem is shared today by many who are highly respected for their academic ability and Christ-centered spirituality. James Packer is one such person whom I know to be a godly, gracious and well-respected academic in the Conservative Evangelical tradition. He proposes, "Eternal punishment, then, as Jesus declares it, is departure into eternal fire."18 John Blanchard, writing on questions of hell, has as his pivotal premise the idea that body and soul are two separate entities. They can be separated; one being physical and the other spiritual. Therefore, he concludes that *death never means cessation, but separation* because Adam and Eve continued to live after eating the fruit.19 But the *Bible does tell us* that Adam and Eve really did die! It just took a little time! They continued in their-God-given *physical existence (body, soul, and spirit) until the natural course of life returned them to dust!* (Gen. 3:19, 5:5) "...for as all die in Adam, so all will be made alive in Christ" (1 Co. 15:22).

The following represents concerns of others *opposing* the view of annihilation. "For the annihilationist, there is no possibility of perfect justice or the righting of wrongs. Good will remain unrewarded and evil unpunished. The serial murderer and the tiny child, the rapist and the kindly old lady, the ruthless dictator and the gentle nurse, everything they are and everything they have been and done will be wiped out of existence"20

CONSEQUENCES DO EXIST FOR THOSE WHO ARE ANNIHILATED

There are equally respected biblical scholars who hold the view that, apart from the possibility of a miraculous rebirth, the ultimate destiny of all people really *is annihilation*. For them, this approach is perfectly consistent with the Hebraic view that we are made from dust, and to dust we shall return. There are instances where this position is advocated. After ten years of study, the Church of England's <u>Doctrine and Worship</u> committee concluded that "a fiery eternal hell speaks of a cruel sadistic God" and so it goes on, "…if a person refuses God's offer of salvation, the consequence is ultimate non-being." 21 This statement actually does speak of God's revealed nature as the criterion for final judgment.

John Stott, another generous and well-respected English Evangelical, offers this thought, "But I do plead for frank dialogue among Evangelicals on the basis of Scripture. I also believe that the ultimate annihilation of the wicked should at least be accepted as a legitimate, biblically founded alternative to their eternal conscious torment."22 In his dialogue with the esteemed liberal David Edwards, Stott agrees that, while a *weeping and gnashing of teeth* should be taken seriously, "…The imagery which Jesus and his apostles used (the lake of fire, the outer darkness, the second death) is not meant to be interpreted literally. In any case it could not be, since fire and darkness exclude each other."23 "…the most natural way to understand the reality behind the imagery is that ultimately all enmity and resistance to God will be destroyed. Therefore, both the language of destruction and the imagery of fire seem to point to annihilation. It would be easier to hold together the awful reality of hell and the universal reign of God if hell means destruction and the impenitent are no more,"24

Although verses of scripture may be bandied about on both sides, let me summarize the question of *conditional immortality* with the suggestion that *both Jesus and Paul were cognizant of the question:*

> **"Do not fear those who kill the body but cannot kill the soul; rather fear him who can destroy both soul and body in hell" (Matt 10:18).**

> *"To those who by patiently doing good seek for glory and honor and immortality, he will give eternal life; while for those who are self-seeking and who obey not truth but wickedness, there will be wrath and fury..." (Rom. 2:7-8.)*

Note the contrast of "eternal life" with "wrath and fury.")

In the second letter to Thessalonica, the Apostle Paul continues:

> *"He will punish those who do not know God and do not obey the gospel of our Lord Jesus. He will be punished with everlasting destruction and shut out from the presence of the Lord" (2 Th. 1:8-9).*

How may *"destruction"* be equated with a form of continued existence?

FURTHER THOUGHTS ON ANNIHILATION

I have to ask the question of how eternal time (i.e. time that never ends) can secure the justice that some feel must ultimately be attained by everlasting torment. Clearly, for those who believe in universal immortality, the underlying *principle of hell's eternal existence really means that no amount of time will bring about the required punishment.* So we are faced with a difficult contradiction. If 100 or 100 million years is not enough (and remember that any measurement of time also requires the dimensions of place and space), then justice seems to tread a very difficult path. There are legitimate ways that honor the required principles of God's justice, and of the consequences that flow from it. They reside both in the realms of the *nature of time and in the nature of God's love*.

God's nature of justice is connected with the free decisions that people make. The *consequences* of those decisions require the involvement of His justice. On several occasions we have noted that the *righteousness* of God is always the determining factor tempering the nature of His justice. The Bible nearly always connects the two. When a person has chosen to live outside the character of God's revealed righteousness (not their own perceptions of righteousness), *then he or she chooses to live outside of life lived in the nature of God.* But the Bible continually speaks of a logical corollary. *The choice is life or death.* What is the opposite of life?

> ***"The wages of sin is death, but the free gift of God is eternal life in Christ Jesus our Lord" (Rom. 6:23).***

In another context, (not one of eternal life) Moses urged Israel to follow God's commands. In that context, He challenges them to choose life (Deut. 30:13, 19).

I am about to make an assumption here that may elicit accusations of sentimentalism. I'll risk them because I see that the Big Story consistently points that way. Throughout this entire book I have spoken of God who honors the dignity of human decision; and that is whether He likes the decision or not! We remember that Jesus sadly accepted the rejection of His loving challenge to the rich man.

> ***But Jesus didn't change the relational conditions in order to include him (Mark 10:17-22).***

Nor did Jesus change kingdom standards in order to satisfy those who didn't accept its high ideals (Matt. 5:48). It would be the grace of God, alone, that would enable people to cross those insurmountable hurdles. The freedom to decide for this relationship with God is vitally important. *But responsibilities are required in making that decision.* The rich ruler knew that he would have experienced great difficulty in following Jesus. We see that Jesus rose above sentimentalism by connecting love for Him with obedience to His commands (John 14:15). God knows best how relationships work. And there are eternal consequences in not living them.

Is there then, as Hugh Ross suggests, some sort of *spiritual existence* for spirit bodies to endure eternal torment? Or, as John Stott suggests; is the New Testament's four-dimensional imagery of hell simply a picture that enables us to understand that the *pain of hell will be experienced by all those who blaspheme the work of the Spirit?* (Matt. 12:31)

Then, are we really thinking of hell as an experience of destruction, and not a material place?

When God raised Jesus from the dead, *everything that constituted His humanity was raised* (i.e., body, soul and spirit). Peter began the Christian apologetic, and risked its entire premise on the *miracle* of God's raising the lifeless body of Jesus from the grave of nothingness (Acts 2:24, 3:15; 1 Pet. 1:3).

And we shall be like Him! The ascended body of Jesus is evidence of how we are to think of our eternal body. "He ...will come in the same way as you saw him go into heaven" (Acts 1:11). It should also be noted here that *the feet of Jesus do not again touch the ground of the old order.* Those in Christ, who are alive and remain, *are raised,* as an act *from above.* They meet Jesus above the old order as He leads the procession towards the order of the new (1 Co. 15:52-53; 1 Thess. 4:16-17).

We see then, as far as humans are concerned, the fire of hell is clearly the torment of knowing that life cannot continue, and that such torment is accompanied by unbelievable spiritual agony! *Hell is mostly all about the conscious knowledge and the horrific terror of separation from Life itself.* It would appear that Jesus is quite deliberately taking this approach in several of His parables. For example, we see it in His metaphors of *weeds and goats* (Matt. 13:30, 25:33); of *one in the field,* or the *one left at the mill* (Matt. 24:40-41). The parable of separation of wheat from tares is particularly helpful:

The kingdom of heaven is not simply about wheat and weeds; it is about God's reign among His people. (Incidentally, in this parable, Jesus speaks of time in terms of kairos, not chronos.) In this analogy, He speaks of weeds being *burned up.* The Greek word that is employed is katakaio. (But katakausai-the aorist infinitive, is the form of the verb which is used.) The verb means, *to burn up, or to consume with fire.* In this present tense sentence, the deliberate use of the aorist infinitive denotes a completed action. Otherwise, the writer would have utilized an imperfect verb. In other words, *the action is complete; it is sealed!* Here, all the parables are illustrative of a personal awareness of *a great separation from life.*

Just to summarize our thoughts on annihilation:
If there is time beyond the grave, there must be the necessary material constituents to make time possible. If not, then there must be a spirit-existence. But this requires a major change in God's sovereign design for human life.

Remember Paradise? Annihilation is really the only credible alternative which gives credence to *God's design* for human existence.

WHAT ABOUT THE RICH MAN AND LAZARUS?

Certainly, it is in this context of time we may consider certain implications in the story of the rich man and Lazarus (Luke 16:19-31). For some, this story furnishes proof of everlasting torment. I don't think so!

> *It is really about separation from the Source of life, (e.g., 1 John 5:12-13) and by choice, that separation is now past redemption.*

In this story the rich man was experiencing his judgment; Lazarus had received his. Here, the rich man received a *Moment* which was neither a good, nor a lasting experience! What we are about to see in this story, told by Jesus, is that the rich man:
Saw what he had missed and would never, by habit of decision, possess. Was already in the throes of hell. Experienced unbearable agony and torment. In his agony, he encountered Abraham, not as judge, but as a forerunner of all those accounted righteous before God (Rom. 5:1-2; Heb. 11:39-40). Having come to the knowledge of an uncrossable gulf between God and his remaining family, could do nothing to remedy *their* situation. Realized the Word of God always gives warning about the consequences of decisions.

> *The redemptive work of Christ takes place within the context of time, and must be appropriated within the context of time.*

The rich man had made his *decision*! It was a decision to gain wealth and maintain it at the expense of the poor. (It was an attitude indelibly imbedded in his character. Satan himself will not repent, even though he knows his future torment!)This attitude also appears to persist in the rich man's family. In those closing moments of time, by experiencing the torment of what his decision had cost him, the rich man called out, *not for salvation or forgiveness*, but for comfort from the torment of knowing what was ahead for him and his family. He seemed to be incapable of serious repentance. *He was already experiencing hell because he was able to see what he had lost!* But what about others who feel they can leave such relational decisions to the very last moment? God, who knows the secrets of all hearts, can not be mocked! (Rom. 2:15-16) At this point, God is looking for the desire of a change in heart and nature.

So we see that the self-centered nature of the rich man remained dominant; it elicited a negative choice in the man (See also Luke 13:24-29). In Matthew 24:30 we see that *there is absolutely no thought introduced which suggests mourning will produce salvation.* (Is this the meaning of Rev. 9:20-21?)

Somehow, *the rich man chooses, or is so conditioned by the past, that he will not come to genuine repentance. (See Matt.18:3)* (Jesus is suggesting here, that *this* condition dominates over the need for penitence. "If they do not listen to Moses and the prophets, neither will they be convinced even if someone rises from the dead" (Luke 16:31).

> *"There is a way that seems right to a person, but its end is the way to death" (Prov. 14:12).*

Incidentally, there is often a great deal of sentimentality associated with biblical understandings of the rich and the poor. It would be right to say that Jesus was always on the side of the oppressed; and that attitude mostly included the poor. However, He did not say that it was *impossible* for a rich person to enter the kingdom of heaven (Luke 19:1-10). Nor did He say that we could get to heaven if we are materially poor. What He was saying was that the attitudes and style of life, which produced certain character traits, made it very difficult for the consumer-minded person to enter, or desire, the character of God's kingdom. (The rich man was experiencing hell, just by looking into heaven!) Achieving wealth to the cost of others is not a kingdom principle. But Jesus did applaud honest enterprise. We see this in his teaching on stewardship in Matt. 25:14-30.

> *We all receive the consequences of the decisions we have made in response to God's decision for us (John 3:16).*

> *It is life in God's grace, or death in oneself.*

The larger meaning of this story is really all about the fate of Israel at the time of Jesus. Abraham, the patriarch of God's chosen people, explains that the story of Israel pointed towards the salvation they (as a nation) had rejected. Like the story of the Prodigal Son, this is also an analogy of the choices that had been made by Israel.

So let's eat, drink and be merry! Some may consider annihilation to be a reasonable alternative. Why not, if that is all it will cost for a self-centered life spent apart from God? That's especially true if I can do it, "My Way!" Clearly, this is *not the position taken by Jesus*, who, in the context of judgment referred to a conscious experience of "weeping and gnashing of teeth" (Matt. 13:42, 50). In this sense, I want to compare *the closing moments of self-consciousness with the terror of hell*. It really wouldn't matter what amount of time we wish to consider. We have noted that time ceases to exist for those outside of its restoration in Christ. However, the *Moment* before that occurs:

> *The torment and terror of hell is experienced in all its*
> *fullness during that awful Moment of personal revelation.*

We see that the rich man experienced a devastating degree of horror. This *Moment* would contain all the experience that was necessary for the awesome realization to occur. A view of chronos (successive, natural time) is telescoped to reveal the fullness of hell's experience. So, whether we prefer to think in terms of seconds or millions of years in the future, it really doesn't matter! It's irrelevant! *Nothing more of hell can be experienced beyond that moment.* The ultimate result is unchanged and is truly horrific to those experiencing it! The fury of hell's torment is therefore *fully revealed* in the closing moments of time. Having said this, I must also note that a case may be made for the possibility that the *degree of torment and terror* may well be more severe for some than it is for others. Jesus intimated this in Mark 12:40. Nevertheless, this possibility in no way deters us from the prospect that:

> *Hell is experienced as an Eternal*
> *Moment of terror and torment!*

> ***"Do not fear those who kill the body but cannot kill the soul;***
> ***rather fear him who can destroy both body and soul in hell"***
> ***(Matt 10:28).***

Here, the writer, penning the words of Jesus, does not make use of the future tense, but his use of the aorist infinitive as a completed act of destruction, *apolesai,* is very clear. Coupled with its association to the condition of hell, it is even more terrifying!

The cruelest irony in the question of evil's existence is that, in the end, there is no one there to reward its adherents for their faithfulness to its perversions. It is easy to understand why ancient Hebrew writers of the Old Testament could only grasp at a description of Sheol. We may describe it as: the nothingness of aloneness.

Clearly, God's offer is one of life or no life at all:

"God gave us eternal life, and this life is in his Son. He who has the Son has life; he who has not the Son has not life" (1 John 5:11-12).

This verse doesn't speak of some Gnostic spiritualization of the separation of body from spirit. It speaks of the wholeness of life as God originally intended: of *body, soul, and spirit living in the fullness of God's "essential relationships of creation!"*

He is the Lord of Life, *and the offer of eternal life must be seen, completely, in terms of response to a generous invitation.*

In the resurrection of Jesus we see that, once more, and through our personal connection to Christ's resurrection, we have now been *gifted* with a life which never ends! Having said all of this, for me, the physical resurrection of Jesus Christ is still a mystery. Let's see why. It's probably a mystery for everyone!

Chapter 10 Eternal Life: Is it for Everyone?

1. Hancock, Graham, *Fingerprints of the Gods, pps. 310-333*
2. Blanchard, John. *Whatever Happened to Hell?* P.37 Crossway Books, Wheaton, Ill. 60187 (1995)
3. Hancock, Graham, *Fingerprints of the Gods,* p.417
4. Dr. Sherman Netland in a television series entitled, *The Unexplained: Immortality,* aired on the A&E Network, March 6th 1997
5. Bartholomew Anita, *Life After Life,* Reader's Digest (Canada) October 2003, p.144
6. Strobel, *The Case for a Creator,* p.249
7. Strobel, *The Case for a Creator,* pps.257, 263

8.   Polkinghorne, John, *The Faith of a Physicist,* Fortress Press, Minneapolis, 1996 p.21

9.   Polkinghorne, John, p.21

10.   The Oxford Dictionary of the Christian Church, Ed. F.L.Cross (Second Edition) Oxford Press 1974, p.1144

11.   The Oxford Dictionary p.1415

12.   Robinson, J.A.T. *In The End God,* pp.91-92

13.   Wright, Tom, *Luke for Everyone,* p.284, SPCK, Westminster John Knox Press, 36, Causton St., London SW1P 4ST (2001)

14.   Pinnock, Clark. H and Delwin Brown, *Theological Crossfire: An Evangelical/Liberal Dialogue.*p.226 Zondervan

15.   Ross, Hugh, *Beyond the Cosmos,* pps. 209-211

16.   Ross, Hugh, *Beyond the Cosmos, pps. 211-213*

17.   St.Cyril of Jerusalem, *Lectures on the Christian Sacraments,* Ed.F.L.Cross, p.62. SPCK Press. London, Fourth Impression 1977

18.   Packer, J.I. *Crux, The Problem of Eternal Punishment.* September 1990/Vol.26,No.3, p.19

19.   Blanchard, John, *Whatever Happened to Hell?* pps. 56-57

20.   Blanchard, John, *Whatever Happened to Hell? p.*67

21.   Ross, Hugh, *Beyond the Cosmos,* p.208

22.   Stott, J and Edwards, D.L. *Evangelical Essentials,* p.320 InterVarsity Press, Downer's Grove,Illinois 60515

23.   Stott, J and Edwards, D.L. *Evangelical Essentials,* p.314

24.   Stott, J and Edwards, D.L. *Evangelical Essentials,* pps.318-319

Chapter 11

THE MYSTERY OF TIME RESTORED

As in Adam all die! (1 Co. 15:22) That's the terrifying reality, *unless some sort of God-given miracle can take place!* When you're dead, you're really dead! The Light of the world had been plunged into the awful abyss of darkness and oblivion. The fact of His death is a matter of historical record. It is found, not simply in the Gospels, but in the writings of the Jewish historian, Josephus.1

"Serious historical research, however, now indicates strongly that the gospels do indeed belong to the genre 'bibliography.' Of course they are not just that. They contain a good deal besides. But they are not less than biographies...There is now, therefore, no reason to say that the writers of the gospels, and their very first readers did not expect them to be taken as accounts of things that actually happened within history...we must not forget that the gospels would have appeared to a first-century reader, whether Jewish or non-Jewish, as books which told the story of an actual person who had lived and died in recent memory."2

Whether we think in Jewish terms of body and soul, or whether we think in Greek terms of body, soul, and spirit, everything in Jesus died! *A soul didn't wing its way up to heaven!* A person didn't go to *sleep* for the next 2000 years or so. The Man, Christ Jesus, had absolutely no power, *whatsoever,* to raise Himself to life. John Robinson put it this way, "There is nothing in man, however noble, which is not subject to death and by nature corruptible."3

But, a resurrection? Surely, that would have to be a miracle; natural immortality had proven to be a noble, but vain hope. It would have to a supernatural accomplishment: from above! And God did it where the Man, Christ Jesus, could not!

At some undetermined, but chronological moment, and at some specific point in the kairos of First Day Light, God breathed into the lifeless body of Jesus.

The Real Adam was reborn and the everlasting time of new creation was restored to a newborn humanity (Rev .21:5a).

Jesus is, "...the first fruits of those who have died, "For since death came through a human being, the resurrection of the dead has also come through a human being" (1 Co. 15:20-21).

In other words, *no one else had been resurrected to the fullness of the new order of life before Jesus.* No one! The great cloud of witnesses (Heb. 12:1) were incorporated into Christ's *Easter Moment*; He being the first fruits from the dead. This Easter moment incorporates all time into it's moment of victory.

For one more momentous time, the passive verb is used in relation to the finished work of Christ. God had said, "Let there be..." and God spoke again into the chaos of humanity's darkness:

"Christ died for our sins in accordance with the scriptures, and that he was buried, and that he was raised on the third day in accordance with the scriptures, and that he appeared to Cephas, then to the twelve. Then he appeared to more than five hundred brothers and sisters at one time, most of whom are still alive..." (1 Co. 15:3-6. Italics illustrating passive verbs are mine.)

BUT SOME DID NOT BELIEVE

Before we go on, we must consider, as the verse above indicates, the resurrection of Jesus is not a spiritual symbol, but *a fact of history*. Paul, who had Luke as a companion, may have considered Peter the first to see Jesus. However, it is more likely that his list of those who had seen the resurrected Christ was not so much one of chronological exactness, but one which lent social credence to the fact of the resurrection (1 Co. 15:5-8). Such names would be those holding a recognizable place of prominence in the Christian community. In Matthew's Gospel, the women see Him first. Both in the longer ending of Mark, and also in

John's Gospel, it is specifically Mary Magdalene. In Luke's Gospel it is difficult to discern who was first. Was it Peter, as Paul thought, or was it the two who walked with Jesus on the road to Emmaus? Nevertheless, that account, *in terms of the Bible being one Big Story, is significant.* When attempting to reveal who He was to the two on the road, Jesus chose to quote Old Testament scriptures:

> ***"Then beginning with Moses and all the prophets, he interpreted to them the things about himself in all the scriptures" (Luke 24:27).***

And later, to the eleven:

> ***"These are my words that I spoke to you while I was still with you - that everything written about me in the law of Moses, the prophets, and the psalms must be fulfilled. Then he opened their minds to understand the scriptures" (Luke 24:44-45).***

When we read resurrection narratives in the Gospels, it is apparent that there may be an ambiguity (maybe even discrepancy) concerning some of the details. Paul actually mentions the Twelve (to represent the Apostolic leadership - which includes Matthias Acts 1:20-26). He knew, quite clearly, that Judas had not been present to witness the event. It was an exciting, surprising, and traumatic time in the experience of all those mentioned. Maybe the differences in written traditions can be compared with the testimony of witnesses to a car accident. Individually, as they recall the event, they do it from the perspective in which they saw the accident. Some of the details may not always dovetail. However, listeners to the stories would not doubt that the witnesses had all agreed that an accident had occurred. One thing is empirically clear in the Bible:

> *All those who bore witness to the fact that they had seen the risen Christ really did speak objectively of the experience as a tangible and historical event.*

To them, the *event* was not a matter of subjective experience, or an allegory, or a poem. It was a real life description of what they saw. Any fuzziness in description of details may have produced skeptics, but the witnesses were convinced of the historical reality of the event. After all, they had witnessed a real-life miracle!

There are presently Christian skeptics who want to interpret the resurrection in ways that are something less than empirical. In John Hick's controversial book, *The Myth of God Incarnate*, a number of contributors add weight to this *Thomas* approach. For example, Michael Goulder offers a *psychological explanation*. For him, Christ's disciples had a desperate need to keep the memory of Jesus alive; even if it meant having to conjure up an apparition which became part of a future tradition. 4 Well, at most, a psychological explanation may possibly last, but no longer than one generation!

In a similar way, others join the fray by suggesting that the meaning of resurrection is confined to some sort of *spiritualized interpretation*; i.e., the triumph of good over evil, or the valor of self-sacrifice, or the victory of hope over despair. It is quite probable that the writer of 2 Timothy was concerned that a Gnostic approach to interpretation was already being considered by some people (2 Tim. 2:17-18). This mode of interpretation is becoming, unfortunately, too common in much of the contemporary mainline churches. As such, it really wouldn't make any difference for those people if someone, supposedly, dug up the bones of Jesus from the sands of the Middle East.

Apart from Judas, all of Christ's apostles had a first-hand experience of their resurrected Lord. Symbolic, spiritual language, or a psychological apparition had absolutely no meaning to them! Together, the apostles had the same experience of the resurrected Christ. In fact they would have laughed at such natural suggestions. Their relationship with Jesus had been restored through the reality of an historical fact, and it is a fact to which they were all witness. This was so important for them, now that they realized that *the very heart of their message could never be simply about the good words, teaching, and deeds of a dead carpenter*. The teachings of Jesus may live on throughout the ages, but they cannot bring with them a personal and intimate relationship with the resurrected Christ. In order to be numbered amongst the chosen foundations of a New Israel, the twelfth person replacing Judas must have:

"....accompanied us during all the time that the Lord Jesus went in and out among us, beginning from the baptism of John until

the day he was taken from us-one of these must become a witness with us to his resurrection" (Acts 1:21-22).

The resurrection is clearly at the very heart of the Christian Gospel. No wonder Paul said:

"If Christ has not been raised, your faith is futile and you are still in your sins" (1 Co. 15:17).

The reality of faith is that, for nearly 2,000 years the intimacy of relationship with the risen Christ has been experienced by those who know God in terms of a personal relationship. For example, we may observe from the call of Abraham (Gen. 12:1-9) that the way of the faith walk (where God sets the goal and the agenda) is actually a complete reversal of the normal ways humanity has chosen to experience knowledge. Here, we see that the normal process is one where knowledge precedes faith: The truth of Christian experience is the very opposite: *Faith precedes knowledge.* (2 Tim. 1:12) However, apart from subjective experience, empirical data is also of the utmost importance:

The wholeness of the resurrected body is the most important sign in vindicating the sovereignty of God's purposes for a restored creation.

From the very moment of Christ's resurrection, the miracle of new creation was poised for a newborn community. The observance of that unique *new creation body* is the most astounding and miraculous sign that has ever happened. In Christ, a reversal of the curse in Eden has taken place. It is in this sign, lauded for two thousand years, that the entire Christian community has rejoiced in the hope of death's reversal. God's purposes do not reside in the vague hope of immortality, but His sovereign miracle of resurrection. It is in this historical sign we all possess the hope that, five minutes after we die, we are already in the fullness of a newly created humanity: Achieved from above, it is with the new born community of Christ; He is the first fruit of new creation (1 Co. 15:20-21).

We won't even bother spending time refuting Gnostic theories that arose from the early *second century*. Nor will we bother with bizarre stories emanating from second century Gnosticism. It would seem that those grasping for such distractive theories just don't get the Big Story. They don't even understand that a miraculous, *physical resurrection* is, indeed, the *only* hope there is. Without it, there is no Big Story! *A miracle, from above, was absolutely necessary to make the Big Story credible.* In deference to those who are indifferent concerning the body of Jesus, I would state quite categorically that:

> *It is absolutely necessary for the world to be granted this one physical sign of resurrection. And this body must be that of the living, physical body of Jesus Christ the Real Adam and*

> **"the first fruits of those who have died" (1 Co. 15:20).**

If the physical resurrection of Jesus was not a reality, then there wasn't a resurrection at all. When Christ was raised, the *whole* of His humanity was restored. Only God could do that! And He did! *The promise of never-ending life was fully signed and restored in the Real Adam.* It is precisely for this reason Paul noted:

> **"If there is no resurrection of the dead, then Christ has not been raised; and if Christ has not been raised, then our proclamation has been in vain and your faith has been in vain. We are even found to be misrepresenting God..." (1 Co. 15:13-15)**

Enough of this! It all seems a far cry from the heart desire of Paul,

> **"...that I may know him and the power of his resurrection" (Phil. 3:10).**

RESURRECTION AND ASCENSION ARE ONE MOMENT

> **"When he ascended on high he made captivity itself a captive" (Eph. 4:8).**

*The Ascension, itself an integral part of the resurrection Moment,
speaks of the hope of all those in Christ following in the train of His
triumph.*

We may say that the Ascension is the *Moment* of being caught up with Jesus
in the train of His victory. In other words, for all who are in Christ, for those,
"... who are alive, who are left" (1 Thess. 4:17) they shall be caught up in that
procession with Jesus leading the way to Zion (Isa. 35:10).

What we see here is the absolute necessity of equating the meaning of
Christ's ascension with the entire picture of Christ's resurrection. The victory of
Christ's resurrection and ascension speak of the victory of God's restoration. It
all sounds very well, but is there any biblical evidence that people, once dead, are
now alive? What I am going to suggest may be a little perplexing. Aren't we all
somewhat restricted by the parameters of our four-dimensional ways of thinking?
What I am proposing, in very positive terms, is that, in the nature of God, *the
procession, which Jesus leads to Zion, consists of all the saints of old who
responded to their Moment of Light,* and of all those *who are yet to receive the Light
and Life of the world, follow in the train of that moment.* All, from every age,
follow in the train of Jesus, the first fruits from the dead. In this sense, past and
future are in God's *Eternal Present.* I'm convinced that there are several very
powerful images in the New Testament which bear out this thinking.

The writer to the Hebrews wrestles with the meaning of restoration for
those who have, historically, walked by faith. In reading this account, we may
glean some theological sense of the strange passage in Matthew that speaks of
bodies rising to enter the holy city (Matt. 27:52-53). Peter also attempts to
describe the restoration of those from the past (1 Pet. 3:19-20). The major
difference in Peter is not that Christ's redemption cannot reach back to the past,
but that, indeed, Christ's *invitation has been extended* to all those who have
longed after God. Peter sees Christ's finished work extending to all people, of all
time.

*But it must be made perfectly clear that the invitation for all is given
in the context of time; not in some after-life of immortality.*

There is no biblical precedent for a belief in purgatory, or for some further opportunity, a million years from now, when the invitation may be accepted. What does a *million years* mean apart from its necessary components of physical dimension? What we learn from New Testament thinking is that *judgment takes place, within the context of time, for all peoples from all ages (John 3:18)*. For example, the writer to Hebrews really does invite us to examine questions concerning the theological and scientific meaning of time.

He invites us to join with an awesome community of saints in worship. Clearly, we are told that, through the finished work of Christ, our *worship is in communion with saints of all ages!* In Chapter 11, the writer mentions some of the great saints who have trusted God in faith, not by sight. Then, he goes on to tell us that they worship the God they formerly trusted, *NOW!* Here, the writer makes use of the verb teleo in the aorist passive tense, and in the subjunctive mood). Clearly, in spite of their great faith, which to this point had brought them nothing of restoration, the passive is used to reinforce the fact that perfection *had been given to them* - but only in connection with the perfection and completion of Christ's work. The Beatitudes can now be understood in this light also. (Matt. 5:48) *The ancient saints are not waiting in a grave for a future moment of resurrection:*

> **"Therefore, since we *are* surrounded by so great a cloud of witnesses...looking to Jesus the pioneer and perfecter of our faith, who for the sake of the joy that was set before him endured the cross, disregarding its shame, and *has* taken his seat at the right hand of the throne of God" (Heb. 12:1-2-present tense italic is mine as is italicization of 'has' indicating the completed work of Christ).)**

Of course, the question must be asked, *"Where is it that the saints of old are worshipping God?"* In 1957 the American physicist, Hugh Everett, (for his Princeton doctoral thesis) may have attempted to answer the question with his original quantum physics thesis of *parallel universes*. The correct answer may well be even more complex than a theory of particle behavior. But it is clearly associated with God's almighty power to control the awesome mysteries of time. Obviously, if all time has been restored through the resurrection of Christ from the dead, then God has completed His work of restoration. He has furnished all believers with a *place* in the fullness of new creation. In the miracle, and mystery, of time's restoration, the newly recreated saints of old are in the new creation - *NOW! At the point of death, we are taken beyond the chronological passing away of the old creation to the Eternal Moment of new creation.*

Clearly, the writer is informing us that this *cloud of witnesses had died in faith*, not having received the *benefit* of God's promises. Yet, they had seen these promises *from a distance* (Heb. 11:13). In fact, they could not possibly receive the fullness of what God's promises meant *apart from the finished work* of Christ! *Jesus is the perfecter of faith* (Heb. 12:2).

He had to die and be raised in faith in order to invite people of all time into the procession and power of God's miraculous work of resurrection.

"Yet all these, though they were commended for their faith, did not receive what was promised, since God had provided *something better* so that they would not, *apart from us,* be made perfect" (italics mine-Heb. 11:39-40).

Why could they not receive this grace apart from the context in which the writer speaks?

When the scrolls of the Bible were written, the separation of chapters didn't exist. So the writer of Hebrews simply continues his thoughts and connects them with the conjunction, *therefore* to Heb. 12:1. What was *promised,* which they did not receive in their day, were the benefits of the kingdom that were gained by Jesus. Just because they had not lived in the chronological time frame of Jesus (or after, as is also the case with us today), did not mean that they were not able to receive the fruit of His finished work. There had to be a "first fruit" of the dead: One who is, therefore, the *pioneer and perfecter* of faith. The writer says that Jesus *completed His work* (which is evidenced by His being seated at the right hand of God) i.e., at His Ascension. All that the ancient saints had hoped for was now possible through Christ's *finished work.* The passage then speaks of the writer's generation by saying, *"apart from us"* those saints of old could not enter into glory, i.e. all those who had *witnessed, and entered into the benefits of Christ's completed work of redemption and restoration.*

Clearly, the book of Hebrews speaks of a multitude of saints worshipping God, not sometime in the future, but *NOW!* As the psalmist reminded us, dead people cannot praise the Lord (Ps. 6:5). The *cloud of witnesses consists of saints of old who presently exist in the power of Christ's perfect and finished work.* (Verbs associated with the worshiping saints are in the present tense.) They *are* living in the Eternal Now! It is not that they *will be raised* (future verbs are not used), but that they *are* raised with Christ who is the first fruits from the dead. They *are* witness to His victory - *NOW*! They join with the thief on the cross, and all who reign with Christ, in the consummated Paradise of the *Eternal NOW*!

JESUS TAUGHT IT

Jesus taught that the resurrection means we may enter into life that never ends - *when it is connected to His risen life!* It is abundant life with Him in the kingdom of God (John 10:10). Plainly, that is the reason why His disciples didn't speak much of an empty tomb, but of a risen Lord. For them, the resurrection signaled an *end of death*. Speaking to Martha, concerning the death of Lazarus, Jesus declared:

> *"I am the resurrection and the life. Those who believe in me, even though they die, will live, and everyone who lives and believes in me will never die" (John 11:25-26).*

It would seem to be a contradiction that people will never die even though, like Lazarus, they had died. But here, Jesus is clearly speaking of a situation where the *conscious presence of relationship with God* never ends for those living in resurrection experience.

Jesus, in declaring Himself to be the resurrection and the life also spoke of ancient saints in a similar manner as did the writer of Hebrews:

> *"Your ancestor Abraham rejoiced that he would see my day; he saw it and was glad" (John 8:56).*

Speaking to Sadducees in the context of resurrection, He quoted a passage referring to *all the patriarchs* in the same way:

> *"I am the God of Abraham, the God of Isaac, and the God of Jacob. He is God not of the dead, but the living…" (Mark 12:26-27).*

And, when some of the Sadducees spoke (as if they believed in the resurrection) Jesus replied:

> *"...I tell you, anyone who hears my word and believes him who sent me has eternal life, and does not come under judgment, but has passed from death to life...the hour is coming, and is now here, when the dead will hear the voice of the Son of God, and those who hear will live" (John 5:24-25; italics mine).*

Clearly, Jesus is speaking of the *now* in terms of His own finished work that was clearly upon Him. It will be in the context of His finished work that the dead are able to hear His voice of invitation to a life that is unending.

In the much-celebrated passage, where Jesus speaks of the destiny of those who believe (John 3:16), He goes on to say:

> *"Those who believe in him are not condemned; but those who do not believe are condemned already, because they have not believed in the name of the only Son of God" (John 3:18).*

These are people who did not believe, in the context of time! We must also remember that there were two real people talking with Jesus on the Mount of Transfiguration. *Moses and Elijah, miraculously connected to the finished work of Christ, were not ghosts talking to a live man!* They faded in comparison with the light of Jesus, but were nevertheless signs of life connected to Jesus.

PAUL BELIEVED IT

We should consider that Paul, raised as a Pharisee, sometimes communicated the meaning of resurrection, particularly to Pharisees, *in terms they understood,* and as he had learned at the feet of Gamaliel (Acts 22:3). In his defense to the Roman governor Felix and Ananias the high priest, Paul replied, "I have a hope in God - a hope that they themselves also accept - that there will be a resurrection of both the righteous and the unrighteous" (Acts 24:15).

Here, there is no contradiction in the case we are presenting. Paul's statement may well be consistent with the approach we have previously considered. This *Moment* is also the horrendously eternal occasion when some realize that they will be forever separated from the Light and Life of the world. However, it doesn't seem that Paul possesses a sense of ambiguity concerning those outside of Christ. Maybe we can clarify this problem in the light of resurrection implications.

It is true that the Pharisees believed in a literal raising of a dead body. This event applied to all people; the just and the unjust. We see this exclusively *chronological view* again in the book of Revelation Chapter 20. Before the judgment seat of God, some would be raised to go to heaven, while others would be raised for a destiny in hell. However, in both cases, resurrection is definitely connected to judgment. The apocalyptic writer speaks of this latter destiny as the *second death*. (Clearly, this is a strict chronological approach to judgment events Rev. 20:14.) Viewed in *the light of restoration through Christ's resurrection,* a chronological time sequence involving a *literal second death* would be difficult to accommodate. Maybe this is one reason why some scholars believe it was a different John who wrote the Book of Revelation. However, we must see this imagery in Revelation in the light of the entire broad picture of the *Easter Moment*.

It is understandable that the above view should evolve as a theological device to explain the meaning of judgment in simple chronological terms. But logically, second death, in successive terms, takes the wrong direction unless we view it within the much *bigger picture of the resurrection moment and of accountability to God for the stewardship of our lives* (Rom. 14:12). It is the need to speak in chronological terms which gives rise to a *literal* interpretation of second death. As we have seen already, this language problem may be resolved when we understand that resurrection and accountability take place for all, within the context of receding consciousness. Within the schema of this Big Story process, both accountability and resurrection of people, from all time, are fully embraced.

People, from all ages, are held to account for the stewardship of their lives.

In the light of other things that Paul says, we may well see that the resurrection perspectives he holds have moved far beyond those he learned in his Pharisaic training. (We remember that the tension between Sadducees and

Pharisees reveals internal disagreement; particularly around the question of resurrection) *Paul's major apologetic for his defense is his complete assurance in the reality and meaning of the resurrection. It is literally the miracle of being raised to new life with a new body.* This is a point that would make quick inroads with some of his Jewish listeners. A deeper explanation, in those volatile circumstances, may have raised unnecessary complications. In contexts where he addresses Christians in particular, we see that Paul is more ready to deal with the question of restored time (of the new order) precisely because of his belief in the end of death (Rom. 8:38-39).

We must remember that Paul had a real and life-changing encounter with the resurrected Christ, the Light of new creation. This was the Light that caused the self-sufficient Paul to be reduced to blindness. It would seem that *his view on time is really dominated by this encounter.* On the one hand, he appears to speak of suspended time (Acts 26:5-6; 1 Co. 15:52) or a falling asleep until there is a resurrection of the body. But here we must caution that the term, *"fall asleep"*(1 Co. 15:51) is used in the King James Version. However, in later translations (and in using earlier manuscripts, e.g., NRSV), a much different interpretation is expressed: *We will not all die.* (Here, it is highly possible that Paul is also thinking of the imminent return of Christ). However, some will most certainly die; and it is in this context that he speaks of *eternal destruction* (2 Thess.1:9). On the other hand, we must recognize that Paul cannot possibly imagine a time, *not any time,* when he may be separated from his beloved Jesus. Just look at a few examples:

> *"For I am convinced that neither death, nor life...nor things present, nor things to come,. nor anything else in all creation, will be able to separate us from the love of God in Christ Jesus our Lord" (Rom. 8:38-39).*

> *"For to me, living is Christ and dying is gain...my desire is to depart and be with Christ, for that is far better, but to remain in the flesh is more necessary for you" (Phil. 1:21, 23, 24).*

An almost identical thought is expressed by Paul when writing to the Corinthian Church (2 Co. 5:6-8).

HOW COULD NICODEMUS BE BORN AGAIN?

Nicodemus was obviously a very religious man; in fact, he also appears to be a member of the highest court in Judaism (John 3:1). Subsequently, he became a follower of Jesus (John 7:50, 19:39). He was a man who had received the visible signs of the Old Covenant and, in the pluralistic society of his day, was one of an entire community that believed exclusively in monotheism! This particular encounter with Jesus took place long before Christ's death and resurrection, so this is a very good question. His conversation with Jesus didn't begin with a question, but a word of affirmation:

> *"Rabbi, we know that you are a teacher come from God; for no one can do these signs that you do apart from the presence of God" (John 3:2).*

Jesus could be addressed (unofficially) as a rabbi because He had met two Hebrew requirements: He was more than thirty years old, and He had garnered twelve male disciples. This constituted the basis for a formal synagogue. Jesus took the opportunity to respond with a puzzling reply:

> *"Very truly, I tell you, no one can see the kingdom of God without being born from above…no one can enter the kingdom of God without being born of water and Spirit" (John 3:3, 5).*

No wonder Nicodemus was puzzled. He couldn't imagine putting his mother through all that again; not at his age! What we shall see is that this language is perfectly consistent with that used by John in his prologue. But first of all, what about that language?

The Greek word, legitimately translated *born again* (NIV) is the word, *anothen*. Its prefix *ano* means *above*. In its qualifying form the word literally means, *from above*. (NRSV) The consistency of this meaning is heralded when John says, "…who were born, not of blood, or the will of the flesh, or of the will of man, but of God" (John 1:13). In other words, *there is absolutely no natural way that a person is able to enter the kingdom of God.* Here is that word *miracle* again! As Jesus was miraculously raised to new life by God, so we have to be *"born again, from above."* In other words, *Nicodemus was to undergo a re-*

creation, and this work, as on the day of Christ's resurrection, would be accomplished by God alone. Basil the Great put it this way, "First, it is necessary that the old way of life be terminated, and this is impossible unless a man is born again, as the Lord has said. Regeneration, as its very name reveals, is a beginning of a second life."5

In some parts of the early Church in Africa, the baptismal liturgy included words such as, "I kill you." These words were spoken at the point when a person was submerged beneath the water (2 Co. 5:17; Rom. 6:4-5).

But now we are back to resurrection again! Jesus, Paul, and Peter connect resurrection with the born from above experience:

> **"By his great mercy he has given us a new birth into a living hope through the resurrection of Jesus Christ from the dead" (1 Pet. 1:3, 3:21).**

Does that mean that Nicodemus would be saved to new life by virtue of *his* decision for Christ? Most definitely not! *Nicodemus would be rescued by God's decision for him, and by God's actions upon him!* (1 John 4:19; Rev. 17:8) The decision of Nicodemus is simply *a response* to God's call, *Where are you?* Response is the human act. Maybe his responsive part can also be described by the word *conversion* to be a process. The Greek word *strepo* is used when Jesus tells a listening crowd that they must be converted (Matt. 18:3). It speaks of a decision to face, or to move in, another direction. In the responsive decision to turn in another direction, God acts *from above* by the work of the Holy Spirit. The term, born from above, is therefore related to time, and God's part in it.

But Jesus had not even died at this point!

Wouldn't it be wrong, and even lacking in integrity, if Jesus had impressed upon Nicodemus the need to be born from above when *it wasn't possible?* Christ had not died, and the resurrection had not taken place! Poor old Nicodemus could have turned up his toes the very next week! Nicodemus could not be born again prior to Christ's becoming the first fruits of the dead. *Now, we are back to the meaning of* the *resurrection Moment and the restoration of time.*

As we have discovered, the saints of old are a cloud of witnesses who worship the Lord, *now!* Similarly, as Christ embraced and restored all time into Himself, then *Nicodemus (along with Old Testament saints of Hebrews Chapter*

11) represents all those who will, and have, responded to Christ's gracious invitation. The power of the resurrection extends to all people from all time. Jesus does not suffer, die, and then is raised again, and again, and again! It has all been done, *once and for all*! All of those who respond, who are, or will, be *in Christ,* are restored to an eternal relationship with God through God's own miracle of resurrection. We remember that Jesus was raised *anothen,* as an act of God from above. The new birth is achieved in and through Jesus, who is the *first fruit* of new creation. It is because of the entire work of God in the Real Adam that humanity may live forever.

Time in eternity has been restored by the resurrection of Jesus!

Those saints of old in Hebrews Chapter 11 most certainly know it! (Heb. 12:1) *That's just what God intended in the first place; and the offer is extended to all people in all times and in all places!*

WITH WHAT KIND OF BODY *DO* THEY COME?

But each in his own order: Christ the first fruits, then at his coming those who belong to Christ." "But someone will ask, 'How are the dead raised? With what kind of body do they come?'" (1 Co. 15:23, 35)

The plural verb *erchontai* is *present tense* and may literally be translated, "With what kind of body are they coming?" If we believe that Paul's dominant theology is one negating any separation from Christ, then we must conclude that his use of the term, *spiritual body,* is a description of the body that is equipped for life in the new creation. We shall soon consider something of the mystery of this *spiritual body* when we make particular note of certain post-resurrection appearances of Jesus.

That brings us to another question: As a pastor, I am sometimes asked about burial procedures. Some people are concerned that their loved one will not be resurrected if their bodies are cremated. Others wonder how God can piece together all the ashes of a loved one that have been scattered over the ocean. Is this really a problem? Paul said that he wanted to show his Corinthian Christians a mystery. The fact is, we really are faced with a mystery here, and the mystery both reveals and conceals our answers in thinking of the resurrected body of Jesus.

Vladimir Lossky may offer some useful insight by connecting the meaning of resurrection with its completion in Christ's ascension. "In his resurrection there was, to be sure, the transition from a physical body to a spiritual body, but in the ascension there was not a further transition into a wholly spiritual entity."6 "At His ascension, first of all He unites the earth to the heavenly spheres, that is to the sensible heaven; then He penetrates into the empyrean, passes through the angelic hierarchies and unites the spiritual heaven, the world of mind with the sensible world. Finally, like a new cosmic Adam He presents to the Father the totality of the universe restored to unity in Him, by uniting the created to the uncreated."7 Lossky may not have delineated the nature of this spiritual body, but he clearly identifies it as one, like that of the Adam in innocence, was intended to unite earth to heaven. Jesus, our Real Adam, did it; and continues to do so!

Nevertheless, we really are confronted with an awesome sense of mystery. How do we glean a seamless answer from the post-resurrection appearances of Christ? The book of Revelation speaks of Jesus reigning with His saints in a real place; *it is the earth of the new order*! (Rev. 5:10, 11:15) But how *earthly* is this place, and in what way is it connected to the old?

MYSTERY IN THE RESURRECTED BODY OF JESUS

Quite probably, *if we appreciate something of the mysterious body of Christ, we may know more about the body intended for a new humanity in the new creation.* Indeed, we may also know more of the nature of the new creation itself. There is no doubt that the resurrection appearances elicit many questions. Interestingly, in the *post-resurrection appearances*, particularly recorded in John, Jesus seems to speak exclusively in terms of His humanity, not His incarnate divinity. For example, in John 20:17 the disciples are now *brothers* and God is equally their God and Father as well as His. Nevertheless, it really takes us into the realms of mystery when we attempt to define the *spiritual* nature of Christ's resurrected humanity. As a matter of fact, when we look at the written accounts, there appear to be contradictions in the way Christ's appearances are described. But the paradoxical accounts are deliberately presented so that we are forced to realize *there is something mysterious about the body that is restored to new creation.* Apart from this body of Jesus, we've never seen anything like it before except, possibly, in the Adam of Eden:

> *In this body, we may be receiving a glimpse of what was once natural and real for the original Adam.*

That is why we are left with just a partial understanding. We may appreciate both the mystery and the paradox in the following post-resurrection appearances:

She knew Him, but she didn't recognize Him. Mary Magdalene thought that Jesus was a gardener - until He called her by name! (John 20:15-17)

There were grave clothes, but no body (John 20:6-7). The one, commonly understood *sign of death* had disappeared!

Don't touch me! (John 20:17) *Touch me!* (Luke 24:39) Surely, this paradox presents us with a mystery of the body we have yet to experience! Thomas recognized Him by the marks of crucifixion. We recognize Him by the marks of a resurrected body.

The doors were locked, but He got in anyway (John 20:19). Will this possibility exist for a new humanity not restricted to four-dimensional activity? Does this seemingly unnatural encounter remind us of natural abilities once possessed by Adam?

He knew where to find fish (John 21:5-6). What does it really mean to have such an intimate knowledge of all creation? This Jesus is really well connected with nature.

They walked for two hours with Him, and still didn't recognize Him, until... (Luke 24:30-31) The mystery of the Word becomes intimate at a banqueting table!

After a whole week, Thomas could still feel the nail prints in Christ's hands (John 20:27). The marks in this bruised and battered body of Jesus, which Thomas recognized, revealed Him to be the One, distinctively displaying the connection with the body of new creation!

Does a ghost have flesh and bones like I have? (Luke 24:39) This *spiritual body* is knowable to the physical senses!

Do ghosts eat fish? (Luke 24:42-43; Acts 10:39-41) We shall eat familiar food (such as God provided in the original, physical creation) in a new creation yet to be experienced!

The disciples knew Him, but they didn't recognize Him (John 21:12). There is something intriguingly exciting about all of our new creation relationships: Puzzlingly, and excitingly, new but somehow and mysteriously connected to the old! "These are my words that I spoke to you while I was still with you" (Luke 24:44). Jesus had already given His disciples a clue that something unusual was about to happen. At the Last Supper, Luke records these words,

> **"Then he took a cup, and after giving thanks he said, 'Take this and divide it among yourselves; for I tell you that from now on I will not drink of the fruit of the vine until the kingdom of God comes" (Luke 22:17-18).**

Do spirits drink wine in the new creation?

This Jesus was not a spirit re-incarnated in another form. The resurrected Jesus was, in whole, *a man of memory!* He brought into the new order common memories of life in the old order. The disciples who followed Him were able to recall, together, incidents to which Jesus related. (Luke 24:44) This emerging principle will be very important to us when we consider the very substantial relationship between the creation of the old order with that of the new order! *Christ's disciples had a common memory of a shared story.*

In all the appearances of Jesus, we realize that the disciples were witness to the mystery of the *spiritual body of new creation.* But somehow, this body had recognizable elements of the physical, and also with personality characteristics they had known in their beloved Jesus. This body was very puzzling! It didn't seem to be subject to physical laws; at least, not as they knew them! (Interestingly, the language of John, concerning Christ's post-resurrection experiences, is very clearly of His humanity, not His divinity.   John 20:17)

For Hugh Ross the idea that a body can walk through a door isn't a scientific improbability at all; at least, not anymore! The fact is many skeptics don't accept this account of His appearing. It's not because of an inability to think scientifically, but an inability to think with a *contemporary* knowledge of science. Our knowledge of scientific laws has dramatically changed. Here, it is worth repeating an earlier quotation from Hugh Ross when speaking of the multidimensional possibilities of the risen Christ. "Though it is impossible for three-dimensional physical objects to pass through the three-dimensional physical barriers without one or the other being damaged, Jesus would have no problem doing this in His extra dimensions. Six spatial dimensions would be adequate."8 Did Adam have this ability? Will we?

> *Was this, truly, the Real Adam with an inbreathed ability to subdue the earth?*

Paul speaks of the body fitted for new creation in this manner, saying:

"It is sown a physical body, it is raised a spiritual body" (1 Co. 15:44).

He is simply trying to say that there is a mysterious *connection* between the person, who is raised with Christ, and with the body that is fitted for new creation. *When connected to the risen Christ, there is no annihilation of the individual personality and, in this spiritual body, the person will be recognizable to others possessing bodies fitted for new creation.* These awesome teaching signs continued until the time of Christ's ascension (Acts 1:3). Whatever the new creation is like, *this spiritual body will work in it very well!*

THE VICTORY OF GOD'S PURPOSES

The cry of the Lover to the Beloved (i.e., to those who are in Christ) is no longer, *"Where are you?" for they have been found by Him!* The prodigal Israel has been invited to return to the forefront of their inheritance. But this intimacy of restored relationships has not come cheaply to anyone who now lives in it. We all have a little idea of what it cost God; we all know that this restoration came by His initiative, not ours. "We love because He first loved us" (1 John 4:19). *We chose Him because He first decided for us.*

The fact is: *We cannot experience the life of Easter Sunday without a death of Good Friday.* "To rise again we must die. Die to our hampering selfishness, die to our fears, die to everything that makes the world so narrow, so cold, so poor, so cruel. Die so that our souls may live, may rejoice, may discover the spring of life.

If we do this then the resurrection of Christ will have come down to us also. But without the death on the cross there is no resurrection, the resurrection which is joy, the joy of life recovered, the joy of life that no one can take away from us anymore."9 The way of Christ's suffering will always be *before* those who love Him, but the hope of eternal life will always be *in* them (Rom. 6:4-5).

That which is being shouted from the rooftops is at the very heart and soul of the Gospel. It is an affirmation that resurrection reality is the beacon sign:

God has miraculously restored all creation's essential relationships.

This joyous affirmation is heralded by saints of all ages because of the intimate power of Christ's resurrection! *And so, the community of the resurrection is called to be an authentic sign of kingdom principles which God instituted in Eden.* But how may this be humanly possible?

Chapter 11. The Mystery of Time Restored

1. Rogers, Cleon L, *The Topical Josephus,* p65. Zondervan Publishing House, Grand Rapids. Michigan 1992.

2. Wright, N.T. *Who Was Jesus?* p.74

3. Robinson, J.A.T. *In The End God,* pp.91-92.

4. Hick *John (ed) The Myth Of God Incarnate,* Michael Goulder, Chapter 3, pp.59-60. S.C.M. Press, London, 1977

5. St. Basil The Great, *On The Holy Spirit,* p.58. St.Vladimir's Seminary Press. N.Y. 1980

6. Lossky, Vladimir. *The Mystical Theology of The Eastern Church,* p.137. St. Vladimir's Seminary Press, New York 10707, 1976.

7. Lossky, Vladimir. *Orthodox Theology,* p.62

8. Ross, Hugh, *The Creator and the Cosmos,* p.111,

9. Bloom, Anthony. *Meditations On a Theme* p.119. Mowbrays Ltd. Printed at Alder Press, Oxford, Second Impression 1972.

Chapter 12

PENTECOST: AN AWESOME MOMENT OF LIGHT

AS IT WAS IN THE BEGINNING?

It really was an awesome *Moment of Light!* We cannot think of the full meaning of restoration unless we include Pentecost into our moments of light. As in the beginning, the power to accomplish the apostolic mandate, given to God's community in Eden, was restored. What we are to observe here is that the anointed community of God was playing out the story of Eden's restoration while inviting the world to participate in the joyous dance. Here, the *Real Adam, the King of creation, is to send His New Israel, His Royal Priesthood, on a universal mission.* All the steps of the dance were in place and the pace had been quickened. They were to be active witnesses and sign-bearers of what they had seen and heard of the good news (Acts 1:8-11). They waited in Jerusalem, not fully understanding why! And then the *fire came down!* It must have reminded them of Moses by the fire of the burning bush.

Inexhaustible flames of Shekina glory seemed to touch their heads *without consuming them!* (Ex. 3:2; Acts 2:1-4) There were about 120 gathered together, and all of them were *filled with the Holy Spirit.* As they were to learn, they would never be the same again! The light of God's fire was an ancient sign that the awesome power of God's Presence would illuminate them in all times of darkness (Ex. 13:21).

Irenaeus, one of the Early Church Fathers, describes the scene in this way, "This Spirit....also, as St. Luke says, descended on the day of Pentecost upon the disciples after the Lord's ascension having power to admit all nations to the entrance of life and to the opening of the new covenant from whence also, with one accord in all languages, they uttered praise to God, the Spirit bringing distant tribes to unity, and offering to the Father the first-fruits of all nations."1

Luke, in his letter of Acts, records that signs and wonders of the kingdom (as Jesus had promised, John 14:12) were first manifested through the Twelve Apostles, the foundational community of the New Israel (Rev. 21:14). *Actually, for Paul, signs and wonders were considered to be a required proof of a person's apostolic credentials!* (2 Co. 12:12) After all, the New Community of Israel was intended to be a sign of what was once possible in Eden. Peter spoke with a new boldness about the power of Christ's resurrection (Acts 2:22-24). He and John pronounced healing in the name of Jesus, and a man, crippled from birth, walked for the first time (Acts 3:8).

"...many signs and wonders were done through the apostles" (Acts 5:12).

Clearly, the inescapable bond between Word and Wonders was not confined to the questionable addition to Mark's Gospel (Mark 16:20).

By God's grace, *the entire community* had entered into a charismatic dimension signifying the recovery of creation's essentials. In character, these realities also encompassed the masculine, feminine, the intuitive, the intellectual and the sensual dimensions, once experienced by the Adam community. With equal integrity, *the intuitive moved naturally alongside the rational.* They were experiencing signs of what it means to be truly human.

Great numbers of men and women were *added to the Lord* (Acts 5:12, 14). Peter had never preached like this before! Clearly, the anointing touch of the Spirit created in this community the deep longing to bring the lost into the apostolic heart of God. In Acts, *Luke does not acknowledge a hierarchy of apostolic leadership.* He tends to emphasize equally that Peter *and* Paul (along with others) were enabled by the Holy Spirit to perform extraordinary signs and wonders. Works of the Spirit included the raising of the dead, as well as freeing people from demonic bondage, and, indeed, the power and authority given to the anointed. (Luke 4:18-19) Luke also records that both Peter and Paul were, themselves, miraculously freed from their own bondage of imprisonment. The ministry of the Anointed Servant (Isaiah Chapter 61; Luke Chapter 4) was surely at work in the community of a New Israel.

WAS THE ANOINTING FOR ORDINARY PEOPLE?

I have often wondered why Ananias (who, very fearfully, laid hands upon Paul) is hardly ever acknowledged in historic churches. (We note that there is a Church of St. Ananias in Damascus.) In being obedient to God, the Holy Spirit was imparted to Paul who also regained his sight. More importantly, Ananias received a word of knowledge that Paul was to be the Apostle to the Gentiles (Acts 9:15-19). Today, in most of the orthodox world, Ananias is thought of as a "layman." Most certainly, neither Peter nor Paul fit into the subsequent hierarchical thinking of the Post-Apostolic Church. Clearly,

The Apostles were not the only believers able to do mighty works through the Spirit. However, the Twelve, representing the continuation of Israel, were the *focus of relational authority and unity* for a new and empowered community of Israel. The faith of the community would be Apostolic! (Jude 3) But the *work* of the Great Commission wasn't given to the Twelve exclusively! The question is: what place did The Twelve hold in the implementation of the commission? In John's Gospel, on the First Day, when the resurrected Jesus appeared to His apostles (probably privately) and having breathed upon them, they received *apostolic authority*. We're back to creation again! (Gen. 2:7; John 20:22) On the mountain of Ascension, they, as representatives of New Israel's tribes, were receiving their commission. It was once given to Adam (Gen. 1:28), and now repeated in the continued community of Abraham (Gen. 12:3, Gal.3:29).

> *"All authority in heaven and earth has been given to me. Go therefore and make disciples of all nations, baptizing them in the name of the Father and of the Son and of the Holy Spirit, and teaching them to obey everything that I have commanded you" (Matt. 28:19-20).*

> *"Go into all the world and proclaim the good news to the whole creation" (Mark 16:15).*

To those who have problems with the authenticity of those texts, we have to admit that all the synoptic writers are in agreement with Christ's purpose:

"...repentance and forgiveness of sins is to be proclaimed in his name to all nations, beginning from Jerusalem. You are witnesses of these things" (Luke 24:47-48).

"...you will be my witnesses in Jerusalem, in all Judea and Samaria, and to the ends of the earth" (Acts 1:8).

And, in the high priestly prayer of Jesus, John records:

"I ask not only on their behalf, but also on behalf of those who will believe in me through their word...so that the world may believe that you have sent me" (John 17:20-21).

God's purposes were to be *heralded and signed by them, as a community, for the sake of the world.* Jerusalem, the Old Testament symbol for Eden, is to provide the starting point of this universal mission. A new community is to be born in Jerusalem; formed and enabled by the Holy Spirit. However, *we must be clear in stating that the authority for this commission was given to the entire community of the Twelve.*

According to John's Gospel, there were just *ten disciples* present who received the inbreathing of *authority.* The text, *on them,* does not make it clear whether the breathing of Jesus was upon them individually, or collectively. (Neither Thomas nor Judas were in the room on that occasion.) However, both Thomas and Mathias were included in the Twelve as having been given apostolic authority. There is no biblical evidence to show that, in post-resurrection appearances, Thomas had been inbreathed individually by Jesus. And, the Ascension had taken place before Mathias was included into the Twelve - Acts 1:20-26. Nevertheless, on the awesome day of Pentecost, the *power* to accomplish the work of the kingdom was given to all 120 assembled believers. Consistent with this view, *the Early Church most certainly honored the relational authority of the Twelve.* Apart from the much-debated (and oft-questioned) passage in Matthew 16:16-18, (e.g., see 1 Co. 10:1-3 and Rev. 1:18 for an explanation of *the rock*) there is *no biblical evidence* to suggest that Jesus ever invested the authority for such leadership in one person, alone.

It looks like the power for an apostolic ministry resided in the entire community, and was historically focused in the commissioned authority of the Twelve. Individual authority, apart from the power and purpose of the entire community, would be meaningless. (Apart from the fact that it also contradicted the nature of the Trinity!)

Quite quickly, in the Book of Acts, we note that Stephen (the first martyr) *did great wonders and signs among the people* (Acts 6:8). Equally, Philip cast out unclean spirits, healed the sick, and was miraculously transported to Azotus (Acts 8:6-8, 39-40). Was this strange occurrence of unrestricted movement yet another *sign* of what was once possible in Eden? Philip made it a family affair. He had four daughters who had an affirmed prophetic ministry (Acts 21:9). In this vein, Peter's quotation of Joel also includes women in the *priesthood of proclamation* (Acts 2:17-18). *Truly, greater things were being done,* not so much in quality, but in the quantity of a new community voluntarily dispersed on its apostolic mission (John 14:12).

It is as if we are hearing God say: *I breathed into you once (the first Adam community), then I breathed into you once again (the Real Adam), and now I am also breathing into you (the community of the Real Adam).* Here, we see a major difference between the Old and New Covenants. In the Old, we see *individuals* (such as Moses, Joshua, Elijah and Elisha), obviously scattered over the pages of Israel's history, but nevertheless, demonstrating signs and wonders of the kingdom. However, in the New Covenant, in this awesome *Moment of Light,* we see *an entire Real Adam community baptized into kingdom power. A Real Adam community was re-born to reflect God's abilities into His creation*

The newly-empowered community of Jesus was enabled to continue, for all time, in demonstrating signs of kingdom *restoration.* No wonder Peter and John (but also Paul) *made certain that well-meaning and repentant converts had received more than an outward sign of the intent to live a repentant life* (e.g., the baptism of John - Acts 19:3). They were all called to be disciples and to live it out in the anointed power of the Spirit. At times, there were apostles who encountered people baptized with water, but not in the Holy Spirit (John 3:5, Acts 19:2). Through the laying on of hands, and effective discipleship, these apostles ensured that:

Word-centered converts also became Spirit-filled disciples! (Acts 8:14-16; 19:1-6.) However, this was not the only way the Spirit came upon believers (Acts 10:44-47). The time had come for an anointed community to demonstrate, once more, what God had intended for His creation. And so:

> *The purpose of this community would be the same as it was in the very beginning: To bring the world into harmonious relationships with God, and to live a life in communal signature of God's kingdom.*

BAPTISM IN THE SPIRIT

In order to provide a framework for questions surrounding Spirit baptism, it is important that a thread be woven into the context of Pentecost.

> ***First, we realize that absolutely nothing of gospel importance occurred unless it was first of all embraced in the Jewish story; for "salvation is of the Jews." (John 4:22; Rom. 1:16).***

> ***"Surely the Lord does nothing without revealing his secret to his servants the prophets" (Amos 3:6).***

Although Peter's ministry was primarily to the Jews, while that of Paul was to the Gentiles (Gal. 2:7), Peter is clearly the first to declare the invitation to the Gentiles. Formerly, they had *not* been included in the lineage of the *sons of God* (Gen. 6:1-2; Isa. 42:6; Acts 10:44-48). And so was revived the universal commission which God intended at the beginning! It was from Jerusalem (the symbolic Eden) that the community's apostolic ministry began. When he was at his best, King Solomon saw the holy city, with its temple, in the same way (1 Kings 8:43).We should not be surprised to read that *Jesus gave a universal commission, which was to begin from Jerusalem.* (Acts 1:8).

> *Second, through Peter, it was to a celebrating Jewish community that the promise of the event was first explained (Acts 2: 1-4, 14).*

Not co-incidentally, Pentecost was actually a Jewish celebration of the first wheat harvest. It was called, The Feast of Weeks! This was a time when, *as in Eden*, the Jewish people acted out their priesthood by offering to God *the fruits of creation*. This feast was not one of blood sacrifice. In Christian terms, it was further transformed to be the offering of a community made innocent. Little did Moses know that, by instituting a celebration of the Feast of Weeks he was presenting a sign of a future priesthood offering the fruit of a restored creation of innocence.

Third, the gospel invitation (proclaimed by Jewish Apostles at Pentecost) received its first and positive response from Jewish people (Acts 2:41, 47).

Nevertheless, as a nation, the Jews did not accept Jesus as their Messiah. But it was from the Jews that God would offer His blessing upon people of all nations (Gen. 12:3, 17:4-5). When speaking to his Jewish listeners on that astounding day of Pentecost, Peter reminded his ethnic kin that God's apostolic purpose was their own inheritance and purpose (as it was prophesied in Joel 2:28-32). *From the stock of David, Jesus was, in person, their long-expected Lord and Messiah* (Acts 2:36).

Fourth, a new community of Eden's line was empowered by the Spirit for the purpose of proclaiming and signing kingdom life to the ends o the earth (Acts 1:8). It was a baptism of fire for proclamation! Fifth, the first thing that the Holy Spirit did was to send the anointed believers out into the street—to market-place ministry! (Acts 2:5-6)

They were primarily an apostolic community, sent out! In other words, the mandate that had been given to Jesus (Luke 4:18-19) was to be exercised *primarily in marketplace proclamation, and in signal demonstration of life in the Spirit.* Signs of the year of Jubilee had arrived (Isa. 61:1-2; Luke 4:18-19).

Sixth, upon receiving the gift of the Holy Spirit, the immediate reaction of the followers of Jesus was to praise God (Acts 2:11).We are back to a community of worship, prior to Babel. Particularly after the destruction of Jerusalem (70 A.D.),

> **Eden is now the New Jerusalem which is above and which is free! (Gal. 4:30)**

The Holy Spirit touched the 120 who were gathered together; they spoke their praises in about sixteen known languages. Each language was clearly recognized by the Mediterranean pilgrims to Jerusalem. The implication is very clear:

> *Pentecost is a signal demonstration of universal unity intended to reverse the catastrophe of Babel.*

For those who understood each language, the implication was apparent:

> **"...in our own languages we hear them speaking about God's deeds of power" (Acts 2:8-12)..**

> *Seventh, we see that all of the believers now spoke in personal and intimate terms of their risen Lord. Through signs and wonders of the Spirit, they were given the power to witness in the medium of proclamation and service (Acts 2:24-26). They weren't thanking God for the memory of a dead rabbi! Jesus was alive, and they knew it! Jesus was right; the Spirit's work is to glorify Him (John 16:13).*

Essential Relationships restored:

The first principle of *Essential Relationships* (i.e., relationship with God) was now possible because the Real Adam had risen. Through His finished work at Calvary, He had secured humanity's reconciliation with God (2 Co. 5:17-19).

The second principle, (i.e., relationships in community) had become possible because the living Lord, through the Spirit, had become the focus and source of their communal relationship (John 14:18). They had entered into the family of the sons and daughters of God! (1 John 1:7) "...this is the moment of the new creation, when a new humanity comes into being through the work of the second Adam."2

The third principle (i.e., relationship with creation) was that He resided in their hearts in a power originally given to the community of Eden. The community was charged with authority, and also the power, to bring all creation into harmonious relationship with God. They were now supernaturally *commissioned to be a royal priesthood, not a priesthood of blood sacrifice, but a priesthood of creation's innocence.* As a communal priesthood, they were called to offer a groaning and rebellious creation into loving worship with their Source (Rom. 8:21).

The fourth principle (i.e., relationship with the self) was possible since they were now filled with the harmonious Light of His presence. If the inner harmony of individual salvation had not been secured, then harmony with the community would also be in peril. Inner harmony had been gifted to them as a result of their concord with God, with others, and with creation. *They were poised to live in signature of kingdom relationships intended for the entire world!*

I suggest, as strongly as is possible, that in order for us to understand the meaning of baptism in the Spirit, we think of it in the context that is described in the *above seven points.* Today's evangelical thinker may describe the term in a way in which David Edwards summarizes John Stott's thinking. Stott is concerned about charismatic-minded people who speak of something extra in baptismal initiation. He grants that growth in Christ is important, (in other words, sanctification) but not a so-called *baptism of the Spirit* subsequent to conversion. To Edwards, Stott seems eager simply to "associate the gift of the Spirit with conversion to Christ." 3 Clearly, on the day of Pentecost, Peter expected the respondents to grow in the fullness of life in the Spirit.

The charismatic-minded undoubtedly acknowledges the Spirit's activity in the conversion process. However, he or she may try to avoid dispute by speaking of a further experience as a *process*; a process of the release of the Spirit's potential. After all, a baptized six week old baby, though now in the covenant, is hardly in any position to embark on a ministry of proclamation! In Orthodox terminology, we may use the term as a description of further releasing of what was promised at baptism. That release is often associated with speaking in tongues or delivering prophetic utterances (Acts 19:6). Some consider it to be the entering into a sanctification of a *second blessing,* which is often associated with the earlier ministry of John Wesley.4 Some Pentecostal churches state that certain signs are *the evidence* of a baptism with the Holy Spirit. For example, at a Pentecostal rally in the Albert Hall, London, I once heard a lady testify that she now knew God loved her because she had just been gifted with speaking in tongues! Hopefully, amid a thunderous applause, some of the leaders at that conference were a little embarrassed.

What we may observe here is that, in general, quite regardless of when conversion takes place, the charismatic-minded may emphasize *power*, while evangelicals tend toward conversion as the beginning of sanctification. However, the *character and the power* of the Real Adam are *both* necessary elements in the entire meaning of Spirit-baptism. Both the *character*, i.e., the nature of God, seen especially in Jesus (Gal. 5:22-23), and the *power* of God (Luke 24:49) are essential marks of the inbreathing of the Spirit. Conversion is not simply a matter of inner spirituality, but the beginning of an outward focused heart. *Nevertheless, leaning on one particular side of that term is a gross understatement of all that it means: At least, not when we associate it with God's original intent for creation.* We must cease our choosing between individual Gospel elements. We are called to be Catholic, Charismatic, and Evangelical!

We have seen that a true experience of Easter means we have a personal encounter with the risen Christ. Jesus told His disciples, "I will be in you" (John 14:18-20), and they clearly knew the intimacy and power of His presence. What this means is, not only the *power,* but the *character* of Jesus grows in those who receive Him. The power of the Spirit and the graces of the Spirit are growing in us as the Spirit is forming Christ in us (Gal. 4:19). Therefore, it really isn't necessary to choose what scriptures should be most important to us. "These texts and others like them lead us to one conclusion: any model of the fullness of the Spirit which attempts to make empowering for service relatively separate from growth in holiness inevitably collides with the truth represented in the very title *Holy Spirit.*"5

A third dimension may be found in historic Orthodoxy, particularly in various arms of the Eastern Church. Although he makes no direct allusion to signs and wonders, or an inward empowering for mission, St. Cyril of Jerusalem speaks of baptism this way: "Great indeed is the baptism which is offered you. It is a ransom to captives; the remission of offences; the death of sin; the regeneration of the soul; the garment of light; the holy seal indissoluble; the chariot to heaven; the luxury of paradise; a procuring of the kingdom; the gift of adoption."6

We must see that the fullness of life in the Spirit has to be *appropriated*. The promise of the Paraclete needs no further additions. When introducing a work of the esteemed tenth century St. Symeon, George Maloney tells us that Symeon is solidly rooted in the theology of the Fathers, "…but he accentuates with great originality the need of a stage in the Christian life beyond the mere Baptism of water, which Symeon calls the Baptism in the Holy Spirit."7 The stage, of which Maloney speaks, is not of a further theological enlightenment, but the *growing appropriation* of all that is promised in the *born again,* Spirit-filled life which is promised in baptism.

No wonder, "The important question that Symeon poses to his readers is not whether the Holy Spirit lives within them, but whether they are consciously aware of this presence within them through a continued penitential conversion."8 Straddling the tension between apophatic and kataphatic experience, it would seem that Symeon would not be impressed by a person simply waving a baptismal certificate. What would that mean if the person knew little of a *substantive difference in his or her life?* What would that mean if the person could not testify to an intense, mystical intimacy with Christ enabled by a heart desire to live in obedience to Him?

What we observe here is that, whether or not a person is baptized as a professing adult or a babe in arms, to be baptized into Christ means that we are called to *grow,* to *sign,* and, through the community of Christ, to embrace the dance as *heirs of the complete story of restoration originally embraced in the dance of Eden.*

THE WORD-SPIRIT DYNAMIC

Clearly, a prophet, when hired and dependent upon the ecclesiastical institution, becomes an oxymoron. He or she cannot be restrained to speaking within restricted parameters of institutional life. *This is particularly apparent once the ecclesiastical institution has become negligent in its primary apostolic purposes.* Often the character of the crowd, or the fickle moods of the culture, take on such importance that the institution will not tolerate the warnings of the prophetic voice (Jer. 23:9-11, 18, 22).

This has profound implications for an empowered community of believers. An old gospel hymn echoes the naïve sentiment, "This world is not my home - I'm just a passin' through." Clearly, in our present context, *this world is our home; it's our Canaan!* In love, we are called to win it for God. The challenging authority of the Word, demonstrated by the enormous life-changing power of the Spirit, is the normal way through which the Church exercises its life.

We remember that in the written Word of God (particularly as presented by Jesus) we see the nature of God best revealed. "Whoever has seen me has seen the Father" (John 14:9). *It is in accordance with God's revealed nature and command (John 14:15) that contemporary issues are addressed.* On the other hand, the scriptures should be a major corrective for flakey expressions of charismatic life. Here, the written Word stands as a beacon illuminating the real nature and character of Eden, i.e., God's kingdom (Ps. 119:105). However, it is vitally important to move beyond current *revisionist theories* of scripture in order that *the power in the Big Story* is not lost. If we have to move beyond such theories then allow me, very quickly, to identify them:

The Bible simply records God's revelation in the context of a particular culture at a specific time. *Therefore, we may ignore or reinterpret it in the light of current cultural principles.* In reality, as we have previously suggested, the fundamentals of present revisionists have *not kept pace* with the implications of contemporary scientific and philosophical progress. Consequently, this position has produced *chaplains to the culture rather than prophetic voices within it.*

It's a bigger story now! But, in reality, for them, it is a much smaller story. The awesome breadth of the Big Story is *reduced to the much diminished experience of the individual commentator; or indeed, any individual in his own time!* The exclusivity of Jesus is denied. *There are many ways to God,* they say. So the power of individual opinion overrides any claim of absolutes.

They tend to view the Bible through the lens of their own cultural perceptions, rather than by evaluating cultural conditions through the filters of biblical revelation. Theology, like Social Darwinism, therefore, evolves through the culture, and so their God also *changes* with the varieties of evolving culture.

Revisionists are disinterested in debating on the basis of biblical authority. And so biblical substance, through the reinterpretation of biblical symbols, has exited the arena of much Christian debate. Here, and very often, substance gives way to sentimentality.

We should note again, as strongly as is possible, that Jesus presented a Gospel that was *Catholic* (one body, one faith), *Charismatic* (focused on the Spirit's character and power), and *Evangelical* (an outward focus in restoring others to relationships in Christ). Unfortunately, for a variety of reasons, and because of particular denominational emphases, church communities and individuals have tended to emphasize one over another. We can't do that. Jesus didn't, nor should His community.

In the Word-Spirit dynamic we must caution against those who display an imbalanced perspective regarding the Bible. Clearly, there are those who hold tenaciously to the authority of Word while playing down the extraordinary power of the Spirit. *But signs and wonders of the Spirit give contemporary and practical credibility to God's spoken revelation* (Heb. 2:2-4; Acts 14:3). *Jesus emphasized both Word and Spirit with equal force!*

Hopefully, you will forgive me for injecting into this section a personal, and admittedly, subjective contribution. Ever since my conversion to Christ, at the age of eighteen, I found myself mixing with evangelical people. They were very helpful in embracing and encouraging me. My language, style, and intellectual curiosity became one with theirs. By the time I entered theological college, the Lord had graciously used me to bring literally hundreds of people to Christ. A singular-focused message of conversion almost consumed my entire ministry. However, after about eight years of ordination in the Anglican communion, there came a point when I realized that *there just had to be more than the persuasion of a well-constructed apologetic!*

I was tired of delving into the meaning of justification by faith to the nth degree. I was disturbed in some groups where some people would effuse their own intellect while hiding themselves behind their Bibles. As persons in need, they rarely raised their heads! I was sometimes disturbed to hear people talk of the dynamic things that Jesus *once did,* but not seeing those things happening in my own ministry. In some situations I was tired of struggling with the propositional approach to sanctification while missing out on the joy and power of New Testament apostolicity. I was a boring and bored Christian! *There just had to be more!*

I knew one or two people who spoke of charismatic experience but I never took them seriously. Arrogantly, I felt I had a theological and intellectual depth that didn't need that sort of thing. It was in the midst of this arrogance and conceit that *God surprised me.* He baptized me in the Spirit! It was wonderful, and I couldn't explain it! But I knew there was something different in me! The next thing I knew was that God used me in the miraculous healing of Bill.

I had visited him many times in the hospital. However, after years of severe heart problems, the hospital doctor had called for his family in order to warn them of his impending death. "I don't expect him to last through the night." Fully respecting that view, and after praying with Bill in the intensive care unit, something happened to him. In four days he was discharged, and three months later, he was dancing. That was just the beginning of a ministry laced with God's surprises. There are many times when I don't appear to see answers to prayer. Indeed, I have known patients die ten minutes after I prayed for them! (Not many families call for me in such a crisis!)However, I do know that, when I stop praying in faith, I rarely find myself to be surprised by God. And that's how I define the meaning of being charismatic:

Someone who is given the ability to be surprised by God!

I remember when, on one occasion, I was ministering in a CSI church in Madras, South India. At the end of the service, the pastor was first in line for prayer (a line which extended right into the street!) He simply asked for prayers for his back problem. About three months later he wrote to me in Calgary. He was obviously very excited in telling me of the happenings subsequent to my departure. I didn't know it, but this pastor had suffered from spinal problems for many years and was due for surgery in two days. First of all, he told me that his pain had immediately disappeared; then after further X-rays, doctors discovered there was now nothing wrong with his spine. He went on to speak of many other miracles that had occurred that day. Quite possibly, in his excitement, there may have been a little exaggeration, but I do know that I have prayed about back problems many times in Western situations with results that are rarely so dramatic. I use these stories, simply to illustrate the following:

"For the kingdom of God depends not on talk but on power" (1 Co. 4:20).

"My speech and my proclamation were not with plausible words of wisdom, but with a demonstration of the Spirit and of power,

so that your faith might rest not on human wisdom but on the power of God" (1 Co. 2:4).

By God's grace I have been extraordinarily privileged to see my ministry transformed by the expectation that God is able to do whatever He wants in me; if I don't get in His way! Along with many others in these days of joy in persecution, I am amazed to witness real signs of the kingdom in our contemporary world. And that, very naturally, gets us back to an apostolic focus.

Interestingly, the writer of Matthew's Gospel (Matt. 28:19-20) uses the Greek word, *mathaeteusate,* which literally means, *be a disciple-maker.* This word is an imperative, active, and aorist verb. The aorist tense, as we have noted, particularly when used in the context of a sentence employing present tense verbs, means that the command is complete, right now! It is sealed for all time! Coupled with the aorist participle *poreuthentes,* which means *to go,* or *from one place to another,* we cannot avoid the charge that the *primary task of Christ's community is that of engaging in a universal, apostolic mission.* And it is non-debatable! In other words, each community of God's Church is commissioned to be in the business of *making* disciples wherever they are.

Many churches know what it means to attract lots of converts to their community, but *do they know how to make disciples?* When conducting conferences in the past, these two questions have motivated me to challenge churches about this imperative:

> *In practical terms, how does your own church engage in a continued process of making disciples? (Deut. 7:6, 1 Pet. 2:9; Matt. 28:19-20)*

> *Is the primary, apostolic focus of your church congregation outward, in terms of service and proclamation, or is most of your energy and resources spent for your own benefit? (Gen. 1:28; Acts 13:1-3)*

APPROPRIATION OF SPIRITUAL GIFTING

The story of the Prodigal Son is a good example of someone (or the nation of Israel) who returned to a *relationship that was already his to reclaim.* In the long-term, that means a cognitive and willing appropriation upon further appropriation; *not a baptism upon baptism!* ("One Lord, one faith, one baptism" Eph. 4:5.) The human decision is always a response to the initiative of the power-giving Holy Spirit. *Genuine Christian experience is truly sacramental in terms of direction; that is, the repentant human response to the gracious touches of the Holy Spirit's initiatives from above.*

Clearly, without minimizing the theological significance of the *initial* Pentecost, the Holy Spirit *continued* to touch the disciples in very special ways (Acts 4:31). Here, the gathered community was filled with the Holy Spirit *again!* These situations must always be seen in terms of response to the *more* of what God promises. Likewise, decisions to appeal to the infilling power of Christ are always ongoing. Spirit-motivated decisions to be conformed to the image of Christ are always ongoing! (John 16:13-14)

The fact is, many people really know little of the Spirit's power until they experience *emptiness in their own life*. It is at this point of *divine dissatisfaction* that they abandon the futility of self-effort; *they risk new possibilities in the Spirit*. Theologies of how much *we possess the Holy Spirit* are really quite ridiculous. The real issue, which becomes a life-long question, is not so much, *How much do I have of the Holy Spirit?* but, *How much does the Holy Spirit have of me?* Again, it is a *decision of faith to risk life in the fullness of God's promises*. The Holy Spirit, as the motivator and enabler of all such decisions, makes possible all that was promised at Pentecost.

The Early Church period was characterized by the *relation of charismatic gifting with that of function and order* (1 Co. 14:40). In the Apostolic period, we see that the Church was not very interested in institutional titles; *they were more interested in the entire priesthood being gifted by the Spirit for ministries of His choosing* (1 Co. 12:4-11). The closings verse of Acts two show the Apostles to be in a process of making disciples. It was a deliberate process. (Many churches need help in engaging with a well-directed process of making disciples.)[xi]

What emerges from this Word-Spirit training is that the priesthood becomes affirmed and authorized in its individual gifting. What we observe is that biblical titles of ministry are associated with spiritual gifting. Offices held in the Church did not relate to institutional position, but the offices tended to be consistent with spiritual gifting.[9] Ignatius was certainly a prophet-bishop.[10] A little later, Irenaeus (c.180 C.E.) speaks of gifts in the Church that include: casting out demons; knowledge; visions; prophecy; healing; and, raising the dead.[11] He also wrote of people who, "...through the Spirit do speak all kinds of languages and bring to light, for the general benefit the hidden things of men and declare the mystery of God." 12 Some time later, Tertullian, a Latin scholar, challenged a sect, called the Marcionites, to produce tongue speakers from among them as a test of orthodox experience!13 However, by the time we get to the fifth century, John Chrysostym of the Antiochene tradition, admitted personal ignorance of the charismatic gifts as listed by Paul, e.g. 1 Corinthians Chapter 12. 14 We have always looked to Science to be in the vanguard of explaining mysteries. However, in relation to spiritual gifting, we see that the gift of *faith* provides an avenue on which to tread the road of *non-rational experience*. It is a way to embrace gifting once normal to the Adam community. Faith and science really are distinct avenues; and each offers its own integrity to matters of mystery.

Most Christians would have little difficulty with spiritual gifts, as listed by Paul in 1 Corinthians Chapter 12. However, *speaking in tongues is a problem* for many. Again, it is one of those gifts which absolutely *requires* faith for its enabling. The negative reasons are mainly psychological; e.g., intellectual, (moving into an area of the non-rational can be petrifying), fear of emotionalism, loss of control, or maybe even of theological positions adopted by particular denominations. Morton Kelsey, a Christian psychologist, describes the phenomenon of tongues as a "...supernatural gift of a foreign or non-human language given at the time of the breakthrough of the Holy Spirit into an individual life. Once this experience has been known, one can enter into it at will, and he finds an immediate way of relating to God and the Holy Spirit."15

From another perspective, Kallistos Ware, a theologian of the Greek Orthodox Church, notes, "When it is genuinely spiritual, 'speaking with tongues' seems to represent an act of 'letting go'- the crucial moment in the breaking down of our sinful self-trust, and its replacement by a willingness to allow God to act within us."16 Personally, I identify very well with this position. I have found the gift to be very powerful in private prayers of adoration and intercession. But it has also helped to loosen up the worship of congregations in which I have pastored.

Many of those who speak in tongues describe it as a key that seems to open up a whole variety of charismatic gifting. Possibly, it is for this reason that Paul (who spoke in tongues *more than all* of them – 1 Co. 14:18) wished that all of his Corinthian readers could speak in tongues (1 Co. 14:5). (However, he never did insist that *the evidence* for having received the Spirit was the gift of tongues.) Obviously, he doesn't want them all to speak in a church gathering at the same time. He made it clear that *gifts of revelation* should be a matter of order (1 Co. 14:40). And they should be tested (1 Thess. 5:19-21). God is not honored by confusion!

BAPTISM IN THE SPIRIT FOR ALL TRADITIONS

Easter, Ascension, and Pentecost are mutually interlocking facets of creation's restoration.

It is in this context that the afore-mentioned seven -point exposition becomes our common focus.

Eden has now taken on more dimension than we first imagined, but nevertheless, from a theological point of view, we are taken right back to the *purposes* of creation. The tenth century Symeon sums up the Baptism with the Spirit in this manner, "The soul through the fire of the Holy Spirit now becomes totally immersed in a conscious way in Jesus Christ. United with Jesus Christ in total conscious surrender of his whole being, the Christian mystic experiences the fire of the Holy Spirit spreading over the human body. Man has returned to the Garden of Eden, integrated in body and soul with God as his center, revealed constantly more and more in the light and fire that is the Holy Spirit of the Father and the Son."17

Clearly, the life of the Early Church community was so attractive that *even priests of the Old Covenant joined it!* (Acts 6:7) In a very short time, the community grew from 120 to 3,000 and then to 5,000! (Acts 2:41, 4:4) Or, as Cardinal Suenens once put it, "Thus we see beyond any shadow of doubt, how the early Church lived by and expressed its faith in the Holy Spirit."18 Not surprisingly, the Apostle Paul considered that significant *marks of apostolic leadership* should be evidenced by demonstrations of signs and wonders of the Spirit (2 Co. 12:12). But is that it, folks? Was all this intended for an age long gone? Does it mean we shouldn't even look for such signs of the kingdom anymore?

ONGOING SIGNS IN THE COMMUNITY

The community of believers experienced kingdom life in a number of ways. They are surely, the very same ways we may observe emerging in the obedient Church of today:

First, *the lifestyle of the community changed from that day on!* In some measure, the Year of Jubilee had arrived. It was not so much about changed systems, but changed lives enabling individual and social change. In their way of dealing with one another they wanted to be a sign of kingdom relationships. With the risen Christ as Lord and focus, they desired to demonstrate to the world signs of Eden restored. They really did care for one another. If anyone was in need, then they could rely on the community for help (Acts 2:45, 4:34). Clearly, this love for one another spilled out. They were not simply a sign of God's justice and righteousness, but longed for it in the life of the world.

Second, *they didn't separate a spiritual gospel from a social gospel.* In other words, they did not separate spirit from body and soul. The power of the Spirit-filled gospel stretched out to the whole person. And so we see today that the saving of the soul is, more and more, accompanied by a *passion for justice and righteousness towards the poor and oppressed.* Robert Webber tells us of a revival of this broader view of mission and style in what he describes as today's 'Younger Evangelicals.'19 Is not this sense of mission consistent with the lifestyle advocated by the writer of First John?

What we observe is an equal concern for John 3:7 (being born again) as there is for Matt. 25:40 ("as you did it to the least of these"). Clearly, the effective outworking of both these emphases requires spiritual gifting as we see in 1 Cor.14:12. If this is not a priority of disciple-making today, then we are left with nothing more than a humanistic desire for self-survival, or a spiritualized gospel with little incarnational value.

Third, *their apostolic focus was nurtured by practical methods of discipleship.* Most of the process of disciple-making did not take place in a classroom, but in real life situations with their training leaders also present. In the West, how much do we see leadership demonstrating what they are teaching? Where this is happening, we can be sure that some sort of classroom evaluation takes place before events of service, and also afterwards.

They loved to fellowship together, pray together, learn together, worship together, break bread together, work together, and to praise God together (Acts

2:42-47). Not surprisingly, the quality of their life attracted a large following (Acts 5:12-13). In many countries of the Southern Globe, the Christian Church is also growing at a very fast pace. One Anglican bishop, answering my question on how such rapid growth was occurring in Africa, simply replied, "Through signs and wonders of the Spirit." Admittedly, effective discipleship for leadership has to keep up with the pace of growth over there. They are aware of their own problems of keeping things together in kingdom fashion. But these are far better problems than we have in the West. We are in serious decline!

Fourth, *they leaned heavily on making disciples who were consciously dependent upon the anointed power of the Spirit.* Where this is happening today, we are likely to observe congregations where a "waiting in Jerusalem" is very important (Luke 24:49). In other words, where basic courses on training and life in the Holy Spirit are offered. And where an opportunity is then given for the expectant learner to receive the laying on of hands. [xii] For many churches, with a meta-mindset, the structures of their affiliations become less important than the discovery of ways in which the kingdom may be served more effectively. This sense of diversity was certainly true of the Church in the Apostolic Age.

The attempt to address the renewal of structure, form, and purpose in mainline churches found some authenticity as far back as the early days of Methodism. John Wesley (1703-91) had enormous difficulty in being acceptable to his Anglican establishment. No doubt, the main problem was his challenging the institution about its impotence and stagnation.

He challenged his own denomination on the need for balance of the institution with the charismatic life of its membership. Forced outside of the established structures, he was moved to *create new ways of developing effective disciples for the Gospel.* We learn some very important principles in the Methodist zeal to present an *unchanging Gospel within new paradigms of a changed methodology*:

First, a whole-hearted acceptance of traditional Christian doctrine coupled with the conviction that such doctrine is useless unless verified in life and experience.

Second, a strong emphasis on the personal relationship of the believer with Jesus Christ as Lord and Savior.

Third, an equally strong emphasis on the work of the Holy Spirit.

Fourth, a serious attempt to embody life in small groups and other communities of committed men and women.

Fifth, a desire for the proclamation of the Gospel to all humanity.

Sixth, a concern for the material well-being, as well as the spiritual needs of the poor.

Seventh, a tendency to bring together lay people and the ordained in new structures of shared life and ministry.20

What was true for his day is equally true for today. The *form and structures* of the Church community become secondary to the *purposes* of the historic and universal community. And that is why we see a diversity of forms and structure in the age of the Apostles. Jesus had appropriated the character of all that it meant to be the Servant of Isaiah Chapter 61 (Luke 4:18-19). By the anointed power of the Spirit, *the community of Jesus is also enabled to be a Servant Church.* Or, as we have noted from the very beginning of this book, the community of God has an apostolic mandate to be the Servant Community *for the sake* of the world; but not the servant *of* the world.

The kingdom has not arrived through the Church, nor will it. Indeed, the Church, in its remaining time, will not win the battle over injustice and suffering. The signature of Eden, sometimes seen through God's ancient community, was renewed on the face of the earth from the day of Pentecost to the present. Nevertheless, Jesus prophesied that the days of struggle would not continue forever. God has appointed an end. And, in doing so, He warns us of signs which will accompany the end. *I think there is a way of looking at these signs in ways that are consistent with the principles God instituted in His creation.* Let's take a brief look at the meaning of latter days.

Chapter 12 Pentecost: An Awesome Moment of Light

1. Kelsey, Morton T. *Tongue Speaking*, p.35. Doubleday & Co. Garden City, New York, 1964.

2. Barrett, C.K. *Peakes Commentary on the Bible, The Gospel of John*, p.867, Ed. Matthew Black and H.H.Rowley, Thomas Nelson and Sons, London W.1. Reprinted 1964

3. David Edwards and John Stott, *Evangelical Essentials,* p26

4. Wellman, Sam. *Wesley,*p.107 Chelsea House Publishers, Philadelphia, 1999

5. Lovelace, Richard F. *Dynamics of Spiritual Life,* p.125. Inter-Varsity Press, Downers Grove, Illinois 60515. 1979

6. St. Cyril of Jerusalem, *Lectures on the Christian Sacraments,* p.50

7.   George Maloney-Introduction, *Simeon the New Theologian, The Discourses,*p.16, Paulist Press, New York, 1980

8.   George Maloney, *The Mystic of Fire and Light,* p.12, Denville, Dimension Books, 1975.

9.   Kydd, Ronald A.N. *Charismatic Gifts in The Early Church,* p.9 Hendrickson Publishers, Peabody, Ma. 01961-3473, 1984

10. Kydd, *Charismatic Gifts in the Early Church,* p.17

11. Kydd, *Charismatic Gifts in the Early Church,* p.44

12. Williams, George and Waldvogel, Edith; *The Charismatic Movement,* p.66. William B. Eeerdmans, Grand Rapids, Michigan. 1975.

13. Williams and Waldvogel, *The Charismatic Movement,* p.83

14. Kelsey, *Tongue Speaking,* p.46

15. Kelsey, Morton T. *Tongue Speaking,* p.168

16. Ware, Kallistos, *The Orthodox Way,* p.134.

17. Maloney, George A. *The Mystic of Fire and Light,* Denville, Dimension Books, 1975.

18. Suenens, Cardinal L.J. *A New Pentecost,* pps.34, 35 Seabury Press, New York, N.Y. 10017, 1975.

19. Robert, E Webber, *The Younger Evangelicals,* p.109 Baker Books, Grand Rapids, Michigan 49516, 2002 (Third Edition 2003)

20. 20 Allchin, A.M. *The Kingdom of Love and Knowledge,* p.38. Seabury Press, NY. 1982

Chapter 13

FROM LATTER DAYS TO THE NEW EDEN

A NATURAL END

Creation's principles are restored! The Big Story of the Gospel is magnificently consistent in its procession through the chronicles of history. In the beginning, the glory and the light of God shone upon a raw creation; it was further crowned in an Adam-Eve community charged with an apostolic mission. In its entirety, it was a mission of kingdom signature. A pattern of harmonious relationships was in place in a paradise where all syntheses of relationships had their focus and source in God. When things went wrong, *God did not give up on His purposes or His principles*. His purposes are sovereign, even if individuals choose to reject them. The methodology of God is one of total freedom; it is always an invitation to accept, or reject, participation in His eternal purposes. Clearly, God is convinced that the *principle of free choice will win out*. We must emphasize again:

"My purpose shall stand, and I will fulfill my intention" (Isa. 46:10).

We have come a very long way from a creation in which God said, *"It is very good,"* to the commentary of the Apostle Paul. He reminds us of the pain of our present creation which is groaning in travail (Rom. 8:18-23). Jesus went beyond this comment in predicting that creation will move toward a *much-worsened state*. His prediction reminds us of a condition of darkness existing before the Spirit breathed on the embryonic creation. Confusion and disorder appears to reign without check. Jesus is really telling us that the natural consequences, through chronological time, must be *worked out* in the desperate and suicidal course of nature's pain and fury.

> *What this means, in terms of chronos, is that the entire creation continues to experience the pain and consequences of its own alienation. The essential and harmonious relationships, which we identified as kingdom-governed relationships of creation, are becoming more and more at odds with each other.*

"And this end must not simply be equated with a cosmic catastrophe and the sudden end of human history. What is old, transient, imperfect and evil will indeed be ended: but this end must be understood as ultimate completion and fulfillment."1 Hans Kung offers a broad theological view of what this ending may mean. Clearly, we must not lose sight of the fact that the Bible provides striking evidence that the *old order* will most certainly pass away; and so this present order will surely come to a *natural end.* However, Isaiah had spoken of a chaotic end many hundreds of years before Jesus:

> **"The earth shall be utterly laid waste and utterly despoiled; for the Lord has spoken this word...The earth lies polluted under its inhabitants; for they have transgressed laws, violated the statutes, broken the everlasting covenant. Therefore a curse devours the earth, and its inhabitants suffer for their guilt...The earth staggers like a drunkard, it sways like a hut...and it falls and will not rise again. On that day the Lord will punish the host of heaven, in heaven, and on earth the kings of the earth"** **(Isa. 24:3, 5, 6, 20-21).**

Amid such chaos, we are to see that *lights of the inbreathed community are being rejected* by a world inevitably plunging itself into nihilistic darkness. There are many who venture to predict the actual time when God allows the chaos to fulfill its natural course. However Jesus isn't counted amongst the foretellers of that day:

"But about that day and hour no one knows, neither the angels of heaven, nor the Son, but only the Father" (Matt. 24:36).

However, Jesus does predict the *signs* of the end. They are consistent with the breakdown of essential relationships which were evident at the time of creation and which were described as being *very good*. Most certainly, He did not predict that existence in this world would get better!

HOPE AMID CHAOS

This disorder signifies the total breakdown of all four elements of essential relationships. However, the chaos in the chronological process is irreversible as it moves relentlessly towards its ultimate demise. Like the totally helpless body of Jesus in the stone-cold tomb, all nature and all human effort cannot reverse its inevitable descent to meaninglessness. Certainly, the point in time will emerge when the Spirit will no longer hover in protection over a rebellious creation. Haven't we seen a picture like this before? Doesn't it resemble the apparent chaos of raw creation prior to its ordering and shaping by the Holy Breath of God? Doesn't it remind us of the similar chaos working out its inevitable destruction at the time of Noah? The major difference here is that one scenario represents the first day of new creation, while the latter is a description of the *latter days connected to the divine process of recreation*. What is abundantly certain is that revisionist hopes for the creation of a better world are nothing more than a naïve dream. Everything will get considerably worse!

At some point, *the sustaining power of God is removed* from a creation that has run its nihilistic course. It will fall prey to the inevitable law of consequence. Indeed, it would appear that, *at this very present, as in no other time in history, we are now feeling the effects of our neglect and plunder of the environment to which we were initially called in stewardship*. It is now possible for us to venture predictions concerning what those ultimate consequences will be in this world. At some point (a moment that is too late-Matt. 25:8-13), many will be shocked to realize that the sustaining Light of God is not shining upon the face of the old order (Matt. 24:22). We have seen this scenario on humanity's behalf prefaced in the death of Jesus (Matt. 27:46).

Apart from Jesus, the first fruits of restoration, all things do pass away! But does that mean that the planet earth will disappear from existence?

We have cause to believe that the old order of the world will certainly pass away (1 John 2:17; 2 Co. 5:17), but there are a few biblical allusions that suggest the physical earth may well continue. At best, it is a meaningless world without end (Gen. 8:21.) But surely, the most significant fact of history leads us to believe that there will always be a tangible relationship with a physical world. As we have seen, the event is the resurrection of Jesus. His resurrected body was certainly surrounded in mystery, but there was a recognizable physical connection of the old body with that of the new.

In the same way, the new creation will hold a certain sense of mystery, but connections with the old world will be apparent. Interestingly, this verse, which appears to deny connection, also affirms it.

"Then I saw a new heaven and a new earth; for the first heaven and the first earth had passed away, and the sea was no more" (Rev. 21:1 - ouranus is used equally for sky as it is for heaven; parenthesis is mine).

If a brand new earth were to appear from above, it would be expected that the writer would have employed the common Greek word for new – "neon." He does not use it. Rather, he employs the word, kainon ("new in species, character, or mode.") It is a word which resembles the English word, *new,* but speaks, rather, of renewal or refreshment. This word may be seen in Romans 12:2 where the Apostle Paul speaks of the "renewing of your minds." The word is also used in Mark's Gospel where Jesus speaks of new wineskins. "...but one puts new (neon) wine into fresh (kainos) wineskins" (Parentheses mine; Mark 2:22). *In other words, there is clearly a physical connection between the world of the old order with that of the new order.*

Recognizing that it is virtually impossible for us to comprehend a complete picture of the chronological process of decay in the old order, nevertheless we may more easily understand the final *result* from the perspective of time's restoration. What we are about to postulate in this area is truly remarkable. It is certainly God's mystery of time's victory:

For those who will die today in Christ, the old order of creation will completely pass away as they enter into the fullness of new creation. Along with other passages of scripture, we have seen that the ancient saints of Hebrews Chapter 11-12:2, have clearly demonstrated that this mystery of everlasting time continues to be enjoyed from the very last moment of consciousness in the old order (John 11:25-26).

Nevertheless, the accounts of Christ's resurrection have left us with paradoxical elements of familiarity tinged with elusive images of mystery. That is the way we must think of the restoration of all things, of the new creation, of the new heaven and earth coming down *"from above"* (John 3:3,7). The gift of being born again, from above, through the resurrection, and, after a death to the old order, is precisely the manner in which restoration takes place. *Creation is born again!*

"And the one who was seated on the throne said, 'See, I am making all things new'" (kainos is used once more Rev. 21:5).

In some sense, there will be recognition of what once was, but also *unfamiliarity with the restoration of what was originally intended. New creation is always seen to be in the context of "anothen"- from above.* When Jesus comes again, "…in the same way as you saw him go into heaven…" (Acts 1:11), *His feet will not touch the earth of the old order!* Zechariah intimates that His feet will touch the earth (Zech. 14:3) but this should be seen in the context of Christ's identification with the new order. Whatever Luke means, it will clearly register an irreversible separation of the old order from that of the new. Those of the new order will be connected to Jesus forever! In the meantime, when we recognize that nearly a third of the teachings of Jesus are prophetic, we will also consider what *chronological signs* are evident in a world of the old order running towards its ultimate demise.

A WAY OF LOOKING AT LAST THINGS

I want to share some thoughts emphasizing the chronological process of viewing latter days from a synoptic perspective. We cannot *begin* our thinking built on *foundations* that are primarily of a symbolic nature, such as are found in the books of Daniel and Revelation. We cannot ignore such books, but we look at them as supports for the bigger story as found in Jesus.

Formerly, we observed a *prophetic principle that the future may unfold a picture bigger than the original context*.2 If we believe we have determined who the Beast is of Revelation, we should also take note that he has been *specifically identified in different ways throughout several periods of history*. In the Early Church, the Beast was the power of Caesar sitting on the seven hills of Rome.3 At the time of the Reformation, the Beast was identified as the Bishop of Rome.4 In much of the contemporary world of fundamentalist Christianity, he has been identified as the power of a European Union. These are theories which remind us to be careful not to develop a biblical theology based on the moods and politics of one particular age. So, in determining the process of latter days, it's not a good idea to interpret scripture with a Bible in one hand and the daily newspaper in the other.

The chronology of Revelation does not always move successively from one moment, or age, to the next. The book invites us to view a big picture depicted in symbolic imagery. It's a bit like looking at the way a light shines on a revolving glass ball. Aspects of the whole picture are observed at one time. Nevertheless, generally speaking, the picture is quite consistent with the Big Story of the Bible. It is difficult to be tied to one view of chronological events. John Robinson illustrates the problem.

Robinson picks up on the difficulty of determining strict time sequences in Revelation by addressing the question of the *second death* in Chapter 20. He has difficulty with the idea that everyone will experience a resurrection, then, after a millennial reign, experience a judgment, then a further resurrection. The destiny of all those raised in this resurrection will be either to an eternal reign with Christ, or to a second death (Rev. 20:14). "The idea of two kingdoms and two resurrections, though common to St. Paul and the Apocalypse, does not appear in the Gospels. It is best viewed as an attempt to harmonize, under the form of successive events, the two elements of the myth emphasized by the prophets and the apocalyptists respectively, namely, that the meaning of history must be vindicated within history and yet that the complete purpose of God must transcend history. The representation of this tension as two stages leads to error if taken literally. For us, the resurrection of the body (an essential element in the total eschatological myth) must be related to the whole doctrine of resurrection which does justice to both these emphases."5

Maybe it is only in this way that we can reconcile passages such as that which speak of the tombs in Jerusalem being opened:

> *"...and many bodies of the saints who had fallen asleep were raised. After his resurrection they came out of the tombs and entered the holy city and appeared to many" (Matt. 27:52-53).*

> *Surely, this is also what the writer to the Hebrews had in mind! (Heb.11:39-12:2)*

We may appreciate Robinson's conclusion, but we cannot completely ignore a chronological process. Apart from his strangely unsubstantiated view of universalism, I believe that Robinson quite rightly places the *resurrection* at the heart of restored time. And, that is paramount when we try to settle the very difficult task of harmonizing scriptures dealing with questions of latter days. *However, it's probably not a good idea to insist on a chronological schema in Revelation.*

The chronological schema of latter day events in Revelation is difficult to harmonize with John's Gospel; that is, unless we view Revelation as part of the whole eschatological picture, and one which is not always interpreted in literal terms.

Because of this difficulty, we will view all latter day literature *in the light of how real events in time are illuminated through the light of the Synoptic Gospels.* After all, the *word of Jesus* must be the criterion by which we evaluate all literature that speaks of latter days. Jesus is the Living Word (John 1:1). Actually, in view of the tension between theological order and chronological events, it is not surprising that many scholars conclude there are two different writers involved in authoring the books of Revelation and John.6

One way of viewing these passages is to recognize that Jesus speaks of a growing chaos and decay from four different perspectives:

Religious, Social, Environmental, and Cosmic.

If we view such passages from these perspectives, *we will note that the process aligns itself, quite naturally, with the unfolding deterioration of the essential principles of creation's relationships.*

What we are seeing throughout a horrific period of irreversible chaos and decay is a frenetic unraveling of the synchronous harmony of those relationships. In the latter stages, creation seems to reflect ever-diminishing signs of God's light and glory, but there are still signs of hope! In the closing stages, creation itself seems to join with the disconsolate train of Adam and Eve departing the gates of its self-made Eden. Therefore, with the residents of Eden, a fallen creation has taken its natural course!

A POSSIBLE SYNOPTIC CHRONOLOGY OF LATTER EVENTS

We can never understand the meaning of events related to latter days unless we are conversant with the essential principles involved in creation's relationships. What we are to observe are events that signal the *climactic reversal* of the relationship between religious, social, environmental, and cosmic elements. To consider something of the chronology of latter days, we will look at the processes of decay in the light of those characteristics. Without identifying the process too tightly, we will easily observe that Jesus' view of latter day events really do signify an immense deterioration of Religious, Social, Environmental, and Cosmic characteristics.

RELIGIOUS

1. False claims to Messiahship (Matt. 24:5; Mark 13:6)
2. Wars and rumors of wars (Matt. 24:6; Mark 13:7; Luke 21:9)
3. Nations rise against nations, earthquakes, famines, plagues (Matt. 24:7; Mark 13:8; 21:11)
4. Possibly, the destruction of Jerusalem should be inserted here (70 A.D.). Matthew records the prophetic prediction of Jesus (24:20-21). Also, there is mention of a great dispersion which takes place at that time (Matt. 24:24). However, there was also a final dispersion in 135 A.D. (which took place as a result of the Second Revolt under Simon Bar-Kochba).7

5. From that time onwards, Jerusalem will be in the hands of the Gentiles; until their time is fulfilled! (Luke 21:24, Rom. 11:25)

<u>Comment on 1</u>: Never, in all of history, have we experienced so many claims to final revelation and messiahship. These signs often seem to appear alongside natural occurrences of upheaval. But there has never been a time when the world has not experienced such natural and social disturbances. Jesus tells us they are just *the beginning of birth pangs*.

However, the rise of individual claims to truth, accompanying the diverse style of a globalized village, *has not, nor could have ever been quite as intense, or achievable, as it is now*. Religion is fine; absolute truth is not. Much of our present media is very effective in presenting this attitude. Paradoxically, and in reality, this unique globalized attitude has actually provided avenues for the license to absolute claims of revelation. Sometimes, the tyranny that is being left behind has led to ruthless pressure for conversions such as has been rarely seen at a global level. Nevertheless, the upholding of individualized religion has indeed given rise to claims that a parade of messiahs have now emerged upon the stage of history. Quite possibly, such repercussions may produce a global desire to do more and more things with a one-world view. The motivation for this desire would not be focused in discovering absolute truth, but in the quest for human survival. Desperation will set in!

<u>Comment on 2and 3</u>: Rumors of wars, earthquakes, famines and plagues are nothing new, nor were they at the time of Jesus. Indeed, seismologists tell us that earthquakes are very natural and that they must happen. Such signs of nature were also present during the time of the Temple's destruction. But Jesus had prophesied it! However, in relation to such contemporary events are the astounding effects they are having *on increasing numbers of people!* We are not just more aware of those happenings; the fact is that *infinitely more people are now affected by them.* Our essential relationship with creation is in the throes of chaotic disorder. Should we be surprised by the results? They produce a chain reaction.

The last century saw two world-wide wars involving the death of untold millions of people, (including six million Jews in the Holocaust). Two earthquakes, one on the twenty sixth of December, 2003 in Bam, Iran, and the other exactly twelve months later in SE Asia exacted a combined toll of more than 250,000 lives. Nature is truly groaning! (Rom. 8:19-21) These astounding events really challenge us not to dismiss the warning words of Jesus. They are a call for the Church to reawaken its sense of urgency to the prophetic and evangelistic purposes of the Gospel.

Comment on 4: This prediction of Jesus proved to be historically correct, but Jesus never associated it as happening near the end of days.

Comment on 5: There is abundant evidence in the Old Testament of a dispersion that will take the Jewish people to the *furthest regions of the world* (Jer. 9:16, 25:33; Ezek. 36:22).

Indeed, such a world-wide dispersion did take place. It began from Assyria's captivity of the Northern kingdom (721 B.C.) to Judah's dispersal (586 B.C.) and from 70 to 135 A.D.

However, there are many biblical allusions concerning *Israel's return to its homeland* (Jer. 12:15, 23:3, 31:8; Ezek. 28:26. 36:24, 37:21-22). After more than 1800 years, in 1948, a Jewish state of Israel was once more established by the United Nations. This event appears to be a major event through which ancient prophets saw the race of Israel coming to some sense of spiritual unity (Hosea 1:10-11). As a nation, Israel, takes its place amongst the major influences of the world.

SOCIAL and ENVIRONMENTAL

1. For the elect, there will be persecution, torture, prison and death. They will be a people hated by all nations (Matt. 24:9; Mark13:9; Luke 21:12). *Obviously, a time emerges when the Gospel of Jesus has traveled around the world in order for the accomplishment of the condition He predicted!*

2. These conditions will give cause for a great falling away from the faith. There will be betrayal by family members, and false prophets will also lead many astray (Matt. 24:10-11; Mark 13:12; Luke 21:16).

3. The despair caused by an increase in lawlessness will be further occasion for a falling away from the faith (Matt. 24:12).

4. There is an injunction that the end will not come until the good news is extended universally (Matt. 24:14; Mark 13:10).The commission to the Adam community has been revived! *This surge in evangelism is recorded as a major sign close to the end of the ages!* The universal commission of

Jesus to His community is to be played out in greater measure than at the time of the Apostles!

5. The desolating sacrilege, standing in the *holy place*, will cause those in Judea to flee to the mountains (Matt. 24:15-16; Mark 13:14).

6. At this time there will be suffering and chaos comparable to *"the beginning of the world,"* and nothing may be compared with it (Matt. 24:21; Mark 13:19).

7. For the sake of the elect, those days of suffering will be *"cut short"* (Matt. 24:22; Mark 13:20). In other words, *the elect will be involved in considerable suffering.*

8. Also, *"at that time,"* as people look for a messiah or a savior from their difficulties, false messiahs and prophets will be capable of producing false signs and wonders. Even many of the elect will be deceived, or seduced by a politically acceptable religious diversity (Matt. 24:23-24; Mark13:21).

Comment on 1-3: Much of this is already happening in the Western Hemisphere, particularly in the falling away from the faith! In these days of political correctness, the rejection of absolutes by a generation rebelling against the values of their parents, and the rise of New Age religions, it isn't difficult to see how conditions would change loyalties. (Obviously, the honoring of absolute values in a globalized economy would cause great embarrassment, and also be a deterrent to the universal goals of a new economy). *Absolutes cannot be tolerated; individual spirituality can!* In much of the western world today, in law, it seems much more likely that individual rights can not only silence those who gave society those values, but now give license for the persecution of the very same people.

The idea that Christians escape persecution has no substance in fact (1 Pet. 4:12). One source estimates that 165,000 Christians are martyred every year in our modern age; that 200 million Christians face persecution, imprisonment and death almost every day; and that more Christians were martyred in the 20th century than in the entire history of the Christian Church.8 In the western world, its obsession with individual rights over corporate responsibility is causing frustration amongst enforcers of law. There is an enormous contradiction of values, and considerable lack of confidence in systems of justice. Violence, a daily delight of the media, and now a paralyzing reality in the West after September 11th 2001, has anaesthetized the sensitivities of a generation now absorbed with the perverse thrill of violence.

As we move a little further into latter days, we are to observe a measure of intense suffering such as the world has never known. It isn't difficult to understand, in our contemporary world, and without discussing the astounding frequency of terrorism abroad, that the chaos which exists has easily discernable roots. (e.g. when individualism is lauded over corporate right and responsibility, and also where indignant petulance emerges concerning the right to possess whatever the individual desires). *The results are leading to a lawlessness of disturbing proportion.* Terrorism, with religious motivation, now springs up in all quarters of our world. (2 Thess. 2:3-4 certainly looks possible from our present perspectives.) In our Gnostic culture, where suffering is rarely granted a realistic place, it isn't difficult to imagine what would happen in the Western world. In sheer frustration, with anger towards God, and in pained disillusionment, *many will turn away from the God of Jesus. They will look for another "savior" who will promise peace and order - even if there is a price to pay for it!*

Quite possibly, the values lauded in a globalized economy (where all absolutes, such as the Lordship of Christ, as well as religious values, are *privatized* and rendered devoid of social context) may easily contribute to well-meaning family members *opposing Christian kin*. This opposition will occur, for the maintenance of universally accepted values! It is also possible that the present failure of historic mainline churches to reject the syncretistic influences of our fickle and ever-changing culture, will also be a contributory factor in this falling away. Such a utilitarian approach may also contribute to the offering of a friendly nod towards other *benevolent saviors*. Whether or not this scenario becomes a reality or not, it must be admitted that, in this techno-communication age, such possibilities now loom much larger than at any other time in the history of the world.

Comment on 4: The universal spread of the Gospel is now technically more feasible in our age of global communication. It is part of the historic apostolic commission that a community be created from all nations of the earth. The *sons of God* are intended to be primary agents in facilitating blessings of universal community (Gen. 12:3; Isa. 49:6; John 1:13). We note that the same technology may also be used by the powers of evil. It is certainly more possible to brainwash the masses than ever before. The purpose of those forces opposing the gospel will be to deceive the nations by producing false signs and values. (After all, so much can now be accomplished through the media and satellite-aided computers!) Nevertheless, although there is presently a great *falling away* in the West, *the Church of the Global South experiences breathtaking growth throughout most of its regions.* Quite remarkably, the primary method of sharing the Gospel in these poorer regions is through the basic and unsophisticated medium of developing personal relationships, and through signs and wonders of the Spirit.

Comment on 5: It would *appear* that Jerusalem (as the material focus of God's dwelling amongst His people) is also to be the focus of a *spiritual conflict* having global ramifications. The idea that the *holy place* is severely insulted (as in the days of Antiochus Epiphanes, 168 B.C.) gives us the impression that the saints of God are now a *globalized networking community. Their primary messianic focus has enraged the universal and controlling powers of the world.* These powers demand a capitulation to their own sets of values. Some Orthodox Jews, and also some evangelical Christians, believe that this sacrilege is The Dome of the Rock - completed 691 A.D. Consequently, it will represent a focal point for global armed conflict. However, for most Christians the idea that another temple should be built in this place makes little sense. They see a spiritual temple in a different light. *Jesus is the temple in a Jerusalem that is above and free! He is the focus, now and forever* (Rev. 21:22).

Comment on 6-8: In the Synoptics, and in John 16:33, the people of God who remain are not spared the pain of persecution, suffering, and death. Isaiah may also have prefigured this suffering to include the elect (Isa. 2:21). We see similar allusions in Daniel 12:1 where it is recorded that *this distress is immeasurably greater than at any time in history.* In Revelation Chapter 13 we also see that there are faithful saints who refuse to buy into the world's new and universal values. As a result, they suffer untold distress. However, as in the Gospels, where Jesus speaks of this unparalleled time of suffering, He intimates that (for the sake of the elect) the time will be cut short. This is quite possibly consistent with the *one hour* (in relative terms) of the suffering recorded in Rev. 17:12, 18:10. Here, the unbearable pain of the saints will end.

The situation described above *may not be too dissimilar* from our contemporary situation. What we are witnessing today is that established historic and mainline churches are falling apart through apostasy and cultural accommodation. Conversely, churches of the Global South are growing at an extraordinary rate. They are no longer intimidated by the heavy-handed and controlling schemes of their founding churches. Clearly, an uncompromising faith has given birth to a powerful mission in evangelism. While the Church of the South is burgeoning in numbers, in many quarters *it is also facing suffering and untold persecution for the sake of the Gospel.* This is a quality of discipleship rarely seen in the West today. What will we trade in the West to secure the absence of suffering? Suffering is the norm for those who walk the Way of the cross.

It would appear that the only hope for the dry bones of the West will be found in the recovery of its apostolic roots, and made possible by the inbreathing power of the Holy Spirit. It will be in the Spirit's power that the Church may stand like a mighty army (Ezek. 37:9-10). If the West is to be part of the continued universal mission, then this courageous stand will be possible solely through the in-breathed revival of the Holy Spirit. *Possibly, the Western mission may be aided and reinforced by churches of the Global South.* God will raise a remnant that is primarily motivated to a mission of evangelism, a mission that will arise from people brought from death to life, and from the powers of darkness to the kingdom of God's beloved Son (Col. 1:13). Surely, the time is right for a Western remnant to *shake off the shackles of the old order* and to recover the mission of Jesus, "...to seek out and to save the lost" (Luke 19:10). Such a return to basics of purpose would constitute an apostolic focus of a *Second Reformation, far surpassing that of the sixteenth century!*

Speaking from perspectives beyond that of a faithless Church, why should we be surprised that our apathy and lack of regard for God's creation results in environmental havoc? This me-focused attitude among nations and individuals is presently resulting in thousands upon thousands who are dying of starvation every year, e.g., the horrific famines of Ethiopia. Our greed for more, and for immediate satisfaction, has produced anti-nature attitudes in the world, but also in the Church itself.

Social conditions appear to be so abysmal that *sheer desperation will be the motivation* for many people to look for a global savior. Possibly, an idolatry of modern technology may produce false promises luring away a self-centered and apathetic Western Christianity from the costly pathway of Calvary!

In our time, we note that there are consequences of a fragile and apathetic democracy pitted against the lawlessness of lustful terrorism. It is not difficult to see why a worsening situation would call for the rise of desperate solutions. *A supposed savior* may well be some sort of charismatic figure, or a universally-accepted political system, or even a religious ideology which *will gain global acceptance for its chameleon benevolence and miraculous ability to ensure political order.* A rise in violence should not come as a surprise. This alluring "savior" would promise to give order amid chaos, but also an attractive means of survival (Rev. 13:16-18). Even saints, people of goodwill, are to be deceived by this pretender's promises. Interestingly, we are already in an age when the overblown claims of New Age religions are being adopted by former members of Christian churches. In the self-perceived notions of justice, the cry, *Peace, peace, when there is no peace,* is being widely lauded from pulpits today (Jer. 6:14). False Christs can now easily find universal adherents through the amazingly sophisticated distortions of our world-wide communication systems.

Having brought about an apparent condition of stability, *possibly by enforcing submission to universal values,* the savior-figure may well replace individual freedom of choice with a further submission to his dictatorial agendas. Is this the *false prophet* of Rev. 16:13-14 and 19:20? Whether it may be *the beast* or the *false prophet,* the writer of Revelation has them working together!

SIGNS IN THE COSMOS AND THE DECAYING EARTH

After that time of suffering, there will be *chaos in the heavens and in the seas.* Clearly, there will be chaotic intrusions originating in the world, and in the cosmos.

It would appear that, despite the advances in technology, humanity is not able to control the chaotic forces from the heavens and below. Quite amazingly, the old order undergoes chaotic situations, such as we read of in Gen. 1:1-2. In creation, order came about when the Spirit breathed upon the disorder. No such thing is promised to sustain the old order.

Clearly, the disordered movement of nature is beyond any human power to control. Such destructive directions may also occur as a result of human failure in its stewardship of the environment. Already, alarming signs of environmental decay are being experienced. In a recent newspaper article, Margaret Munro cites reputable sources when warning of the massive escape of methane gases at the top of our planet. While, "Polar ice has been shrinking at a rate of 74,000 square kilometers annually for the past 30 years...The Arctic ice is withdrawing so fast...that by 2050 it may be non-existent in the summer...But there is little anyone can do for the animals and other life forms that will be stranded as temperatures climb and the Arctic's icy cloak lifts. If you live on the sea ice, like the polar bear, you are in big trouble - your habitat is disappearing." 9

Natural catastrophes may well effect changes in the sun, moon and stars (Matt. 24:29; Mark 13:24-25; Luke 21:25; also see Joel 2:31). On the Day of Pentecost, quoting from the prophet Joel, Peter reminded his Jewish audience,

"The sun will be turned to darkness and the moon to blood, before the coming of the Lord's great and glorious day" (Acts 2:20).

(In some parts of the world, it is already difficult to see the sun! And when we consider the results of the rape of the Brazilian rain forests, the polluted air emanating from the industrial world, and the terrifying results of global warming, we may also observe the stark and brutal consequences of *humanity's failure* to live in harmony with God's creation. That's not all! There is a major problem looming, which for a variety of reasons, is not receiving its deserved attention: "Water is not a renewable resource!" The commentator in this television program goes on to say that about two million children die every year from water that is unfit to drink.10 Massive famine will surely result. There are other factors beyond our control. Certain cosmic actions will proceed, indicating humanity's failure to maintain its creation charge:

1. 1. *Then*, the Son of Man will appear in the heavens. With His angels, He will gather the elect who remain on the earth (Matt. 24:30; Mark 13:26; Luke 21:27). Does this remind us of the *translation* of Enoch and Elijah? We noted in an earlier chapter that, at the Parousia, the feet of Jesus did not even touch the ground of the old order. However, the saints *who are alive on earth* do meet with the Lord in the context of chronological time. *It will be a Moment of great separation.* Theirs will be an experience similar to the translation experienced by Enoch and Elijah. "We will not all die, but we will all be changed, in a moment, in the twinkling of an eye...and we will be changed" (1 Co. 15:51-52). The dead in Christ are changed already (1Thess. 4:15-17; Heb. 12:1). No doubt, all of this will

occur when the time of persecution and suffering has been cut short. But none of this will occur until there has been a massive grafting of Israel into the vine of Jesus (John 15:1; Rom. 11:11-13, 23). This will surely be an astounding move of the Spirit.

Quite regardless of interpretation, one thing is certain. As the destiny of the two thieves on their crosses signify:

> *There will be some determining point of eternal separation between those who are alive in the relationships of the new order of creation and those who are not (Matt.13:30).*

Possibly, this separation will somehow coincide with the *Moment* of the final conflict recorded in the symbolic literature of Ezekiel Chapters 38-39; Zech. 12:9, 14:3; Rev. 16:14-16). Here, the powers of the earth have, together, been seduced.

2.   As in the days of Noah, much of the earth's population will revel in an orgy of self-centered abandonment and drunkenness. They will live as if nothing could go wrong! On that day, as it was in those days, and that of the Rich Man and Lazarus (Luke 16:19-31), *the people who choose to remain outside of Christ are those who will see and will mourn* (Matt. 24:30, 37). At this point there *will be weeping and gnashing of teeth* (Matt. 25:30).

3.   Each of the Gospels includes a severe warning in its commentary. *It is a call to be ready,* because it will appear like a thief in the night. We will all be taken by surprise! And those who are *not ready will not be included* in the life of the new creation (Matt. 24:36-44, 25:10-12; Mark 13:32-36; Luke 21:34-36).

4.   In each of the Synoptic Gospels, Jesus warns that this generation will not pass away until all things are fulfilled. Heaven and earth *(the old order of fallen creation)* will pass away, but God's Word will remain forever (Matt. 24:34-35; Mark 13:30; Luke 21:32 - see also Isa. 40:8; 55:11).

Comment on 1: Many of the natural, *cosmic calamities* appear to extend beyond the control, or even the cause, of human endeavor. They will cause terror on the earth. However, the disasters are fully representative of the fact that *nature itself will turn in on itself (comparable to the end of the self-destructive Judas)*, and it will take down our known, natural world with it. (This principle of consequence and subsequent impotence was established by God in the Old Testament; e.g., in Lev. 18:24-25.)

Comment on 2-4: The Ascension of Jesus (the Real Adam) signaled the discernible end of the old order, but the chronological race to destruction had not yet played itself out. Clearly, the Resurrection of Jesus, Ascension and Pentecost should be seen together as part of the whole eschatological picture. Together, they present to the world an astounding, *Moment of Light.*

The final battle of Armageddon may best be viewed as the *climax of the spiritual battle* between the forces of good and evil. In this context, it may best be understood in the context of a *Moment of Light,* rather than one physical battle of armed conflict. In this latter imagery, the elect of God are pitted against opposing forces in armed battle. *The idea of winning spiritual battles for truth by the means of force of arms is not consistent with the eschatological (or any) teaching of Jesus.* Paul agrees – 2 Co. 10:3-4. We may discern how the nature of this battle is played out in both the Old and New Testaments:

In Daniel 12:1-3, the haughty arrogance of the Oppressor is quashed, *not by the armies of the elect,* but by the forces of heaven! In the *passive* mood, it is revealed to Daniel that, "your people shall be delivered, everyone who is found written in the book." We should note here that, in a later part of Daniel, the final battle is *connected to some form of resurrection.* (Maybe it represented a later hope for the revival of Israel's autonomy). Clearly, *the battle is the Lord's! It has been won on the cross and is consummated in His resurrection.*

"…the first fruits of those who have died" (1 Co. 15:20).

In 2 Co. 10:3 the Apostle Paul speaks of the *nature of our warfare:*

"…we do not wage war according to human standards; for the weapons of our warfare are not merely human, but they have divine power to destroy strongholds."

Nowhere in the New Testament are we told that the purpose and nature of God's kingdom is won by employing the same destructive tools as the *enemy*. The final battle is the Lord's, and He has won it in the resurrection of Jesus!

In Rev. 20:9 we observe a picture of those opposing God's purposes, who are also attempting to overcome the saints of God. But they are thoroughly consumed; not by superior armaments of the saints, *but by the light and fire of God's glory!* This may be the most significant *Moment of Light* of latter days. *As in the beginning, the light of God shines upon creation, but in cleansing and restorative power!* (Gen. 1:3) The kingdom belongs to the sovereign God!

This *moment of God's sovereign triumph* has been seen to have an extraordinary parallel in the Old Testament. As Enoch and Elijah are translated (Gen. 5:24; 2 Kings 2:11) so the *faithful on earth* are raised to meet Jesus in the translation from the old order to that of the new order (1 Th. 4:17).

The gathering of the remnant from a decaying earth will not go by unnoticed. Again, this teaching of Jesus most certainly denotes some noticeable form of *separation*. When there are two in a bed and one goes missing, that will be noticed! The whole world will see His sign and, consequently, many will mourn over the nature that gladly accepted such loss. *At this time*, those of His elect, who are remaining, will *be caught up to meet Him into the new order of creation's restoration*.

In this big picture, we see that Jesus has taken *all His people who are alive* (including the great saints of the ages) or who have lived in the old order of time. They have gone to the new creation that He won at Easter. So the meaning of being caught up in the air is clearly connected to the fullness of new order of restoration. At some *Moment* in the dying embers of a decadent order, the victory of Easter Sunday is fully experienced by those who remain, and who are *in Christ*. The event clearly emphasizes that, at that moment, *there is no ending of time for all who are in Christ*. What remains of the old order will be left to suffer the fate of its inevitable demise. *How could it possibly endure, once the Light and Breath of God's sustaining love has departed?*

The word, *generation*, (genea) is often used in a simple chronological sense, i.e., Matt. 1:1, but it is also used to describe the moral condition of an entire community (Matt. 12:39). Here, Jesus describes a *generation* as being *evil and adulterous*. In the Matthew Chapter 24 passage we see a clear identification with a generation of people who, in latter days, morally identify with the apostate at the time of Noah. However, those who are identified with the *Word* are they who will endure forever! Not surprisingly, in Matthew's Gospel, Jesus ends His discourse on latter days with the following warning:

> **"Therefore you must also be ready, for the Son of Man is coming at an unexpected hour" (Matt. 24:44).**

In His finished work, Jesus holds together a Big Story of a new creation, which moves in opposition to the course of destruction. The old order of creation will most surely pass into nihilistic meaninglessness! (Rev. 21:1) Of course, as we have noted, this does not mean there no longer remains a physical connection between the old and the new order. Indeed, the mystery of the resurrected body of Jesus allows us to ponder such a possibility. Jesus also offers this connection *by basing His teachings in the meaning and purpose of creation.*

> *Not even for one moment does Jesus doubt that God's sovereign purposes will be accomplished. (Isa. 46:10, 55:11). God's purposes have surely triumphed, while He has maintained a self-imposed vulnerability to His principle of free choice!*

The power of Evil is defeated! Yes, the Lord did speak of an eternity for certain beings which would continually remain in an eternal state of torment (Matt. 25:41*). But these entities were created as spirit beings!* They are not creatures consisting of the elements comprising body, soul, and spirit. As such, they are not constrained by the dimensional elements that constitute the existence of time. *As spirit-beings,* the Beast and his angels and also the False Prophet remain in an eternal state of *fiery torment* (Rev. 20:10). *Here, we see that hell is forever and ever living with beings having the same perverted nature as the instigator.* However, we hasten to note that the God who created life in a spirit condition can also destroy it. But the *destructive power* of the same fire (where death itself is destroyed (Rev. 20:14) is promised for all whose names are *not* found in the book of life (Rev. 20:15; 21:7-8; 2 Th. 1:9; 2:3, 8). Incidentally, God doesn't need a book if all time consists in Him. The old order of creation is clearly over! So what we glean from the highly symbolic character of Revelation is:

> *Fire is the appropriate symbol for both total destruction and eternal torment.*

However, as we have seen, fire may be experienced one way or the other! It represents extinction for mortal beings while it is seen as eternal torment for spirit beings.

But, what about the Jews - where do they fit into this eschatological picture? Quite honestly, there is no Big Story unless it includes the Jewish people at the beginning and at the end. The mandate, given to Abraham, demands that the Jews be a significant part of the entire story. (Their purpose is to *unite* both Jew and Gentile in God.) It may not be politically correct to go this way, but the one Big Story compels us to seek consistency in the telling.

"ONE NEW HUMANITY"

Wasn't this God's purpose from the very beginning? (Gen. 1:28) When Jesus spoke of the times of Gentile fulfillment, quite probably, He had in mind a period when *significant events of history* would not revolve around the Jewish people. Not, at least, until the Gentiles had enjoyed their day in the sun! Both Jesus and Paul pick up this theme with the phrase, "until the full number of the Gentiles has come in" (Luke 21:24; Rom. 11:25). What does *"full number"* mean? Is it the right number of people for the new creation? Is it the right number of Gentiles being led by Jews into, and beyond, the days of the old order? For some, the full number means the end of the leading influence by the Gentile Church, and this apostolic role being, once more, headed by a Jewish community having recognized the promised messiah to be Jesus.

Quite apart from a small number of orthodox Jews (and some fundamentalist Christians) the hope that a temple would be rebuilt on Mount Zion is not widely held. The entire point of a temple would mean the restitution of a sacrificial system (abhorrent to most Jews and totally obsolete in orthodox Christianity). For Christians, the work of redemption, and of ransom, has been completed on the cross of Christ. Therefore, the latter day procession to Jerusalem, probably headed by Jewish people, (with Jesus at the head, Eph. 4:8) would *not be for the purpose of offering sacrifices, but to enter into the very focus of First Day Light; God's Shekina Presence.* The mighty work of the Spirit would have ended; the times of the Gentiles and the leadership of latter days might therefore be headed by Jews eager to see their beloved Messiah (Isa. 35:8-10).

Maybe the idea really does relate to the right number of people populating the new creation! Whatever it may mean, we may easily see that:

> *It will probably relate to a latter history of the Jewish people, who, as God's original community as "sons of God," now provide an even clearer understanding of the meaning of eschatos.*

The most significant moments of latter-day history will be focused around them, *as a people!* Nations that do not know God will be attracted to them! (Isa. 55:5; Zech. 8:22-23) God had allowed for His chosen people the consequence of being scattered among the nations of the earth. They had lost their identity as a resident nation in a land containing the old Jerusalem! But through the prophets, He promised that they would return to their homeland. (Does not the promise go even beyond this to a New Jerusalem above?)This would not happen as a reward for anything they had done. The event would be signatory *evidence of God's sovereignty upon the pages of human history.*

"It is not for your sake, O house of Israel, that I am about to act, but for the sake of my holy name" (Ezek. 36:22).

The Apostle Paul does not see the grafting in of the Jews to be the result of any human effort. It is a mighty work of the Spirit. This miracle will require nothing less than the mighty and sovereign breath of God sweeping over His ancient people, again! Indeed, the entire sovereign plan of God is at stake here. He uses the Greek word, "egkentridso" (to be ingrafted) in a future tense, and in a passive mood. It is God who does this astounding work! It will likely be a massive and sudden move of the Holy Spirit upon His ancient people. *Clearly, the most significant sign of latter days will be when this miraculous work of God is accomplished.*

One commentator bemoans the fact that very few Christians really have an understanding of God's plan for Israel. "It is also a fact that prior to 1948 hardly any of the mainline Christian denominations publicly stated or believed that God would raise Israel again in fulfillment of scripture."11 Israel was intended, and understood itself to be, a people that would focus a world in unity under God's anointed One:

> *"...and he is named Wonderful Counselor, Mighty God, Everlasting Father, Prince of Peace. His authority shall grow continually, and there shall be endless peace for the throne of David and his kingdom" (Isa. 9:6-7).*

Clearly, the fulfillment of all that is meant by restoration will not happen apart from Jesus. His place is at the head of the kingdom. Jesus made it clear to the Jews that He was the real David of prophetic fulfillment (Mark 12:35-37). Ezekiel, in his eschatological message of hope to an inbreathed people, and restored from dry bones, (chapter 37) looks forward to a time when the Real David is King:

> *"My servant David will be king over them, and they will all have one shepherd" (Ezek. 37:24).*

Of course, in the context of which Ezekiel speaks, this will not take place until Judah and Ephraim become *one stick*. (Ezek. 37:19-22).

How all this fits together in chronological fashion is something known only to God (Mark 13:32). It will most certainly not be fulfilled because of any human effort. Obviously, Ezekiel had spoken in agreement with the sentiments of Isaiah regarding God's sovereign purposes:

> *"The zeal of the Lord of hosts will do this" (Isa. 9:7).*

In other words, the restoration of the Jews, as a people under the headship of Jesus, will be the major sign of the long-awaited Parousia. Jesus once said to His own disciples:

> *"When the Spirit of truth comes, he will guide you into all the truth; ...He will glorify me..." (John 16:13-14)*

As an apostolic community, *it may also be* that the picture of consummation is *prefaced* in a united Jewish-Gentile mission inviting the world to unity in Jesus Christ! (Gal. 2:8, 3:28-29) But, as we have intimated, according to the Big Story, doesn't this mean that Jesus will be at the forefront of one Jewish and Gentile community? Yes, it does! The Old Testament clearly points to One who will sit on the throne of David, and Jesus saw Himself in that picture of kingdom rule. (We saw this bigger story where Jesus is shown to be the Real Adam-King, and the one riding triumphantly *on a donkey* into Jerusalem.) *The one Big Story really does come together in Jesus.* How could any Christian (out of misplaced sentimentality) negate the biblical hope that the Jewish people will, one day, realize their own calling? It will be through *their* Jewish Son that *their* apostolic purpose, promised through Abraham, finds complete focus (Gen. 12:3). Paul, a Jew who saw completion of the nation's story in Jesus, also saw Jesus to be at the very centre of its entire story.

We should now have enough confidence in predictive prophecy to believe that, somehow, *God will achieve His stated original purposes* through His ancient people. When that occurs, the Jews may once more be at the latter-day vanguard of an apostolic mission to the world!

> *"For nearly 2,000 years the Promised Land lay desolate. Where once great forests stood, the hills were empty of trees and covered with rocks. 'The land was under Turkish control from 1517 to 1917, and Turkey destroyed this land thoroughly. The rulers enacted ridiculous laws; for example, one that required taxes to be paid for live trees. The people cut down the trees so they wouldn't have to pay taxes! This country, therefore, ended up in a truly wretched condition.'"12 But God promised that, on the return of Israel, the deserts would once more blossom like a rose, and forests would return to their former glory (Isa. 35:1-2).*

With a charter of statehood in 1948, the astounding miracle of the Jewish return continued. Thousands of Jews were released from places like Russia and other parts of Europe and North America. Upon arrival, they began the laborious work of restoring the land. In spite of continued conflicts, the country flourished. Massive amounts of money and expertise were exported to Israel from Jewish people of countries around the world. Great waves of immigration took place, and the miracle of restoration amazed an astonished world. Israel now sends agricultural experts to consult with leaders of the world's developing nations. Yet, there are distinctions of belief within the nation. For example, many are atheists; a great number are agnostics. There are liberal Jews; also, there is an influential segment of Orthodox Jews. *Their sense of commonality is ethnic, not religious! They have become one stick in law, but not in heart.* Of course, they are no longer separated into people of the North and South. They are all Jews (fulfilling the astounding prophecy of Jacob to Judah - Gen. 49:8-10).

> *"I am about to take the stick of Joseph (which is in the hand of Ephraim) and the tribes of Israel associated with it; and I will put the stick of Judah upon it, and make them one stick, in order that they may be one in my hand" (Ezek. 37:19).*

Many years later, the writer to the Ephesians uses the language of a *commonwealth of Israel* (Eph. 2:12). Indeed, he may well have built upon a similar theme found in the book of Zechariah (Zech.12:10). Further, he goes on to speak of the breaking down of a wall of hostility that exists between Jew and Gentile. Then, he makes this most astounding statement:

> *"He has abolished the law with its commandments and ordinances, that he might create in himself one new humanity in place of the two, thus making peace, and might reconcile both groups to God in one body through the cross..." (Eph. 2:15-16)*

However, this unity of Jew with Gentile could not have happened until there was some form of unity within Israel itself.

The tribes of Israel are no longer separate. Inter-marriage has formed Jacob's descendants into one group called the Jewish people, or Israel. Today the names "children of Israel" and "Jewish people" are synonymous. This must surely be considered to be miraculous. Amazingly, the Holocaust, which was dastardly, and ruthlessly designed to cleanse the world of the Jewish race, became the very instrument to shame the United Nations into bringing Israel to nationhood!

Clearly, Israel now stands as a focal point of controversy and of conflict upon the stage of world history! Somehow, there appears to be no enduring solution to this present conflict. But one thing is clear: *It is perfectly legitimate to raise questions of justice to both sides of the present Jewish-Palestinian dispute.* Indeed, the Lord had revealed to the Jewish Patriarchs His desire for a benevolent relationship with other Semitic nations -Gen. 17:4-8! Has the hope of *one new humanity* become more possible now than in any previous age? Only God knows, and only God knows how that may be possible. Surely, such a union could not happen apart from some sort of divine involvement. And that would certainly be considered to be one more *Moment of Light* in the prophetic story of restoration.

The thought that Jewish and Gentile people, coming together under the lordship of Christ, and sharing a common destiny, does not sit well with present-day Dispensationalists. (They are a faction arising from millennial thinking.)Their idea is that Jews and Gentiles have two distinct destinies in latter days, *as well as in eternity*! As such, the Church and Israel are not united in a common future.13 Of course this entire reasoning does not fit into the Big Story at all! The first Adam was given an apostolic commission, which was certainly passed on to Abraham and all of his successors, *including Jesus, the kingly son of Judah.*

One thing is very clear: From a theological perspective, *it is inconceivable to think of a joyous and triumphant procession to a New Jerusalem (Isa. 35:8-10) which is not led by Jesus (the remnant figure of Judaism)* and also of great masses from among the Jewish people. This glorious procession must be led by Jesus because He is the Real Adam. He is reclaiming, by resurrection, a better Eden. The old Jerusalem will not do. He is the One who leads from captivity *one new humanity* that is brought together in Him through the power of the cross. Maybe it isn't coincidental that Charles Ryre (an exponent of dispensationalism) in his summary of its major tenets, omits the crucial revelatory moment of all restoration history: *the resurrection of Jesus Christ!* 14

A BETTER EDEN?

Initially, there was nothing wrong with the old Eden; after all, God said that it was *very good*. The dance was a warm embrace of all Essential Relationships. However, in the light of God's redemption and restoration in

Jesus, the question may well be posed. The New Eden is the focus for a redeemed community, which once more is united with God. Its gates have been reopened! The biblically consistent picture is one where the Groom and the Bride dance and fellowship together at the eternal wedding feast where all eternal relationships are restored. Whatever difficulties we may have in interpreting symbolic, biblical literature, the common imagery of God's triumph is very apparent to one Jew of ancient antiquity:

> *"For I am about to create new heavens and a new earth; the former things shall not be remembered or come to mind. But be glad and rejoice forever in what I am creating; for I am about to create Jerusalem as a joy, and its people as a delight" (Isa. 65:17-18).*

From a scientific point of view, Hugh Ross tells us that God didn't just pick the best planet from all the space junk that existed; He fine-tuned His creation to make our planet a fit dwelling place. "...the remoteness of the probability of finding a planet fit for life suggests that the Creator personally and specially designed and constructed our galaxy group....and Earth for life....While there is not the remotest chance that the natural conditions and physical laws of the universe will spawn a planet capable of sustaining physical life, there is nothing to stop the Creator of the universe from miraculously designing several planets, rather than just one planet, with the capacity to support life."15

> *"Then I saw a new heaven and a new earth; for the first heaven and the first earth had passed away, and the sea was no more. And I saw the holy city, the new Jerusalem, coming down from out of heaven from God, prepared as a bride adorned for her husband" (Rev. 21:1-2).*

Much of the imagery in apocalyptic literature is highly symbolic; it is therefore open to a wide variety of interpretations. However, our primary purpose in examining such imagery is to glean from it a picture of how *the original purposes in creation* have been restored. Clearly, much of the imagery provides an impression of how the restoration may appear. Our struggle is also one of discerning how such symbolism is consistent with the Big Story. This imagery is often a *poetic way* in which to illustrate the reality that *God has* secured His purposes. *The Lord is sovereign and His purposes have not failed.* God has placed Jesus, the Lamb and the Real Adam in the central position of the restored creation. We will look briefly at eight biblical images of consummation:

First: Jesus, the Real Adam, reigns with His saints in the new heaven and earth. His work is complete and the victory has been won. *The human community has been restored in order for it to take charge of a Garden that will, once more, be the focus for a universal priesthood of worship* (Isa. 65:17-18; Dan. 7:13-14, 22; Zech. 14:4-5; 1 Co. 15:24-25; Rev. 5:9-14; 11:15). Clearly, its inhabitants are not spending eternity learning how to play harps. Once more, they are embracing the *dance of innocence* in a worship that is the work of sustaining Essential Relationships. The apostolic mission is now complete, and the full number has been gathered in! (Rom. 11:25) Interestingly, the *manner* in which final restoration is secured is the same as it was in the beginning. *It is the power of the Word!* (Gen, 1:3; 1 Thess. 4:16; Rev. 19:11-16) Restored humanity returns to the open gates of a new Eden to delight in the *majesty of God's light and glory* (Zech. 14:7; Rev. 21:9-11).

> **"And I saw no temple in the city, for its temple is the Lord God the Almighty and the Lamb" (Rev. 21:22).**

Truly, our Jerusalem is above and is free! There is no longer need for the focus of God's presence to be centered in a building; it is in the living Shekina Presence of God and the Lamb.

> *No longer do we hear of Moments of Light;*
> *Restoration heralds an Eternity of First Day Light!*

First Day Light now saturates everything, including all people dwelling in God's restored creation. The sacrificed Lamb, the Real Adam of creation, takes the seat of royal authority, and He reigns with God in the new creation. The One Human, (the One who has proven His submission to God) becomes Zion's assurance that God's haunting question of the old order:

> *'Where are you?' will never be posed again.*

As it was on the First Day of creation, the Light of God's glory baptizes the everlasting dawn of creation's new day. The prophet Isaiah had already anticipated that there would be no longer need for natural light of the fourth day! (Isa. 60:19) Time would no longer be governed by Fourth Day Light, but by First Day Light of glory. Somehow, the direct Presence of God's light and glory is all the energy needed to keep the new creation in light forever. In the vision recorded in the Apocalypse, *there is also no more sea*! (Rev. 21:1) Disorder and disobedience no longer dominate the passageways of life. For Habakkuk, the waters of tranquility cover a troubled sea in a world that is filled with the knowledge of God's glory (Hab. 2:14). It is a picture of order:

> **"And the city has no need of sun or moon to shine upon it, for the glory of God is its light, and its lamp is the Lamb" (Rev. 21:23; Isa. 60:19).**

Second: *Where the Lord reigns there is no place for tears, death, pain or sorrow* (Isa. 61:1-2; 1 Co. 15:25; Rev. 7:15-17, 21:3-4).

Although a theology of eternal life is underdeveloped in all of Isaiah, the third Isaiah receives a glimpse of *some form of a* New Jerusalem existing in a condition of exquisite concord (Isa. 65:20). However, the New Testament shows us clearly that citizens of the kingdom live without sorrow forever! *Time is no longer an enemy; it never ends!* Its ability to spawn the terror of decay has been defeated. Humanity now receives possession of the newly-created DNA of life in a dimension of time that is now a restored friend!

Third: *Dysfunctional humanity, once driven from Eden, is now redeemed, restored and unified in a community of the New Jerusalem.* The dream of the psalmist has been realized. Even beyond the parameters of his vision, everyone will be in a unity focused in Christ (Ps.133:1; Rev. 21:22). Jesus, the *royal judge*, as in days of Israel's kings (2 Sam. 15:2, 9:8), now *reigns at the seat of justice* (Ezek. 34:23). The prophetic vision of Isaiah may well possess far more ramifications than he had envisaged:

> **"In days to come the mountain of the Lord's house shall be established as the highest of the mountains, and shall be raised above the hills. Many peoples shall come and say, 'Come, let us**

go to the mountain of the Lord. To the house of the God of Jacob; that he may teach us his ways, and that we may walk in his paths.' For out of Zion shall go forth instruction...He shall judge between the nations and shall arbitrate for many peoples; they shall beat their swords into ploughshares, and their spears into pruning hooks; nation shall not lift up sword against nation, neither shall they learn war anymore" (Isa. 2:2-4).

In order to enter the city of glory, reconciliation and justice have first been secured at its gate by the royal watchman. This situation was secured on a hill outside of Jerusalem; it was called, Calvary! But imagine being in a situation where everyone you meet has a heart desire to serve you; even Jesus, *our Lord and Brother!* (John 13:14) Maybe the great arbiter of justice has very little to do! After all, the primitive impulse to settle disputes through means of warfare has now been abandoned (Isa. 2:4). The Lord reigns, and He sits as the focus and source of love and unity for His beloved Bride.

As on the day of Pentecost, all the saints sing the songs of praise (Rev. 7:9-10). They focus on the Lamb of God. *Jerusalem is truly above and is free.* Its paths are trodden by the redeemed. There are no ravenous beasts of prey. The lion lies down with the lamb. Singing and everlasting joy reigns in the hearts of Zion's people (Isa. 35:8-10, 65:25; Rev. 21:27).

Fourth: *The New Jerusalem has twelve apostolic foundations and twelve gates inscribed with the names of Jacob's sons.* Surely, the twelve by twelve (144 in Rev. 7:4 and 14:1), represent a perfect number of the new Israel who are all redeemed by the blood of the Lamb (Rev. 14:3). Together, it is they who are worthy to lead:

"a great multitude... from every nation, from tribes and peoples and languages, standing before the throne and before the Lamb, robed in white with palm branches in their hands" (Rev. 7:9).

The pivotal foundations, *and the ever-open gates*, bear the name of Jew and Gentile as one, all being of the *sons of God.* New Jerusalem's gates of pearl indicate that the redeemed of Israel hold a place of glory while connected to the city's foundations. Universal unity has been restored in a reconciled body of one single humanity (Matt. 19:28; Jude 3; Rev. 21:12-14). Through this body, focused in Jesus, the Real Adam, the apostolic commission of creation has been completed.

> *Once more, we may hear God's triumphant shout of joy, "It is very good!"*

Unwavering recognition of Christ, as Lord, is the premise upon which the *entire community* of the redeemed enjoys unity with God and with each other. Jesus, the Lamb of God, is indisputably the focus of unity in the New Eden.

Fifth: *There is but one tree here: It is the Tree of Life which holds enormous significance for the universal community*. It lies, mysteriously, on both sides of the river flowing from the throne of God; East, West, North and South. As in the beginning, every part of the new creation is fed from this tree (Gen. 2:9; Rev. 22:2). The Tree of Life produces twelve kinds of *fruit* (the entire year is filled with abundance for the whole community), and the *leaves of the tree* are for the healing of the nations. It represents the apostolic community which offered healing for all peoples. (Once again, humanity has an intimate knowledge of, and relationship with, creation). From this tree, all creation is nourished from its Source. All creation is dependent upon it! Of course, this imagery belongs to the original Eden. (It is also envisioned by Ezekiel as an ideal temple of hope for the people of Diaspora - Ezek. 47:12. However, the apocalyptic vision of restoration in the New Testament shows the temple of Ezekiel to be neither ideal, nor yet complete.)

Admittedly, and in hindsight, we realize that the Jerusalem which comes down from heaven, really is free (Gal. 4:26). *The restoration of the Old Eden is deliberately incomplete* in the vision of Ezekiel. Its primary purpose is to offer hope to a beleaguered people bereft of their focus in Zion. In the New Jerusalem, *there is no need for a temple* at all! (Rev. 21:22-23) God and the Lamb become the temple, its light and its glory (Rev. 22:5). Also, Ezekiel's temple of hope continues to require a priesthood offering now redundant sacrifices of redemption. Only in the obedient sacrificial work of Jesus may it be said, "It is finished!"

Sixth: *The imagery of Eden's river of life is now replaced by an undivided river flowing through the New Jerusalem.* (Ezek. 47:1-9).

Zion's river of life has no streams branching from it. It is a single river providing everlasting sustenance to a city that is at unity in itself (Gen. 2:10-14; Zech. 9:10; Rev. 22:1-2, 14). But this river flows out from the throne of God, and through the streets of Zion. The purpose of the river is to feed the entire new creation stretching from East to West (Zech. 14:8). The worship of Jerusalem's citizenry is never exhausted because the worshippers possess an everlasting thirst for the inexhaustible riches of God (Rev. 7:15; Eph. 2:7). Interestingly, Jesus waited until *the last day of the festival* to invite the celebrants to drink:

> *"Let anyone who is thirsty come to me, and let the one who believes in me drink" (John 7:37-38).*

> *"...but those who drink of the water that I will give them will never be thirsty. The water that I will give will become in them a spring of water gushing up to eternal life" (John 4:14).*

Jesus is the River of Life! Basil the Great may well be correct in suggesting that eternity will never be exhausted by our desire to know Him.

Seventh: *In the original Paradise, Eve was presented to Adam as his bride. Now, the Real Adam is the Groom who presents His Bride, the Church, to God.* Christ's offering is one of praise and thanksgiving because He also presents a new creation back to the Source and Author of life (1 Co. 15:23-24). Once again, a royal priesthood, fitted for the new creation, walks in harmony with its Creator, and in the garden He has prepared for them (John 14:2; 1 Co. 15:44).

Eighth: *God has restored a people to the realities of a new creation, which constitutes God's original meaning and purpose for humanity* (Rev. 5:10).

Here, the citizenry of the new creation can touch, taste, see, and smell. This is no Sheol! The creation story tells of God creating physical beings fashioned from clay who were intended to be at home in a *physical world.* If the restoration of our humanity is to be something other than as physical creatures touching the earth of new creation, then God would surely have *failed to demonstrate His sovereign purposes.* His involvement upon the pages of history would not have achieved what He intended at the beginning. But through the death and resurrection of Jesus, God has insisted in playing out the entire duration of the dance. Once again, there is communal, environmental, cosmic, and personal harmony. *The inhabitants of the new creation are fully in step by embracing the eternal dance of creation's innocence!*

> *Once again, the essential relationships of creation are working together in an awesome dimension of praise and worship.*

How can the Jesus, the very heart and life of this Big Story, ever be compared with any other figures of any other religions? "...they saw no one with them any more, but only Jesus" (Mark 9:8).

> *In the light of God's activity throughout our biblical view of time's seasons, Jesus Christ cannot simply be considered to be the best news on the block; He is the ONLY news on the block!*

CONCLUSION: ETERNITY IN FIRST DAY LIGHT

The Lord reigns! His sovereign purposes for harmonious relationships in creation have been accomplished in Jesus Christ. This Big Story has not been a fairy tale! How dare we arrogantly compare it with Camelot? *Didn't God have all His desired elements in place at the beginning?* This is a real story emerging from *real facts concerning God's involvement in history.* The beginning of creation's story, and its meaning, can now be understood in the very life, death and resurrection of Jesus Christ; the One who leads the dance for all ages! Just because God is omniscient, and because He is our omnipotent Lord, doesn't mean that what He won in Jesus didn't come at considerable cost to Himself. God became vulnerable for us! Camelot left us with a vague and fruitless hope of better things in a younger generation. Latter days have proven such a naïve hope to be fruitless. But in God's Big Story, the zeal of the Lord Almighty has accomplished this! (Isa. 9:7). God has secured His eternal victory of reconciliation in Jesus Christ (Phil. 2:6-8, 10-11; 2 Co. 5:19).

Satan, the spiritual source of perversity in the old order, is now destined to spend all eternity in the company of other spiritual creatures who share his self-perverted, and ego-centered nature. What an indescribable hell that must be! Satan has lost his place in heaven (Rev. 12:7-9) and, *because he is a spirit-being, is destined to spend all eternity in that everlasting torment of fire* (Rev. 20:10).

We have seen clearly that *freedom of choice is at the very heart of kingdom life*. It is a vital principle of life in a creation dominated by the power of love. There can be no love where there is no freedom! The tree, which represents the knowledge of good and evil (Gen.2: 17), no longer appears in the new creation of Revelation. *But this doesn't mean that the ability to make choices has gone!* True and loving relationships must entail the freedom to choose. Surely, without this ability, an important principle of creation would have been abolished! If Satan has lost his place in the new creation, does that mean its citizens are no longer tempted? Where love is, there is freedom! Surely, we must assume that, *having once seen the horrendous consequences of self-motivated decisions, all citizens of the kingdom would ensure that the power of love is sought above all.* Jesus, the Real Adam, is there. And, because He is acknowledged as Lord, we see that He does reign in the awesome power of love! "If you love me you will keep my commandments" (John 14:15). That's a matter of choice! Having been redeemed, restored in Jesus, and now tasting the unimpeachable joy of Essential Relationships being played out, we will *eternally remember* the awesome penalty and futility of resisting the irresistible love of God.

While we are in this present time, all people are invited to *choose Christ* in response to His finished work. Clearly, we understand that there are consequences associated with the choices we make. If the Church is truly to be a prophetic voice, and a light to the nations (Isa. 49:6; Matt. 5:14), then, at every opportunity, *the primary apostolic invitation must be extended*. But, in the new order of restoration, we realize that God's purposes for His creation have been secured in Jesus, the Lamb of God.

The Lord's sovereign purposes have been accomplished! The wolf lies down with the lamb (Isa. 65:25). All creation is once more in a perfect state of *harmonious relationships* under the lordship of the Real Adam! No longer are citizens of the new order separated by the barriers of language. The calamities of Eden have been reversed in the finished work of Christ. And, as the Light of God's glory was the manifest sign on creation's First Day, so it is the everlasting Light on the *endless First Day* of restoration. There will be a profound reality of a continuing priesthood operating in the ministry of innocent worship and praise! The full number has been gathered in! All of the redeemed are eternally free to make *creative choices* under the loving lordship of Christ.

We have not been called to be mindless, moronic robots. Here is an astounding paradox: When our hearts are primarily set on love for the Lord, and the glory of His kingdom, questions concerning our trust for God are subsumed in *the astounding truth that God really trusts us!* Yes, at the present, inferior decisions may be made; prideful motivations may surface; sin will surely creep in; but the Lord Jesus is always with us (Matt. 28:20). Presently, in the power of Christ's love, the Real Adam's recreated community is called to be a continuing sign of hope to a floundering world. *Love is Life, and Life is Love; and the greatest of all is love* (1 Co. 13:10, 13). Love is the overriding force that permeates everything associated with the *perfect*. That is, the new creation under the headship of Jesus.

After embracing the vision of God's holiness, His majesty, and His awesome Presence, was it possible for Isaiah to say, *No,* to the Almighty One? Undoubtedly, he could have responded negatively, or else there would have been no need for the question to be posed (Isa. 6:8). However, what we learn from this encounter is that *the closer we abide in the Light of God's glory, the less likely is the desire to make self-centered decisions.* In the new creation, the Man, Christ Jesus, forever points to the awesome, holy, and majestic presence of God's light and glory.

The Big Story of creation, redemption, and restoration, has been presented in the analogy of a collage. An impressionistic Picasso may have left us with a story that was vague, and open to an infinite variety of interpretations. The Big Story may have appeared too elusive to discern clearly. A Constable may have left us passively with so much detail that little room is left for questions, personal choices, or meaningful involvement. Some people may prefer that easier and stifling approach. But what we see in God is the Creator who doesn't offer Abraham a blueprint. He offers a Way, a direction, and a Presence! (Ex. 33:13-14) The fact is, *the story of a pilgrim people was often very untidy and wayward, but the prophetic sign of God's original direction was always apparent before them.* Just as there was need for a Good Friday in order to experience Easter Sunday, the corollary was that the path of the Way had to be walked by faith in order for the full picture to appear.

The idea of putting together the pieces of a *collage* reminds us much more of the picture into which Christ came. Sometimes, there are bits that don't contribute to making sense of the Big Story. But then, how do we know how to extricate those bits from the panoramic arrangement? In this book I have pointed out, very strongly, that the criterion for evaluating each piece of the picture is when it contributes to a focus declaring *Jesus Christ to be the meaning and focus of all history*. He is the beginning and the end! (Rev .1:8, 17) He is therefore truly our Savior, Lord, and King. He is the Way, the Truth, and the Life (1 John 4:1-3; John 3:16, 14:6). *If any piece doesn't contribute to the development of this picture, then it doesn't fit the Big Story at all!*

With questions on their minds, and with faith in their hearts, martyrs of old died in the belief that God, *in Christ alone*, made sense of history. They died with the word, *"Maranatha"* on their lips. It was not a whimpering cry of defeat. It was a triumphant affirmation of hope in the ultimate meeting with Christ - the Lord of new creation. "Maranatha, come quickly, Lord Jesus!" was the summary statement of lives offered in thanksgiving for God's salvation. It was also a cry of thanksgiving because creation's entire meaning had been restored in Jesus, the Alpha and the Omega of life (Rev. 22:13).

Paradoxically, the garden where we presently walk is both tragic and beautiful. On the one hand, it is racked with the ravages of death and decay. It groans in travail while it also pants in the memory, yet glorious anticipation, of new creation. Although the signs of glorious light seem to be fast diminishing in a return to darkness and chaos, there still remain magnificent icons of God's sustaining love and glory. We have not yet arrived at the point where we cry in desperation for the mountains to fall on us (Luke 23:30). But the signs are ominously near! As servants of the Lord Jesus, we have yet much to offer God through the glorious freedom of loving and joyous stewardship. In the process of trusting that the sovereign God is victor, with martyrs and confessors of every age, we are given the assurance that, "...we are more than conquerors through him who loved us" (Rom. 8:37).

Our goal, our prize, and our joy, will be God Himself, God alone!

Harmoniously, and in faith, we resonate with all creation in a Benedicite of praise, "O all ye works of the Lord, bless the Lord. Praise Him and magnify Him forever."16

"The Spirit and the bride say, 'Come.' And let everyone who hears say, 'Come.' And let everyone who is thirsty come. Let any one who wishes take the water of life as a gift" (Rev. 22:17).

And so, in this *eternal outburst of praise*, we who are alive and remain join with all creation in our longing for the Sovereign One who says:

"'Surely I am coming soon.' Amen. Come, Lord Jesus" (Rev. 22:20).

"God saw everything that he had made, and indeed, it was very good" (Gen. 1:31).

Like the poor man who was invited to stand at Abraham's side (Luke 16:23), we are called to live in the promises given to all of Abraham's descendants (Gen. 12:3; Isa. 27:6; Gal. 3:29).

AND SO, BY GOD'S GRACE, WE ARE INVITED TO ENTER INTO THE GLORIOUS LIGHT OF NEW CREATION'S ETERNAL FIRST DAY! (Rev. 21:23)

Chapter 13 From Latter Days to the New Eden

1. Kung, Hans, *Why I Am Still a Christian?* p.142
2. Ladd, George E., *A Commentary on the Revelation of John,* p.14. Eerdmans Publishing. Mich.,1972
3. Ladd, George E.., p.11
4. Ladd, George E., p.11
5. Robinson, J.A.T, *In The End God,* p.105 Collins Fontana Books, London, 1968
6. Ladd, George E., p.7
7. Tenney, Merrill C. *New Testament Times,* p.368. Eerdmans Publishing, Mich. 1965 (reprinted 1984)
8. Voice of the Martyrs Web Page, www.vom.com.au/default.asp (2001)
9. Munro, Margaret, *The Times Columnist,* p. A2 "Escaping methane adds to Arctic's climate worries." March 8th 2006
10. *Water, Water:The Water Apocalypse.* The Discovery Channel, April 14th, 2006
11. Doron, Reuven. *One New Man,* p.31 Embrace, P.O.Box 10102 Cedar Rapids, IA 52410. 1993.

12. Archbold, Norma. *The Mountains Of Israel,* p.25. A Phoebe's Song Publication, Third Edition, 1993

13. Ryrie, Charles *Dispensationalism,* p.39. Moody Press, Chicago. 1966

14. Ryrie, Charles p.212

15. Ross, Hugh, p.198-199, *The Creator and the Cosmos*

16. Book of Common Prayer, p26. General Synod of the Anglican Church of Canada, 1962

AN INVITATION TO ACCEPT JESUS CHRIST AS SAVIOUR AND LORD

Please read the following and, when you can make these words your own prayer of commitment, offer it to God. This, or a similar prayer, is one of dedication which you will repeat many times in your relationship with God.

Heavenly Father, I thank you for loving me. Thank you for sending your Son so that I may enter a new life of relationships. Lord Jesus, I come to your cross, the place where I may begin again. I ask you to forgive me for all the sin of the past; for all that has offended you, and hurt others. Please forgive me, and set me free from the pain of broken relationships. Thank you for your forgiveness! I ask you to come into my life to be my Savior and my Lord, now and forever.

Thank you Lord Jesus because you are now in my life. By the power of the Holy Spirit, and through your Church, enable me to be conformed to the image of Christ, to follow and serve you all the days of my life. Amen

The following verses of the Bible are *assurances* that God has heard and answered your prayer: 1 John 1:9; Rev. 3:20; John 15:14; Acts 2:38. May I urge you to join a church where the authority of the Bible is held high, and where *a home group-based congregation* provides an avenue for a life of growth in discipleship and in your priestly service to Almighty God.

---

c

b. The concept of there being two gods is based in Dualism. This idea took different directions and was conceived in various philosophies. For example, not only were there two 'first causes' but these forces represent, on the one hand, the idea of pure spirit being good while, on the other hand, matter was essentially evil. Mind and matter are both distinctly unconnectedly real and opposite

[iii] Gnosticism has many ramifications. Basically, it attempts to deal with questions of evil by separating pure existence (pure spirit) from matter (which is evil). Gnosis, or knowledge, is the key that liberates the soul on the path of perfection. Mind and matter are distinct entities. This knowledge is not commonly possessed, but is secret and passed on through ritual and secret ceremonies.

d.In the belief that the soul is immortal, Universalism holds the idea that the love of God is ultimately irresistible to everyone. Some even assert that Satan will also be won over by God's love-eventually!

[iv] John Calvin was heavily influenced by Augustine who developed the thought that humanity was totally depraved-therefore not capable of responding to good, moral choices apart from the prevailing grace of God. This thinking led to a theory of Predestination whereby he held that there were certain individuals who were 'elected' to salvation. Of course, this led to serious questions regarding the human capacity to exercise free will. However, many of his followers went further by developing a theory that all others were excluded form this salvation. (Double Predestination).Jacobus Arminius, another Dutch reformer, reacted "against the deterministic logic of Calvinism."" The Arminians insisted that the Divine sovereignty was compatible with a real free-will in man; that Jesus Christ died for all men and not only for he elect." The view in the book is not consistent with any found in the 16th century reformers ie, a predestined and individual salvation. It takes root in the apostolic calling of an entire community.

.v Pelagianism is the heresy which holds that humans can take the initial and fundamental steps towards salvation by their own efforts, and apart from Divine Grace. *Oxford Dictionary of the Christian Church.* (1957) The teaching of Pelagius (late 4th-early 5th century) took root in Britain where many spoke of 'lifting up oneself by one's own bootstraps.' And, in this vein, and in the North America of today, some of the more Gnostic-inclined are offended by a language that speaks of the need for salvation.\

[vi] "Destroy this temple, and in three days I will raise it up…But he was speaking of the temple of his body." (John 2:19,21) Note, Jesus said this in the context of His cleansing the old temple, which He correctly predicted would be destroyed. In John 11, after the raising of Lazarus, Jesus connected the new temple, in his body, with the resurrection. From that time on, the religious establishment "planned to put him

to death." (v.53) In Rev.21:22 there is no temple in the vision of restoration. "...for its temple is the Lord God the Almighty and the Lamb." The Temple doesn't *contain* the glory; the Temple (Jesus) *is* the glory!

vii The author's book, There Must Be Another Way, is a call to Reformation in practice. It speaks of how churches may make disciples for a 21st century world. Published by Essence Publishers, Guardian Books, Canada, 2006. Or see web page: www.timothyministry.ca

viii The Greek word eis is used to mean 'one.' The KJV translates this as, 'one blood,' meaning that, through Christ, we are all descended from the stock of Adam-Eve relationships, i.e., "Sons of God."

ix There have been a number of attempts that try to show how Jesus never really died. They range from recorded accounts in Matthew 28:11-15 to Hugh J. Schonfield's, The Conspiracy of the Empty Tomb

x In the Book of Revelation this raising from the dead is for the purpose of a second death. (Rev.20:14)

xi See courses by Charles Alexander; click "Resources" www.timothyministry.ca

xii One such effective course, produced by the Timothy Institute of Ministry, is entitled, "Growing in Christ." Click on Resources at: www.timothyministry.ca

For congregational resources in developing effective disciples, and for useful aids in developing church-planting congregations, please see the author's web page:

www.timothyministry.ca

Other books by Charles Alexander:

There Must Be Another Way: "The Gospel never changes, but the methodology must." Honoring five essential principles of apostolicity in these days of Second Reformation, the result is a pointed way of making disciples, and a relational way of re-structuring ministry for a twenty-first century world.

Angels Don't Wear Shoes: This is a very simple and often humorous apologetic for the ordinary person in a 21st century , post-modern world. It is an effective tool of evangelism for the friend at work, a relative, or a casual acquaintance.

Published by:Essence-Guardian Books, Canada / 20 Hanna Court, / Belleville, ON, Canada K8P 5J2 / Ph: 1-800-238-6376

For further contact, and other resources for ministry, see web page of Charles Alexander: www.timothyministry.ca Email: info@timothyministry.ca

To purchase additional copies of this book or other books published by Advantage Books call our toll free order number at:
1-888-383-3110 (Book Orders Only)

or visit our bookstore website at:
www.advbookstore.com

Longwood, Florida, USA
"we bring dreams to life"™
www.advbooks.com

LaVergne, TN USA
05 August 2010
192267LV00002B/1/P